FROM JAVA
TO NAGASAKI

THE COMPLETE
SECRET WARTIME DIARIES
OF A PRISONER OF THE JAPANESE

1942 -1945

To the Brixnis Association

Best wishes

Greg Lewis

Kind regards

Jeremy Stewart

19/1/18

LES SPENCE
EDITED BY GREG LEWIS

From Java to Nagasaki
By Les Spence
Edited by Greg Lewis

First published in 2012 by
Magic Rat, 12a Lansdowne Avenue West
Canton, Cardiff, Wales CF11 8FS
magic.rat.books@googlemail.com

A catalogue record for this book is available from the British Library.

ISBN: 978-0-9562722-2-5

Typeset in Adobe Caslon Pro by
Steven Levers Book Design, Sheffield

CONTENTS

PROLOGUE

This is the diary of Leslie Magnus Spence. It was kept secretly for almost four years while Les was a prisoner of the Japanese in Java and Japan.

It was written in three small books and hidden from his captors. Les faced punishment and possibly death if his secret diaries were discovered.

Les served in the 77th HAA (Heavy Anti Aircraft) Regiment of the Royal Artillery. This was a TA regiment from South Wales comprising three batteries: 239, 240 and 241. It was established to provide air protection for Cardiff, Newport and Barry, and surrounding districts. The regiment was to include many sportsmen - county cricketers, footballers and rugby players. Les himself had spent many seasons playing for Cardiff Rugby Club and been captain during the 1936-37 season. He and his team-mates had joined the TA unit together. In August 1941 they left Cardiff for Frome and then, in late October, they were sent north to Scotland in preparation for serving overseas.

The 77th had trained to fight the Germans in the deserts of the Middle East but the Japanese attack on Pearl Harbor on December 7, 1941, meant they were diverted to the Far East.

The diaries open with Les Spence aboard the ship, 'Warwick Castle'. This ship was part of convoy WS14 which assembled off Oversay on December 9, 1941, and arrived in Freetown on December 21, 1941. The convoy was to split up off Durban with 'Warwick Castle' becoming part of a sub-convoy designated DM2. It arrived in Batavia (now Jakarta) on Java on February 3, 1942. Before they even arrived on Java Les confided to his diary: "It will be no picnic. I am afraid some of us will not see the end of next month."

What follows is a remarkable testament to courage and endurance in the face of hardship and cruelty – and a first-hand account of how to hold onto hope when all seems lost.

A NOTE
ON THE TEXT

Considering the extreme conditions in which Les kept his diaries, they are remarkably tidy and well-written.

I have been unable to make out the occasional word and have noted that in the text by way of the entry [illegible].

I have tried to keep to Les' punctuation but, on occasion, have added punctuation points to assist the reader.

None of the words have been changed except to correct a common error in Les' writing where he repeatedly writes 'has' as 'as'.

Some of Les' language is indicative of the time. The use of the term 'Nips', for instance, was commonplace. Les occasionally uses other terms relating to the racial background of people. These have been kept to maintain the integrity of the text.

Diary entries with an asterisk next to the date have a corresponding note at the back of the book. Where possible I have included short biographical details on those mentioned by Les.

1942

Thursday January 1*
Cooler, sea moderate, should be in Capetown Sunday or Monday.
Ear painful. Orderly says very quiet compared with last one. Beautiful night.

Friday January 2
My ear very painful, hoping it will not interfere with my shore leave.
Tempers are getting frayed and rows becoming more frequent.
Beautiful night. Listened to Churchill's speech. Really good.

Saturday January 3
Flag at half-mast on one of the boats. It makes you think.
The news seems to be better. What a speech from Churchill, it was magnificent.
Last concert before we arrive Capetown. A very poor show. Spoilt by the officers. Pity.
Wait till we arrive in Capetown. We'll paint the town red.

Sunday January 4
Went to communion. A very nice day. Towards tea-time the convoy spilt up, one going to Durban, we off to Capetown. Everybody excited. We should have a good time.
Played cards in the evening.

Monday January 5
Arrived Capetown 9am. Glorious view from the sea. Lovely day.

Friday January 9
Left quayside early in morning. Jack Lewis missed boat but caught [illegible] boat and came aboard 7.30am.
Everybody onboard feeling depressed after such a glorious four days ashore.
Mac talked of getting engaged last night. She was a charming girl.
Weather was very bad. Raining and cold.

7

Saturday January 10
Weather much warmer. Started swimming again.
Much speculation as to our next port of call, maybe Rangoon. A deep depression seems to have settled over the boat. Everybody feeling affects of Capetown hospitality. Played cards in evening and had a bit of luck. Bert seems to be worrying about his wife.

Sunday January 11
Went to communion in the morning. The weather certainly much hotter. Will probably meet Durban convoy tomorrow. Peculiar dream last night, dreamt that Bert's wife had a baby boy. Have noticed that dreaming every night. Must be climate. Played cards. Won.

Monday January 12
Weather becoming hotter. Went swimming. Food much better.
Suppose [sic] to meet convoy from Durban tomorrow. Maybe we will then know where we are going.

Tuesday January 13
Still darned hot but no sun. Had a tropical downpour of rain in the morning. Saw convoy. A lot of new boats, other boats missing. Saw shores of Durban. Burma seems to be popular rumour.

Wednesday January 14
Lovely day, going faster than previously. I think we will go to Mombasa and then maybe India.
Lightening terrific in the evening and all through the night.

Thursday January 15
Had a shock this morning about 6am. The alarm went for boat stations. What a rush. It was only a short in the wires.
Rumour is that we are going to an island.
Phew it's getting hotter. No cards.

Friday January 16
What heat. It's over 90 in the shade. You can't even keep cool swimming. Nobody seems to know where our ultimate destination is.

Saturday January 17*
Its darned hot and it is still over 90 in the shade. No parade because of the heat. Japs 110 miles from Singapore. Situation looks serious. Why o why have we not learned the lesson of Norway and Crete. Lack of air force.

Wrote letters, 2 to Capetown, one to Ken, one to Bateman. Stayed on deck all evening.

Sunday January 18*
Went to communion in the morning. Still over 90 in the shade. And am getting a bit fed up. Rumours run over the ship re our ultimate destination.
Wrote to mother. I should say we will soon know our destination.

Monday January 19*
Well at 7.30 this morning we said goodbye to half of the convoy and the Ramillies. They're off to Middle East. We were met by another warship and away we went with 8 other ships. It's now obvious it is Singapore.

Tuesday January 20
It is still hot and the news still bad. I think we are bound to go to Singapore if it does not fall before we can get there. Did quite a lot of swimming. Heading N.E.

Wednesday January 21
Mailbag planes today. It looks as if will arrive at Colombo on Sunday. Have wrote to mother, Ken, Cherry, [illegible], Marjorie, Babs.

Thursday January 22
Still warm. Arrangement being made for disembarking at Colombo. I understand I will go on the quayside and be in charge of our baggage.

Friday January 23*
Orderly Sergeant. Still warm. We are not going ashore on Sunday but calling for water then on to ? [sic]. Singapore I fancy. We are still going slow by N.E. Clock half hour.

Saturday January 24*
Still going N.E. by E. Have now been told we're not going to call at Colombo. Calling instead at [illegible], south of Ceylon. We seem to be slipping up in this war with the Japs. It looks very serious for Australia. I still think Singapore is a good bet.

Sunday January 25*
Went to communion. Clock half hour. Well we will be in port tomorrow. Wonder if it will be Colombo or that island.
Took Fryett to church in the evening. News from the [illegible] it's Singapore after our port tomorrow.

Monday January 26*
What a day! Informed by steward at 7am that we would not be calling at port but would be sailing another nine days. Went on deck and we were going west. Changes course to E [illegible] 8 o' clock [illegible]. E of A left us about 9pm for water. Convoy all to hell. Still think it's Singapore.

Tuesday January 27
No sign of E of A. Still very hot. Are putting up more guns. Still think we will go to Singapore. News getting lousy. Hope at home seems to be [illegible] over for Far East.

Wednesday January 28
E of A back with us. Change our course S.E. Definitely Singapore and it will be no picnic. I am afraid some of us will not see the end of next month. Met another convoy, also cruiser. Churchill seems to be having a rough time.

Thursday January 29
Still on S.E. course. Must be near Sumatra. Boys are not so sunny and bright. Many serious faces. Still very hot. Water becoming scarce. None to boil potatoes.

Friday January 30
Still on S.E. course. Big pay. We had a full week instead of [illegible]. I wonder where we will have our next week's pay, if any. What a mess we've made of Far East.

Saturday January 31
We have not had one bit of good news since leaving England. Benghazi has now fallen. We've withdrawn all our troops to Singapore and we will defend it to the end. Reinforcements are on the way so the BBC tell us. I don't think many of us will live to tell the story of how we saved Singapore.

Sunday February 1
Went to communion. We heard at noon today that our destination was Batavia and that we would arrive on Tuesday. Personally I think we will call there and go on from there to Singapore where they badly need reinforcements.

Monday February 2
No more news except that it's doubtful whether we land tomorrow. The heat terrific. It is very doubtful whether we land. A rather heavy night in the mess. I still say Singapore.

Tuesday February 3
Saw my first volcano this morning off Sumatra. Nobody knows anything. Convoy split at 1 o'clock. Arrived at Batavia and docked at 7pm. One hour later we were told to be ready to move off ship in the morning. Great excitement. Everybody looking forward to being on land once more!

Wednesday February 4/Thursday February 5*
This day marked the commencement of a terrible tragedy. We left by train for Surabaya at 6.30am, all in wonderful spirit. We were welcomed all the way and great reception at all the stations we stopped. We stopped at our last station at 11pm and on leaving we sang Cwm Rhondda. Then at 3am in the morning a terrible catastrophe befell us.
A head-on collision with a goods train loaded with bombs and petrol. It was terrible. I found poor old Ken dead. Jimmy Boxall, Stoodley, and Capt McMillan. Some had terrible injuries and I do not think they will live. Ainsley, Bill Black and George Lock. Jonny Milligan also dead. Arrived S at 12am by bus.

Friday February 6*
Went to hospital to see the injured and bury the dead. Had a great shock, a few more dead. Horace Evans, Ron Shrine and Bill Black dead making death roll 18. Nine [from] 240. John Ainsley, G Lock will soon be dead.

Saturday February 7*
Poor old George Lock passed away and was buried today making death roll 20. Capt McMillan, Jim Boxall, Bill Black, John Ainsley, Stoodley, Ken Street, Horace Evans, Ron Shrine, George Lock, Jonny Milligan all dead. Harvey Hardacre, Pat Cox, M O'Fitzpatrick, are seriously injured. Mac Weeks, Dai Grandon, Fred Woods, Hughie Edwards slightly injured. I am feeling very miserable especially at night.

Sunday February 8
First Sunday in Java. No communion but I think of last Sunday when most of the boys were attending church service. I am afraid the food question is not so good.

Monday February 9
Still no news of our guns. Our sites are not so good either. The heat is very [illegible] and we have heavy thunder storms in the afternoon and evening.

Tuesday February 10*
I am acting BSM but do not feel any joy at holding the position. We move tomorrow to our own gun site.

Wednesday February 11
What a day. I feel absolutely all in. I think the site is putrid and our food arrangements leave a lot to be desired.

Thursday February 12
Settling down but have very little money. We are paid far too little. I heard a whisper today that I may get emergency commission.

Friday February 13*
Unlucky day. HRH with Wilf visited our camp and seemed rather pleased. Heard from Wilf that my name had not been submitted for commission – HRH the rat.
Had a good night.

Saturday February 14
My birthday – not a greeting. Still no news of the guns maybe tomorrow.

Sunday February 15
We had an order to camp in the mountains. It was very pleasant and the war seemed to be miles away instead of on our own doorstep. It was very quiet at night.

Monday February 16*
News of the convoy. First part will be in tonight. About time. I am feeling very tired. It must be the heat. Major G told me that I had been recommended for a commission.

Tuesday February 17
The guns arrived today. Johnny Probert was made an officer. It was a great disappointment to me after being told I would get a commission. I can take it but I shall never forgive HRH for this.

Wednesday February 18
No chance to rest, work, work and more work. No time for meals. Still sore about commission especially after being told by Major Gaskell that I had been recommended. HRH will regret this.

Friday February 20
Pay day and I did not know it was even Friday until I looked in my diary. I am feeling very tired and went to bed 8pm.

Saturday February 21
The hard work and poor food is telling on the boys and we must have more food if we stay here. Went out for first time in the evening for three nights. This has been a week of very hard work. Airmail was received from England by some of the boys.

Sunday February 22
Today we had a visit from the Brig Colonel and fired our first round which was not very successful. I can't see the Dutch holding on to this island.

Monday February 23
Now we are certainly seeing things and I must say the Japanese are darned accurate in their bombing. Our firing is poor, no doubt due to the ammo and climate. Fighters are the only answer.

Tuesday February 24
We've been here 3 weeks and I reckon within the next 3 weeks we [will] either be dead or prisoners of war. The boys laughed and said I was a Jonah but we wait and see. The Japanese bombing is too darn accurate for my liking. I had a good night at the club.

Wednesday February 25
What a day of bombing. They just came over and bombed hell out of us. No fighters and we could not touch them with our guns. Had a narrow escape when shrapnel fell near me and went into the ground 3ft. This bombing can't go on.

Thursday February 26
Another heavy raid today. Docks badly damaged. I get knocked off my motorbike. Not badly hurt. The raids are terrifying native population. I wonder if we will see the end of next month. Maybe if we are lucky.

Friday February 27*
We left today for Tjilatjap, a port. It looks as if we are making a dash for a boat to Australia. I think the Japanese will soon take this island. What a rush today, only half the battery able to move and rest follow tomorrow.

Saturday February 28
Well on our way to Tjilatjap, should make it tomorrow. Nasty accident with one of the lorries. We lose Lock and Stiles with injuries, taken to hospital. Heard that the Japs have landed and are advancing quickly. A lot of Americans pass us on their way to Tjilatjap.

Sunday March 1
We arrived at Tjilatjap in pouring rain. After a terrific soaking in rainstorm on arrival had to put guns in action. Worked till 4am in the morning. Absolutely dead beat. We do not run anymore but have a go.

Monday March 2
Very busy day putting guns in action. Have not seen any planes yet. Most of battery arrived in great haste. Am at RHQ, not too comfortable, may be worse. Plenty of boats in harbour.

Tuesday March 3*
We were paid today. I wonder when we will get our next pay?
Ted Sumption has arrived with only half a battery. It looks as if we will soon see the Japanese.

Wednesday March 4
We had it today. The Japanese absolutely knocked hell out of the docks and sunk most of the ships. The bombing was deadly. Couple more raids like this and we can pack up. Where are the fighters!

Thursday March 5
Bad day for the 77. 241 lost several good men when the Japs dive bombed the gun site, missed the guns but hit houses nearby. I had a crack with the Bren gun but did not hit anything. Planes too fast.

Friday March 6
We left the barracks in the morning to escape the bombing but nothing happened. I damaged my ankle on motorbike. Hear that our position is hopeless. We left Tjilatjap at 7pm for some place on the coast. Don't think we will make it. Said farewell to Wilf, Padre and rode with the Major to what fate had in store for us. Maybe this will be the last entry in my diary.

Saturday March 7*
What a night. Last night we travelled throughout the night and made the crossroads before the Japs got there. We are now in Tasikmalaya and everything looks hopeless. We blew up our guns yesterday and we are now trying to make

for the mountains. Met the 239 with their guns. Put strong patrols out in the night. The Japanese are expected any minute. We left at midnight. Is there no end to this running away? Something bound to happen soon.

Sunday March 8
What a day. A day that will live in my memory. The Dutch army surrendered and we were left with the baby. We were ordered to fight on but later on the order was countermanded and we made our way to Tjisompet. What a journey and what chaos. I never thought I would live to see this day out.

Monday March 9*
We've surrendered after being on this island for 6 weeks and without even seeing the enemy. So the war is over as far as we are concerned. Just prisoners of war.

Tuesday March 10
We are being treated very well and if rumour is correct we stay here and look after our own administration. It sounds too good to be true.

Wednesday March 11
It is very cold in the evening and have not yet had a good night's sleep for 10 days. I wonder how they are at home. I expect they are very worried. Poor mother, I wish I could cable her.

Thursday March 12
We seem to have settled down very nicely but I think it's too good to last. I have a feeling we will not be long here. What next!

Friday March 13*
A day of rumours, now stated that we stay here but I have my doubts. It's too simple. Grub is still fair. BHQ and RHQ seem to be living in luxury.

Saturday March 14*
If I could be certain that we stay here I could be quite contented. Have started a magazine going. First issue will be next Friday if we are still here. Have now been told we move six miles away. It's a great pity because we've worked darned hard at this place. My foot is giving me trouble. I think I shall have to go quiet for few days.

Sunday March 15
Had our first service as prisoners. It seemed unreal. Another day of rumour and we now await more news of our departure to a prison camp. Visited our supposed new home. It left me cold. We had quite a good concert. We were

aroused at 11.30pm by Major Gaskell and given some bad news – leaving for Batavia in the morning marching all the way. Shaken the boys.

Monday March 16
What a journey and what a day. We arrived at G about 4. Raining in torrents had to sleep out in it for the night. I had a hell of a job finding shelter for the boys.

Tuesday March 17
Rumour says that we will not now march to Batavia but will go by train. After over a week I finally meet the Japanese, the people who we surrendered to. It's a funny war.

Wednesday March 18
What a day. It rains and rains and rains and I get soaked three times, eventually sleeping in Woolsey [sic] car. I am fed up. Issue the boys with rum.

Thursday March 19*
We arrived at [illegible] where we catch train for Batavia maybe. Didn't it rain? It just came down in torrents. We don't know how long we shall be here.

Friday March 20
Still it rains. In the afternoon many rumours where we are going in Batavia. I am not feeling so good.

Saturday March 21
Another Saturday. I wonder how they are at home. I hope they will soon know that I am still alive. I think this war will go on for years. I think we will be kept captives in Batavia and many of us will go down with sickness.

Sunday March 22
Another church service by the Padre. Still no news of moving. Rain still comes every afternoon. Maybe the dry season will soon be here.

Monday March 23
First day not to have rain and also sent letter home to mother and Ken. I wonder when they will get it. Not before July I suppose.

Tuesday March 24
No rain again today. It looks as if the dry season has commenced. Advance party to Batavia leaves on Thursday. We shall probably go Sunday. Feeling ill today. Have not felt worse since been in Java.

Wednesday March 25
Magazine came out today, appears to be a great success. Take poor view of the attitude of officers since our surrender. It seems that the men are completely forgotten.

Thursday March 26
We definitely move on Sunday to Batavia. What next! I think it will be for the worse. The rainy season seems to have finished, now for the heat.

Friday March 27
The boys are going down with fever and sores and bites. One must look after himself in this country. Had a lovely swim in the river. Was really lovely afternoon.

Saturday March 28
Very busy day getting everything ready for the move. Rations are still scarce and the men doing a lot of grumbling. Maybe it will become worse. I hope they are OK at home. I always seem to think of them on Saturday.

Sunday March 29*
Palm Sunday. We left for Batavia at 5.30am, arrived at Batavia 10pm and went to a prison. It was terrible. The RAF were there and they said as we came in, 'God help us'. Now we are prisoners.

Monday March 30*
It is said that we will be here only a few days but I doubt [it]. I think this is our home for a long time. Much to my regret HRH arrived and will be staying with us. Am now in the OM with Wilf.

Tuesday March 31
As I thought, we are staying here and the food is terrible. Rice, rice and more rice. Thank God I can eat some of it. Some of the boys will not eat it. But I am afraid the time will soon come when they will crave for it.

Wednesday April 1
Working parties started today and went to the aerodrome. They came back very tired. We have a wireless and the news is not so good.

Thursday April 2
Another working party went out today. We are lucky to be able to supplement our food with some of our rations otherwise we would be very hungry. I am rather enjoying myself in the mess. Am afraid HRH does not like it.

Friday April 3
I went out on a working party and thought of home most of the time as it was Good Friday. Some of the boys are ill through not eating the rice. You must eat to live.

Saturday April 4
The Japanese had an inspection today. Took wireless, helmets, gasmasks etc. It was all done very nice. My thoughts today are back home. I feel a little miserable. I wonder how long we will be here. Wilf and I weighed ourselves today. Wilf 90kg, 14st 2lbs. Me 84kg, 13stone 5lbs. I have lost little weight so far.

Sunday April 5
Went out to aerodrome once again on working party. Communion was held for the first time in prison. I was very sorry that I missed it. I enjoyed the march to the aerodrome. It's a pleasure to be out of prison.

Monday April 6*
Stayed in prison. Many boys are sick. Hawkins being very ill. It seems pretty hopeless for him. News not too good. I wonder how long we will be prisoners.

Tuesday April 7*
Attended this morning having missed Easter Sunday. A very quiet day. More men sick. I think Charlie Hawkins doesn't want to live. Played cards in the evening.

Wednesday April 8*
Went to the aerodrome today, not so good. Felt very tired and gee was it hot. Poor old Charlie dead. Who next?

Thursday April 9
Went to the drome once again. Blimey it was hot. Had many interesting chats with Wilf, Frank and the boys. More aerial activity today than any day since we've been here. News very bad. Gloom over the prison. Hawkins buried today.

Friday April 10
Had a quiet day in camp. Three RAF boys escape but are captured. Hell of a row. We do not get any rice. It looks as if we may leave here for Formosa. News bad. I hope and pray that the time will soon come when we are released.

Saturday April 11
Not much doing. Stayed in prison. I am feeling a little groggy. All the prison is talking about the escape. The nips say that they will be shot and that the whole

camp will lose 14 days privileges. They started by stopping the concert. I think the time will soon come when we wish that we were with the others.

Sunday April 12*

Went to service and communion this morning. Still feeling groggy. I think I have a fever coming on. Another one of our boys died today. Thompson from C section. He was buried today. Went to bed with temperature 101.

Monday April 13

I had a bad night, have got the squitters. Went four times to the lav in ½hr. Am feeling very groggy. Have not felt as ill for years. My temp is 102. I feel like I am in for a rough time. MO says I must take no food.

Tuesday April 14

Feeling lousy. Temp 102. Thanks to Noel I had aspirin and quinine last night. They seemed to have helped to keep fever down. MO says I'm unlucky. Have got fevers and touch of dysentery.

Wednesday April 15

Feeling better. Thank God. Was getting worried. Temp down to 100. One must keep fit or else.

Thursday April 16

Another bad night. Went to the lav many times and sweated terrifically. Told to sleep outside because nips said they were locking all cells. Am feeling better today and think I have got over the fever. My temp is now 100.
Played bridge in the afternoon with Major G, L Hunt, K Taylor.
News not so good.

Friday April 17

Feeling much better today. Temp down to normal. However had a really bad night. Had to change my pyjamas twice, wet through with sweat. The nips want return of our money, books and clothes. It looks as if they will now take our [illegible]. Played contract with Wilf, Major G and Ken Taylor.

Saturday April 18

A very quiet day. My temp down to normal. Also did not have to get up during the night. Through Nip kindness or heart? [sic] we had our concert, it was not brilliant but had to be curtailed as the nips were taking a roll call at 9.15. It was a b- nuisance. We had to stand for nearly two hours. I wonder if they now know at home that I'm a prisoner.
Poor mother!

Sunday April 19*
Went to service, also communion. Quite a fair number present. Capt Birch comes out of hospital looking very thin but better than when he came in. Now that I'm fit again I must look after myself. I think that I can stick this life for a long time as long as my health stands up.

Monday April 20
Went to the docks on a working party and had a most enjoyable time. Got soap and cigs for the boys. I wonder what will happen when all our surplus grub goes and we are not able to buy anymore.

Tuesday April 21
A very quiet day, not much doing. RW is still sick, also [illegible] and Blakey. They don't seem to improve. B called in the mess, and is extremely pleasant, the big conceited fool. He will have a lot to answer for at the end.

Wednesday April 22
Yesterday was bad day for the boys. The nips stopped buying. I was going on working party but felt lousy and cried off. Have got a hell of a cold and also passed blood when on lav. Put wind up me.

Thursday April 23
A very depressing day. Working party on drome got soaked and had to return. No buying. Noel went down with fever, also Major G. Our surplus rations nearly finished, just 3 more days. Went to lav. Seemed to be ok. NFG.

Friday April 24
Working party went out to drome. No buying. Great disappointment. Have definitely decided to get married if I should return to England. I do wish we could get some books. More men go down sick. NFG.

Saturday April 25
No working party today. Very hot. Played chess and bridge most of the day. Passed a very pleasant hour with Wilf reminiscing on our past exploits. Three years ago today we were playing 7s at Twickenham.
Felt rather miserable at night. Thoughts were of home, wondering how they were. Wilf and I got in rather hot water over the rations. I think we were in the right. I am told that I am pessimistic because I have made up my mind that I am serving a sentence of 500 days. The boys just laugh but I think I will laugh last.

Sunday April 26
Went to communion – quite a large attendance. All privileges are restored and a promise of better food. Working party not allowed to buy.

Monday April 27
Went on a working party with Wilf and had a quite interesting chat with Nip. Hell I've got a fever coming. My temp 101-2. I will be down and out tomorrow.

Tuesday April 28
Really and truly got this cursed fever again. Temp 103. Feeling lousy but have not got diarrhoea like last time. MO says it must take its time.

Wednesday April 29
This is the time when I miss home most of all, when I'm sick. I miss all the little comforts. Temp varying from 100 to 103. I am not feeling at all well, I'm rather constipated. Yesterday Wilf was placed under arrest on a charge. The CO dismissed case today.

Thursday April 30
Yesterday was the Emperor's birthday. Temp 102, still not feeling any better. Am getting worried at my constipation. Will take laxative tomorrow. Feeling tired. NB Had to change three times during the night because of fever.

Friday May 1
Another month starts. I wonder what it holds for us. Temp 101 – 102. Another lad died today making a total of four. Took pills today, no effect.

Saturday May 2
Temp normal in morning. Getting desperate re constipation tried castor oil and other medicines, but no effect. My cheeks are getting sore through being in bed. This is a bl- terrible climate! I wonder how Mother and Dad are and whether Ken is now a proud papa. Poor Mother she must be very worried. I hope I will soon be free to cable her.

Sunday May 3
I think this is the first communion for me to miss. Am feeling much better had the use of my bowels – whoopee. I feel like a new man. I must keep my bowels open. My temp went up once again in the evening.

Monday May 4
I got up today. My temp now normal. Col down with fever, very very few have escaped. If only we could get some decent food we would be able to stand up to this climate.

Tuesday May 5
Feeling rather faint so am taking it very quietly. The men are getting more food from the Dutch people outside. However it's very very small in quantity. I'm feeling very depressed these days.

Wednesday May 6
I feel certain that it will be at least two years before we can hope to be released. It's rather a black outlook but I cannot honestly see what hope there is of getting free before end of next year.

Thursday May 7
Had a hell of a shock when I weighed today. I have lost nearly a stone. I now weigh 78kg, 12st 7lbs. Wilf lost 6lbs now weighs 88, 13st 12lbs. Wilf, Ken and FF go down sick. I think everybody has now been sick.

Friday May 8
I'm still feeling rather weak. The Dutch people continue to send fruit and food to us which is very [illegible]. [Illegible] refuses to do pack drill and is placed in solitary confinement. I hope I do not get another attack of fever. NVG.

Saturday May 9
The food question is becoming acute as our little syndicate have practically eaten all the ration. The Padre has gone sick. We have got a football field just outside the prison and we start playing on it tomorrow. NVG. I am very worried regarding my health. I feel so weak and I'm losing a lot of weight.

Sunday May 10
No communion today because the Padre is sick. We had a full parade this morning for the camp commandant and stood in the sun for over an hour. I went out on working party and got nothing. We are all feeling very hungry and are all losing weight. NFG.

Monday May 11
I went out on a working party but got nothing to eat because we were only on half day. I still feel weak. I think HRH wants to get the officers out of here should the Aussies leave prison. NG.

Tuesday May 12
A nasty shock today we are moving from here on Thursday. Nobody can understand reason for move, nobody knows where we are going. I am very sorry to leave the prison because I think we will have a much worse place.

Wednesday May 13*
Unlucky day. I played football and got nasty scrape on my knee. We ate and ate all we could and went to bed feeling very full but sad. It seems that we will be going to a much worse place called Priok, a mosquito infected area. I think I will be separated from Wilf and co.

Thursday May 14
We hear that we move at 1 o'clock, going by train. What next? We arrived at Priok at 6pm and met most of the regt. The prison camp is more open than the jail but I'm afraid we are not going to enjoy this place as much as the jail.

Friday May 15
The first night was lousy and also the first day. The rice is much better but very much less and the food is less than we had at the jail.

Saturday May 16
What a night last night. We were up nearly all night with the Nips taking a roll call. The food is very bad compared with the prison and at the moment I prefer the prison. The sanitary arrangements are ghastly. I'm much afraid of dysentery. The Nips here are not as friendly as the jail. NG.

Sunday May 17
Had nothing but parades all day long. Had no chance to go to communion. My knee which I cut on the 13th playing football is very painful and turned septic. I have Bert Evans sleeping with me.

Monday May 18
We have been 50 days in Batavia and the boys are looking the worse for wear. Black market is prevalent in this camp and buying so very expensive. My knee is very painful. Wilf and I have managed to get some [illegible].

Tuesday May 19*
The food is not so good here as the prison and working parties going out to the docks have to work like hell. I do hope and pray that we can keep down this epidemic of dysentery. My knee is getting worse.

Wednesday May 20
Have had a terrific week and have not had a moment of rest. I think we will start offensive in Europe within the next 10 days. I do hope the war will soon end.

Thursday May 21
Had a rugger match this evening but did not take part owing to my knee. I think I will like this place except the sanitary arrangements are bad.

Friday May 22
My knee is still bad and I think I shall have to lay up. I have now a lump in my groin. Food is much better but not so much.

Saturday May 23*
My knee has got considerably worse and I have decided to lay up. Doc Lloyd's put some special treatment on it and I've left it for 48hrs. I do hope it will soon get better. Whit Saturday. My thoughts are of home and of the good times that we had on Whitsun. I get my Nip number and the number adds to 13. I do not like the number. NVG.

Sunday May 24*
I could not manage to go to church or communion. My knee very painful. Another fellow died here today, total of eight, heard that Stan Street was dead. Hope it's not true. I am certain that we will be prisoners for at least 18 months. I dreamt Mother was dead and it made me feel very sad.

Monday May 25
So this Whit Monday my mind goes back to last Whitsun at Nottingham. What a change in a year. The weather today is typical Whitsun weather at home. My knee is still painful but I think Doc Lloyd is doing his stuff.

Tuesday May 26
My knee is better. Another fellow dead. This dysentery is getting serious. I am afraid we will lose a lot of men if it's not immediately stamped down.

Wednesday May 27*
Another one of our boys died in hospital at Tasikmalaya. Poor old Stan Street. It's very sad when you hear of someone dying who you know very well. I am still laid up with my knee.

Thursday May 28
Had a good night last night when we had a debate – very interesting. My knee is very much better. Another death occurred today. It's very very serious this

dysentery. I think we are in for a very rough time and many good people will die with this disease. I pray to God that I will come out safely.

Friday May 29

My knee much better, will be able to walk on it tomorrow. Bad news re dysentery. It seems that 710 are affected. Stated that 75% of camp will be wiped out if we don't get it under control. I am very worried.

Saturday May 30

The dysentery position becomes more serious. Have a shock when I find I have a touch of diarrhoea. I feel rather shaky and am worried. The camp played its first league match tonight and won 4-2, Wilf scoring the lot. I do hope that I will be spared to go home to Mother and Dad. That is all that I am living for. What a grand day it will be when peace is signed. I do hope and pray that the day of release will soon come.

Sunday May 31

Went to early communion. Not many present. My knee is much better also had no trouble with my tummy. Went to service in the evening, did not think much of it.

Monday June 1, 1942

My knee is much better but my toes are really bad. I am still unfit for duty and feel rather weak after a week in bed. Maybe I will get stronger. NVG.

Tuesday June 2

Toes are still sore. Doc did his stuff on them today so am hoping that they will soon be better. What a waste of time this life is.

Wednesday June 3

Had a long chat with Wilf and came to the conclusion that prison life makes a man forget all his principles. He becomes mean and selfish. Very very few people are able to rise above it. It makes one feel very miserable. Wilf and I wonder what will be the result of all this.

Thursday June 4*

Toes and knee better. Called on 241 and had a chat about old times with Griff, Allan and Ted. Another death from dysentery today. It appears that the MO has got down to the job because there are fewer people down.

Friday June 5

Six months ago was in England on the eve of our departure. I am afraid it will be another 18 months before any of us return home. I wonder how many of us will survive.

Saturday June 6
We played 239 at soccer and won 3-0. I am having a crack at some more food but it costs too much. This selling of men's food is terrible. It should be stopped. Dysentery down from 80 to 18. Am now feeling much better. Knee and toes properly healed. A rather heated debate last night on whether England will be a better place to live in after the war. I can't see how we can hope it to be.

Sunday June 7
Went to early communion. Very few present. It's rather funny that we don't notice the heat but it's probably 90 in the shade. I wonder if Mother and Dad are healthy. I do hope they are well and not worrying over me. Lovely tea, boiled some potatoes that I had from Wilf.

Monday June 8*
Ice-cream good but must not be too optimistic. Long argument re what we should do to Germany after the war. I think we should spilt the country up and put a government in charge of the state. I think we will be here at least another 12 months.

Tuesday June 9
Ice-cream fairly good but not as good as yesterday. Wilf has made contact re food. It looks good to me, had oranges and a real luxury – a bar of chocolate! I was hungry last night. I don't think I've been so hungry in all my life.

Wednesday June 10
I did not play again this evening much to the CO's disgust. However we won but it was a very poor game. Doc Lloyd has gone down with a sceptic throat, he looks rather groggy.

Thursday June 11
I miss communion this morning because of the Col's parade. It seems very stupid to have a parade in a POW camp. The "old boy" was pleased so everything was ok. Wilf is all for moving. I'm doing my best to get it cleared.

Friday June 12
A very quiet day. Ice-cream not so good. Boys are getting depressed. Money is now getting short amongst the officers. My foot is once again bad. Doc Lloyd is still rather ill.

Saturday June 13

I must say that I feel that we are here for a long time and am feeling today a little depressed. Two of the boys were caught last night pinching from the Nips. Lucky for them our own people spotted them. We played soccer match this evening and drew 2-2 after a very hectic game. Another death today from malaria. My toe is very painful.

Sunday June 14

No communion today because the two Padres thought it was too wet! People wonder why the churches are empty! We honoured the King's birthday by singing God Save the King and giving three cheers. Ice-cream NSG.

Monday June 15

Wilf is now laid up with bad foot through football on Saturday. The Nips are annoyed over yesterday's celebrations and have cancelled all meetings until further notice. My toe is still bad.

Tuesday June 16

HRH spoke to me today re my presence in the OM. Said I must not visit same. He also told me that if there had been any vacancy I should have had a commission. The B- liar. He promised that I should be commissioned as soon as there was vacancy.

Wednesday June 17

I'm keeping well away from HRH. All the old 242 think he's a perfect -. I shall build a small place for me to see the boys privately. Rugger match this evening. Ice-cream fair.

Thursday June 18

The Nips sprung a surprise visit to 1,2,3 camps and carried out a search for arms. Tobacco came in today and the boys were able to buy it at 22 cents an ounce. My toes are still sore, so also is Wilf's foot. Got some "dope" from Wilf. Ice-cream bad.

Friday June 19

The more I see of HRH the more I dislike the man however he's more to be pitied than hated because if ever a man is living in a fool's paradise he is. Ice-cream bad. The weather is much cooler.

Saturday June 20

Another Saturday. I wonder how many more we will have in captivity. My toes are becoming better. I am determined not to be depressed and counting all my blessings which are many. I am starting my personal record of my experience since joining up.

Sunday June 21
Went to communion this morning and we had one of [illegible]'s special church parades. Very dull day. I am noticing that I am apt to get rather short-tempered. I must try and stop it because one must not grumble to the men.

Monday June 22
A year today Russia entered the war. I was at Nottingham. We had issue of sugar. Our camp only done this evening. Wilf was not fit. I hear that dysentery is on the increase. I think it will be ever with us.

Tuesday June 23
I saw today a wonderful performance of Merchant of Venice given by the POWs. It was a really good show and held the audience for two and a half hours. Rice is getting scarce and our rations are very small. Noel James was taken into hospital with dysentery.

Wednesday June 24
Went to communion, only five present. Weighed myself today and was agreeably surprised. Found that I had gained 5lbs. Weighed 81kg, 12stone 11lbs. Am now buying sugar on the camp at the correct price.

Thursday June 25
Played soccer this afternoon in goal. And scraped both knees once again. I hope they won't turn septic. Nasty incident on parade very nearby me. Managed by a little tact to squash same. Ice-cream bad.

Friday June 26
Dysentery on the increase. Another death this evening. I thought one could now be cured. I was wrong. Hell of a fuss about agreeing document swearing allegiance to the Nips. I would not sign anything unless threatened to be shot. I bet we all sign within a week.

Saturday June 27*
Saw a few guns go by today and within 10 minutes they were having a go. Seemed to be something like French.75. I cannot see how we can possibly hope to be out of here for another 12 months. Fryett seems to think Sept. I feel rather depressed over the war but feel certain that we will push through. The singing this evening made me think of home. Poor Mother, I do hope and pray she is well.

Sunday June 28*
I gave up tobacco. Went to communion today. Also two other services. HRH birthday. I had a drink with him, a small tot of whiskey. I think he is getting worse. He told a deputation that he only had 7G left and he spent 6G on a hat while I was with him.

Monday June 29
We were able to buy tinned fish, tobacco, pepper, salt, curry and coffee. I bought coffee, curry and salt. The Nips have now stopped the buying because of our refusal to sign the form swearing allegiance to the Emperor.

Tuesday June 30
Ice-cream has been very bad for two days. Hope it will soon change. Another death in Batavia hospital. Dysentery is still on the increase and malaria will be very prevalent in the next five weeks and can easily become fatal.

Wednesday July 1
Ice-cream bad and food problem is becoming very acute. A rice shortage and today more than 50 men went short. Welsh rugger trial this evening. Wilf nor I played. Not much talent. I wonder how they are all in Cardiff. They must be very worried. Poor Mother.

Thursday July 2
I slept very badly last night. I think I had a few mosies in my net. Played soccer for the camp (my first league game) and beat number 3 camp 4-0. I did not enjoy the game. I lost my gold identity disc. Am feeling very despondent. I do hope I will find it.

Friday July 3
Good news. I found my disc. I am very relieved. Another death. Chap died suddenly last night while walking to his bed. Must have been heart. Have started new abode doubt whether I will use it. Sorry to leave Bert.

Saturday July 4
Had our concert this evening. Not much of a success. Had a hell of a row with Wilf re chess. I thought he was most unreasonable in his demands. Will see the Colonel about it.
Am not sleeping too well these nights. Am afraid some of the boys are getting depressed. I keep on telling them it might be worse and that I'd rather be here than Germany but would I?

Sunday July 5
Went to communion in the morning, only five present. Terrible storm during the night. Consternation in the camp. Nips threatened to shoot anyone if did not sign form re obedience. 1,2,3 camp have signed. HRH and all the Colonels were the first to sign. Ordered to sign by Major Gaskell.

Monday July 6
Well we all signed a form today swearing obedience to Nippon Gov. It was humiliating. I wonder what it portends. It may be nothing. The food is getting scarcer and I am feeling hungrier. My funds are running low. Ice-cream not so good.

Tuesday July 7
It may be coincidence and it may not but they took 62 malaria and dysentery cases from here today and sent them to hospital in Batavia. The sickness in the camp is increasing. Sores and boils are very prevalent. I don't think we will be out of here for at least a year.

Wednesday July 8
Have now made it up with Wilf and had a good laugh. Col sick but not serious. Large number of Nip generals visit camp today. Haven't been to lav for four days, must do something about it. Am feeling hungrier.

Thursday July 9
Saw Padre last night re confirmation. He said that he would take Wilf and I together. Told today that we have been allowed privileges of buying eggs and going swimming because we are the best disciplined camp in the prison. Nice work, no doubt we will get our legs pulled but we have got the goods.

Friday July 10*
Played chess tournament yesterday. Won my game but we lost match against camp 7. Ice-cream bad. My toes are bad and have now got Singapore toes. Eggs supplied today. We go bathing tomorrow. I wonder how they are at home. I wish we could hear from them.

Saturday July 11
Today was grand. I spent one golden hour swimming and sunbathing. It was the most enjoyable hour spent on the island during the day. I hope we will soon go again. League match cancelled this evening because of sickness in number 10 camp. The 77th played the 6th and won 4-2. Felt very tired in the evening. A day that will linger in my memory.

Sunday July 12
Went to communion. A very good sermon by the Padre. I feel a bit stiff after yesterday's swim. Ice-cream fair. Dysentery and malaria are both on the increase. Some of the boys look really ill. I do hope and pray that with God's help I will keep my health.

Monday July 13
Two more deaths today. It makes one think maybe you will be the next if it is God's will. Sugar and bread sold today. Wilf and I weighed today. W 87kg, me 81kg without boots and [illegible].

Tuesday July 14
Ice-cream bad and lads becoming depressed. Many are now agreeing with me that it will be another year before we get free. Rice being cut down, quality instead of quantity. We won 7-0 this evening. Did not play toes are really bad.

Wednesday July 15
60 coffins arrive in camp today. I suppose there's nothing like being prepared. My toe is bad. I have to lay up. Rice is becoming very short and today we only had two meals. All games stopped because of food shortage. Ice-cream bad. We've refused to go on working parties but five men later agreed to go.

Thursday July 16
My toe is bad and I have to lay up. Most annoying. Last night's speech by the Colonel was ridiculous re working parties. Corned beef 95 cents, marg 55, jam 25, on sale but very few buy because little money. Feeling slightly miserable. I wonder how long this cursed war will last.

Friday July 17
Still laying up with my toe which is extremely painful. Have also got a frightful cold. Eggs again on sale. Nasty incident at docks through some of the boys stealing. Deserve all they got. Debate rugger v soccer. I did not go.

Saturday July 18
The weather still is hot but not too oppressing, in fact I think the climate could be a lot worse. My toe is still very sore, swollen and septic. Went to the show, had a good turn-out. HRH taken ill, slight appendix trouble. The boys go bathing again and have a whale of a time. Unfortunately I could not go because of my toes. Ice-cream not very good. I do hope and pray that they are all well at home and that they are not too worried.

Sunday July 19
Went to early communion, just managed to hobble along. It's a delightful day just like English summer. Had quite a long chat with the major. I must say that we are being well treated by the Nips. I keep on telling the chaps it might be a lot worse. NB.

Monday July 20*
I've got a terrific cold. I hope and pray that it will not turn to malaria. The JJ out today and is quite good. Will not be able to play in England v Wales rugger match on Wednesday. Pity. Am in mock trial.

Tuesday July 21
Have still got a lousy cold and my toe is still painful. Played in chess match, won my game. We also won the match. Big parade on Saturday. It makes one very sick, such baloney!

Wednesday July 22
Terrible night last night. Rain came down in torrents and I got soaked. Did not get to sleep til 3am. Felt lousy throughout the day. My cold is no better. Rugger match cancelled, also mock trial. I wonder how dear old 'Jo' is keeping.

Thursday July 23*
Another terrible storm last night but rain did not come through. My cold appears to be better, very little improvement in the toe. Phew it's hot and close. I'm worried about home and what they are thinking after hearing swen*[sic]. Ice-cream bad. I wonder if I shall ever see home again. Sad thoughts.

Friday July 24*
Another death today this time from our own battery – Knight. Malaria victim. Everyone preparing for big parade tomorrow. All bull!! I've still got a chill, am rather worried. My toe is much better.

Saturday July 25
Old Jo's birthday. I wonder how he is and how his baby and Joyce are keeping. My thoughts are full of home today. I think I will write a letter to Jo wishing him many happy returns of the day. I wonder if I will see him again. I do hope and pray that I will. We played number 10 this evening and won 1-0. Rather rough. My toe is better. Bad cold. Ice-cream good.

Sunday July 26*
Went to communion and attended the dedication of the new church called St George. I feared that I would not see it but I am grateful to God that I am able

to do so. Maybe I lacked faith but I feel that I now have faith more than ever. Stayed up til gone midnight with Wilf and [illegible].

Monday July 27
Went to the lats today. Have still got lousy cold. 77th played 6th AA and won 2-1. A very enjoyable game. [Illegible sentence]. New Jap Commandant arriving, seems to be ok. NF.

Tuesday July 28
Still have a cold and my toe is still bad. Six of the seven MOs are sick so 200 sick in hospital are going to Batavia. I read a book today and was struck by the word fortitude and that's what we must have. NF.

Wednesday July 29
The days are becoming very boring with nothing to do. Rugger match again cancelled. Mock trial held in the evening and was quite a success. Wilf, Frank and I took part. Good fun. Wilf went on a working party and brought back some bread, giving me one loaf.

Thursday July 30
Another visit by big Nip general. Rumour in camp that we will be put on island south of Java. All baloney. Eggs and soap for sale this evening. My toes are getting better, still have a bad throat. But my [illegible] noticed how thin my blood has become.

Friday July 31
Rumour continues but I turn a deaf ear. I only wish the boys would do the same. Sugar and eggs for sale. I manage to get two eggs but no sugar. My cold is still bad but toes seem to be improving.

Saturday August 1
Went to the lats. Had a real clean out. Rumours very strong re leaving island. Of course they are all baloney, presumably all internees will be leaving on 14th August. Macbeth was played today. Not as good as Merchant of Venice. Wilf took part of King Duncan. Played number 8 and drew. I could not play owing to my toes. I cannot get rid of my cold.
I wonder if Jo has gone home for Bank Holiday. I hope that Mother and Dad are feeling ok.

Sunday August 2*
Went to early communion. Padre Phillips preached a good sermon in the morning. No doubt the weather is becoming warmer, temp is now over 100 in

the shade. We had 25 cigars, also a darn good tea. Went to church again in the evening and then read some old letters.

Monday August 3
Thought of home all day today. I wonder if they are all well at home. I do hope they will soon get news of me. My toes are now ok. Still have a cold and a stiff neck. NFG.

Tuesday August 4
Another death today from bronchial pneumonia. He was playing football last week, poor lad. Practised air-raid warning lasting for an hour. NF.

Wednesday August 5
Went to the lats today. Another practice raid alarm. My toes are nearly ok but my cold is still hanging on. Nip hospital ship arrived with wounded. If only we could read the future. I can see no hope of an early release and we still have another 350 days to make our 500 as a POW.

Thursday August 6
Went to communion only six present again today. Weighed myself in the morning. Am now 82kg without boots etc. 13st 3lbs. Three years today I was called up. I wonder how much longer. Played camp 1 and won 2-0. I played and damaged my foot again. We now have one more match to play, number 9, and if we win we become champions.

Friday August 7
My foot and knee are now bad through last night's match. Will probably be a few weeks. What a life. Managed to hobble to a concert at number 1 camp in the evening. Excellent show. Strong rumours that we are moving – NVB.

Saturday August 8*
My foot is badly swollen but have Ernie Curtis massaging it twice a day and it seems to be doing some good. Concert in our camp last night was poor. Match played this evening resulting that our camp or 9 must win outright to win championship. Rumour is still strong that we will shortly leave this camp. I think we will.

Sunday August 9
Went to communion but not to morning service. Had my foot massaged in the morning. Some good ice-cream. I think we will be POW for at least a year. I am worried about my pains in my head. I wish I knew what they were. I don't think I will be fit for Thursday night.

Monday August 10*
Another visit from a big Nip general. All building stopped. It looks as if we will be moved shortly. Nip tells Frank big battle in Pacific, we lose many ships. Still have pain in my head. Friday night is the night for the big match. Went to lats.

Tuesday August 11
I am feeling a trifle depressed but I try and remember that there are thousands worse off. I keep on wondering whether I shall ever see home again. I do hope and pray that I will be spared. Went to lats.

Wednesday August 12
Am feeling a trifle fed up and not so good. I hope I'm not sickening for something. 77th played the rest and drew 1-1. Rumours still going around that we shall soon be leaving. Played chess match and won my game.

Thursday August 13
My unlucky day maybe. The mosquitoes are becoming very prevalent. There are hundreds of them. This camp will be full up very soon with malaria. I'm sure of this. The weather becoming warmer. One egg issued and pineapples for sale. Tomorrow night's match cancelled.

Friday August 14
My foot is much better. Think I would have been fit if match had been on. 77th played rest and won 3-2. Good game. Ice-cream fair. Went for a swim and thoroughly enjoyed it. This was the second I've had. Bought apples and oranges.

Saturday August 15
I thought we might of [sic] left this camp by now – still there's plenty of time. Air-raid practice alarms are becoming a nuisance. Light went out tonight at 8.30 and did not come on again. Many fellows are sick, mostly with sores. I wonder how they are at home. I often think of my dear Mother. How she must be worrying with no news from me.

Sunday August 16
Went to communion early. Morning church cancelled because of practice raid warning. Have been told that we must play final match tomorrow night or lose the points. Went to church in the evening. Another raid warning 9.30pm. My one toe is still sore. Went to lats. NF.

Monday August 17
The final match of the league ended tonight in a draw 0-0. It was a very even game. I played but had few shots to deal with. Went to the lat. Les Hunt is sick.

I think it is malaria. We were ill together at the jail. I wonder?

Tuesday August 18
Am now completely out of sugar. Makes a big difference to the eating of rice. Saw big flight of Nip bombers today – looks rather significant. Les Hunt is in a high-fever. It's amazing how soon you go down. My new abode is nearly finished.

Wednesday August 19
We had eggs today. Much against my wish I played rugger for Wales against England. We won 8-0. I injured my knee and toes again. I played centre ¾. Did not do much. NVG. The match was a complete flop.

Thursday August 20
My knee is gone again after last night's match. A year ago today we left Cardiff for Frome. What a contrast today and a year ago. We were all excited and wondering where we were going. Today all excitement gone and we have lost many friends.

Friday August 21
Les Hunt taken to hospital last night. He certainly looks groggy. Ice-cream very good. Boys becoming resigned for at least another six months. My knee is sore. I will probably move into my new home next week.

Saturday August 22
My knee is sore but I am now wearing boots. If I keep fit I may go out on working parties. I wonder how they are at home and if they are all alive and well. Poor Mother she must be worrying herself to death. Many of the boys are down with malaria. The mosies are becoming worse. Ice-cream fair. I think death will increase in the camp with the malaria because we are all becoming weaker.

Sunday August 23
Went to early communion and also church at 10am. A very good address by the Padre. Wilf and I weighed. Wilf 88.6kg. (14st). Me 83kg (13st 4lbs) with boots on. It's becoming hotter. I am afraid we have yet to have the bad moments.

Monday August 24
My bed full of bugs so went bug hunting. I must try and get in my new home. We played number 2 for the final this evening and drew 1-1. I made a big mistake and let in a soft goal. Wilf was badly fouled on umpteen occasions. Ref was bad. Number 5 camp not popular.

Tuesday August 25
Very fed up over last night's match. We now play number 9 Thursday. Another death today – only in hospital 2hrs. Played number 1 in chess and lost. I lost my first match and played last night's referee – such is fate. NF.

Wednesday August 26
Played Scotland and Ireland and drew 3-3. Wilf did not play. Will have to play them again. My first game in the pack. Very depressed this morning. Feeling cold and temp 82 in the shade! Another death today. Malaria is becoming worse.

Thursday August 27
My bed made today. First time since Mar 1 that I have slept on anything but boards and concrete. Another death today from malaria all from number 3 camp. Situation becoming serious and alarming. Two men got out of camp and were captured by wogs. We were out at 12 o'clock for roll call. Ice-cream good.

Friday August 28
The two fellows who escaped are not in jail. The Major got five days solitary and the camp got five days working parties. A grand concert, night really first class. Nips cutting down rations and stopping rugger. NG.

Saturday August 29
Ice-cream good. We played number 9 camp (241) in the final this evening and got a terrific hiding losing 4-0. This is the first match which we have lost. We were simply outclassed. I do not think I was to blame, maybe others do. L Hunt seems to be better so does [illegible]. I am moving tomorrow to my new home. I feel sorry to leave Bert – he's not a bad sort. His only fault he's too military for me.

Sunday August 30
Went to communion 8am and also morning service. Today I moved into my new home. It's a most delightful and cosy room. I only wish Mother could see it. The Colonel spent the afternoon in it with me and later on Wilf came to tea, providing the goods to provide a really good tea. A very happy day.

Monday August 31
I slept very well last night in my new abode. I am having pains in my back due to my kidneys and lack of exercise. Another death today making six deaths in five days. It certainly makes you think and thank God for your own good health. NVG.

Tuesday September 1
So another month has gone. How many more before we are released? Wales play the rest on Saturday. Wilf playing. I only wish Mother could see me in my new home. I think she would weep.

Wednesday September 2
Malaria and dysentery on the increase. I am afraid we will lose a lot more men before we get out of here. Number 9 and number 2 played for the league final and drew. But number 9 went on top. Number 2 runner-up. Own camp being third. Went to lats.

Thursday September 3
Went to early communion, about 20 present. Another death today from dysentery. He was only ill for one day and was from the 240 battery. He had never been ill previously. Poor boy. Went for a bathe. It was so invigorating. Another death. Two today. It's serious.

Friday September 4*
My little home is becoming popular. Alan R Smith, Wilf, J Rutter, Ken V and others have dropped in for a game of chess, cards and a chat. We played infantry in first round of the cup and lost 4-3. I played a lousy game. Rugger international match cancelled for tomorrow night.

Saturday September 5
Phew! It's becoming hotter and hotter. The temp is over 100 in the shade. I played rugger in the evening for Wales against a scratch side winning 5-0. Wilf did not play. I'm firmly convinced that the European war will be finished before this one and that we will not get released til July 1943.

Sunday September 6
Went to early communion and also to 10 o'clock church. We have now been exactly half a year prisoners of war. What has the next six months in store for us? Had a great tea. Alan Smith, Griff Davies and Wilf came to my abode and we had eggs, sausage roll, onion rice. It was the best meal I have had since POW.

Monday September 7/ Tuesday September 8
It's hotter and hotter. Slept well last night despite attack of indigestion through my tea. I've got all my photos up on the wall. They help me to live again in my memory those wonderful times. I have Mother's photo over my mirror so that every morning when I arise I say good morning Mother. I do hope and pray that I will soon see her once again. I had a lovely swim yesterday and we had a wonderful concert in the camp this evening. It was great. Went to the lats.

Wednesday September 9
I am having many visitors to my new home and it is becoming a popular rendezvous. I think it is the best billet in the camp and its great charm is its privacy.

Thursday September 10
The boys are becoming depressed and are making up their minds that our release from POW will be some time. In fact my 500 days is not laughed at as it was when I first said that we would be prisoners for that length of time.

Friday September 11
Have now got a septic toe, very painful. Cookhouse stores again broken into. Nips taken strong action. Boys are very depressed and fed up. I'm trying hard to keep up their spirits. I count their blessings. Had Les Hunt to tea, eggs and milk.

*Saturday September 12**
We are becoming more than ever resigned to the fact that it will be a long time before we are released. I say good morning to Mother every morning when I get up and see her photo in front of me. It makes me feel better. We played sapper row and lost 2. Not a bad game.

*Sunday September 13**
Went to lats. Went to early communion and morning service. Les Hunt came to tea. Sensation. Number 2 -8 camps to move out at 7am tomorrow. Destination unknown and nobody is certain if they will come back. Probably we will all go sooner or later.

Monday September 14
Went to lats. WP left at 5am. I went on WP 10.30am. First time for me to leave the camp for four months. Worked very hard. Nips very active shipping booty from the island. Return to camp 3pm. Very tired but feeling grand, thank God! Wilf was on the same WP. No news where 500 went. NF.

*Tuesday September 15**
We hear today that we are going to be paid for WP – 10 cent a day. No news of 500. Rumours say Singapore, Sumatra? I think still on Java. We may be allowed to write home soon. I wonder if they know at home that I am POW. We are having new numbers. My new number adds up to 13 same as my old one still unlucky.

Wednesday September 16
A lot of movement going on with the Nips. They are probably preparing for attack on some new places.

Thursday September 17
Went for bathe, got inoculated and played football all in one afternoon. I got a few nasty cracks playing in goal. The rainy season is approaching as we are now having rain in the afternoon. We are definitely getting paid. Rugger international on Sat.

Friday September 18
My feet are sore after yesterday. I see a lot of Alan, Griff and Wilf and we are together quite often, much to HRH disgust. We got paid today but I did not receive a sou. Wilf feeling pretty low, also general feeling of pessimism in the camp.

Saturday September 19*
Very warm. Went to the lats. Played rugger in the evening for Wales against the rest. We won 7-3. Wooller dropping a goal last minute. It was the best game of rugger seen on this ground. We had a big parade in the morning and were inspected by Col Lane who was very pleasant with the parade.

Sunday September 20
Went to early communion and also morning church. New guard take over from old guard who have not been as bad. Alan, Griff and Wilf came to tea today and thanks to Alan we had the best meal yet in the camp. New guard are not so good.

Monday September 21
This new guard are very annoying and are making our life miserable. We had a parade for the new Nip commandant. Another 500 are moving on Wednesday. Lights went out at 10.30 tonight and have to be out at 10 tomorrow night. This lousy guard.

Tuesday September 22*
500 moved off today at 7pm. Number of friends gone. Camp becoming desolate. Feeling acute depression. It appears that this camp will be next to be spilt up and sent away. Sad thoughts. Colonel ill, suspected appendix going to Batavia.

Wednesday September 23
Colonel did not go to Batavia, feeling better. The camp looks more deserted. A good concert in the camp this evening. Nips behaving better. Went for a bathe. All hair must be shaved from head at once. Wilf and I had long chat in the evening, rather pessimistic.

Thursday September 24
This is the 200th day we've been POW. I do not think we will be out for another year. Weighed today. Me 85kg, 13st 7lbs. Wilf 89kg. 14st 1lb. Wilf's wedding anniversary. I wonder where we will be in a year's time. I think we will be moving in a few days time for better or worse.

Friday September 25*
Rumoured that the boys have gone to Borneo – not so good. I am dreading the day when we have to split up. I can't make up my mind whether I want to stay or go. Wilf, Les Hunt and Frank had a long chat in the evening.

Saturday September 26
Went to lats. Feeling rather depressed and so are the rest of the boys. This moving business is getting the boys down. Wonder if this camp will move. Personally I think that we will be from here next week. My 500 days imprisonment forecast looks as if I was optimistic. Wilf, Les Hunt and Frank spent the evening playing cards and chatting. Dysentery on the increase. Poor Jack Lewis went to hospital today.

Sunday September 27
Went to early communion and morning service. I am now going for a bathe every afternoon with Wilf and Alan. We have great fun in the water with a football.
I wonder how they are at home. I do hope and pray that they are well and that the day will soon come when we will be united once again.

Monday September 28*
I am now preparing for a move at any moment. I have got a touch of Java balls. This bathing in the afternoon is great fun. The boys are earning about 20 to 30 cents a week. I am not going out so I'm not getting a cent.

Tuesday September 29
Well still no news of moving, though we will be/are prepared for it at any moment. It's amazing how everybody has become so pessimistic, no doubt due to lack of news. I would give anything to hear from home.

Wednesday September 30
Life is made easier in this camp when you have such good companions as Wilf, Alan, Griff, Ken, Frank, Noel and all the remainder of the 242. Good news for officers who are getting paid. 450 Aussies arriving tomorrow.

Thursday October 1
900 Aussies arrived today from Timor. They looked rather rough but seemed to be a rather pleasant lot. Had some good fun bathing and spent some time in number 9 camp with Alan and Griff. Received my second inoculation.

Friday October 2
The Aussies settled down very well. Wilf got a goat yesterday and I had a little share of the stew. I was rather disappointed over the whole affair.

Saturday October 3*
Nips have got a bee in their bonnet re news and the whole news position is grave. Rumour of a plague in Badong have not been confirmed, thank God. Number 9 won the knock-out cup. Now that the officers are getting paid I hope I will be able to borrow some money. Have now got into habit of late nights through Wilf and Les Hunt coming down for a yarn. Still sore about the goat.

Sunday October 4
Went to communion but not to morning service owing to extra duties through taking over RSM. Another death today, a chap dropping dead in Number 3 camp. Many rumours about the war but none authentic. Lovely in the sea. Up til midnight chatting to Wilf, Frank and Les.

Monday October 5
Got inoculated for third time in 10 days. This time for bubonic plague. Life is made more pleasant for the chats that I have with the old 242 boys especially Alan, Griff, Wilf, Noel, Ken, Frank, Doc and Geoff. We had heavy rain this evening – damp season commenced?

Tuesday October 6
Not feeling so good today. I think it must be inoculation. My ear is also very painful. Rained again at 6.30pm. Terrific storm. Many boys got soaked. Australian fractured his skull. A very good tea.

Wednesday October 7
Australian dead – who fractured his skull. My ear is painful so do not going swimming or play football against camp 9. We lost 2-1.

Thursday October 8
These Aussies seem to be a very decent crowd. We had concert here this evening, it was not so good as the others. Food seems to be better but it's still not enough. I wonder how's Mother? Does she know that I am POW? I do hope and pray that she is safe.

Friday October 9*
A year ago today we arrived at [illegible] where I spent 10 happy weeks before leaving for this lousy island. Our talks at night are becoming very keen and are most instructive and frank. Received fourth inoculation in 10 days.

Saturday October 10
My ankle is swollen. I suspect beriberi. 500 men are from the jail en route to Japan. I saw many old friends and it was quite a happy party in the evening. Rugger trial but did not play. I do hope we stay here but I'm afraid this month will see us move. I look back on my past life and deplore the time I've wasted.

Sunday October 11*
Went to early communion – most enjoyable. Sermon by Aussie padre. Lads from jail left early. I do hope they arrive safe. Listened to Evensong and felt very homesick. Had long conversation with Wilf, Frank and Dusty Forge on our personal lives.

Monday October 12
I am having trouble with my ankles. They are still swollen and I am feeling very tired. The officers are having only 10G a month which makes it rather hopeless proposition to do any borrowing. I still think we shall move.

Tuesday October 13
Reported sick with my ankles but MO unable to diagnose trouble. Had long chat with HRH who seems to be very distressed and pessimistic. He has got some plan but I think it all baloney. Very good evening.

Wednesday October 14
A very enjoyable swim. I am certain that we will move within a few days. It will be Japan. I wonder how they are at home, they must be worrying a great deal.

Thursday October 15
A hot day and many rumours. I feel certain a move is imminent. Saw Twelfth Night performed by Camp 1. It was brilliant. At last we are losing 30 odd men. Mac Weeks left. Also Les Hunt and Dusty. A sad party this evening.

Friday October 16
A very busy day. 1100 are now leaving the camp and some of our officers will be going. I wonder if Alan, Wilf and Griff will be in our batch. I hope so. Though afraid not.

Saturday October 17
We get lists made out for departure. 4,5 and 9 together. Padre not coming. All 242 boys going. It should not be long. Only 17 left in camp. Pleased that Alan, Griff, Wilf and Frank are all together. I have made up my mind that it's Japan, our destination. That will prolong our stay as POW for at least another 500 days.

Sunday October 18
Went to early communion but not to morning church because of conference called by HRH. Had a very busy day getting parties ready for move. Had Wilf, Griff and Alan to tea. A very excellent meal. We are all fortunate to be in the same party when we move.

Monday October 19
37 men are leaving 240 and the time of their departure draws near. M Mitchell, Fawcett, Probert and [illegible] are all going with second batch. They are moving off with the first batch. Our batch, the third, moving later.

Tuesday October 20
Enjoyable swim. 1 and 2 groups full dress rehearsal, probably moving tomorrow. I am certain it's Japan. We will be moving in a few days. Quiet evening, with Wilf, Alan and Griff.

Wednesday October 21*
Well they left today. Les Hunt and Dusty and over 1,000 others. It was very sad to see so many friends leave. We will be certain to leave within next few days. Enjoyable swim everybody very pessimistic.

Thursday October 22
We hear today that they sailed 9.30am this morning. My contention is that we will all go to Yokohama by easy stages. A good concert at the camp. Frank was very good. Stayed up til 1.30am chatting with Wilf and Frank. Wilf states that we will not be home before '45. I agree with him but did not tell him so.

Friday October 23
My ear is becoming painful. Am now learning to float. A really good supper this evening of goat stew with Wilf, Frank and Bert Evans. Hear that we will not be moving this month and maybe not next.

Saturday October 24
I see the MO about my ear and it appears that I have Singapore ear. No bathing but I go in today but do not enjoy it. We hear today that we will not leave this month and maybe not next.

Sunday October 25
Went to early communion and also to church in the morning. For the first time for many weeks did not go bathing. Had treatment for my bad ear which is very painful. Slept very badly. I have been to the lats three times in three hours, am afraid I might have dysentery. I pray that it is not.

Monday October 26
Today I go out on my first working party from this camp since I have been here and get my leg pulled by Wilf, Alan and Griff. Yesterday 500 Dutch troops came in, not one English. I did not go to the lats.

Tuesday October 27
Am still having treatment for my ears which is very painful. Will not go swimming until they are better. Take poor view of Bert, he is scrounging.

Wednesday October 28
Am not going to bed til past midnight any night through Frank and Wilf arguing. We had a very strong argument this evening re the man who is always [illegible].

Thursday October 29
Went on my second working party today and had a very quiet day. Another death today, a corporal from Number 2 Camp. Wilf, Frank and I have a long chat re a play and have decided to have a shot at writing same.

Friday October 30
The question of a typewriter has arisen. I have decided to sell it but HRH disputes my ownership. Alan, Griff and Wilf and I have a long chat re my next move. It looks as if it's going to be a big row.

Saturday October 31
The 242 in this whole camp played Number 9 and lost 2-1. The typewriter has become a very sore subject and I think it much wiser to drop it altogether.

Sunday November 1
I go to early communion and also to morning church. I hear quite a good sermon by Aussie padre. Alan, Griff and Wilf came in the evening. I went to recital with Griff.

Monday November 2
Went on working party to Coconut Grove, a very easy day. Feeling very tired but still go to bed very late. Alan, Griff and Wilf come in for the evening. Weather very wet.

Tuesday November 3
Go swimming today but my ear is still painful. Many rumours re our departure. I think we will move this month or maybe next week.

Wednesday November 4
A very hot day and my ear is very painful. Had a grand concert in the evening. Fryett excelled himself. Some of his cracks are superb. Thought one was meant for him but Frank said nay. Wilf and I have a good laugh over Frank's recital.

Thursday November 5
On working party to Coconut Grove and got into conversation with a very pleasant Nip officer. It seems that we are bound sooner or later for Tokyo. Have long chat with Wilf and Frank re my supposed hypocrisy which I fully deny.

Friday November 6
We had the first of our three Nip parades. We were on the football field for 2 1/2 hours. About 80 English and American sailors arrived today. Nips will not allow anyone to speak to them though we understand they were sunk in the SA!

Saturday November 7
Went on working party again to CG, was with Wilf and the Nips gave us bread, buttered on both sides! Rained like the devil in the evening. Went to bed earlier than usual. Nips are still keeping strict guard on the new arrivals. Nobody allowed to communicate with them. Good news. We are being allowed to write home.

Sunday November 8
I went to early communion and to morning services and visited Griff who is down with dengue. Am now completely broke and will have to rely on my WP pay to buy extras. Frank is not one of Alan's agents and is doing good. We may write a letter home.

Monday November 9
Went on WP so missed big parade by Nip general which was very good. Rugger match between Aussies but did not play. Alan has settled my little debt and has promised to buy any extras we need as Wilf is also broke.

Tuesday November 10
I wrote home today but am not very hopeful of it being delivered. Griff came over in the evening, first time for six days. He is looking ok. Ice-cream extremely good. I think we will soon be moving.

Wednesday November 11
A year ago today I was in [illegible]. I wonder where I will be in a year's time. Short impressive service in our church. We get several messages from sailors.

Thursday November 12
Went on WP. Pity concert wasn't held last night. Australians are more popular with Nips than we are. We play sapper row, lose 6-2, poor game. Long arguments with Wilf and Frank in the evening re my supposed hypocrisy.

Friday November 13
Friday the 13th and we have done 250 days as POW. Sailors are allowed out today. We find three Welshmen. They have very interesting news. Good concert. Frank very sentimental. I get very annoyed with Wilf over 55 [sic] for the typewriter.

Saturday November 14
We hear from sailors that Ken [illegible] reported killed, also Wilf, but it appears there is some misunderstanding. I borrow 55 from Major. Hand over to Wilf. HRH, on warpath again re my friendship with officers. This time I shall have no option but to tell him that I will not let him interfere with my friendships.

Sunday November 15
Went to early communion and church. I feel very sore over HRH and his action in trying to stop me talking with Alan, Wilf and Griff. Chat at bathing, decided to tell HRH that I will do as I please.

Monday November 16
Went on WP. Very easy. On return from WP many events happen which were very annoying. HRH saw Alan, Griff, etc at Number 9 and said I was not to be seen over with them and he told me that I was not to be seen with Wilf, Alan, Griff or any other officer. I told him I would do as I pleased in POW camp.

Tuesday November 17
Last night's events are sole topic of conversation today and I see no reason why we should not carry on in the same old way except that I will not go to Number 9 Mess in the afternoon.

Wednesday November 18
I understand HRH is going to speak to me again. I hope he does. I'm ready for him. Wilf, Alan and Griff come over and have a chat. Wilf and I play [illegible] and [illegible] at bridge. Ice-cream excellent.

Thursday November 19
Went on WP, a very quiet day. I have further interview with HRH who states that he does not want in any way want to upset my friendship with Alan, Wilf or Griff but I must be discreet. I think he's still just a big - .

Friday November 20
Went on another WP to the [Illegible]. Not too bad was back about 3o'clock. Wilf, Alan and Griff did call though. HRH does not like it. We have some really good ice-cream.

Saturday November 21
No WP. Nippon holiday. Have good day. Swimming and sleeping. Frank, Wilf, Alan and Griff, call in the evening. We have a long chat finishing off with the usual cup of cocoa. We never go [sic] to bed before midnight last night because of wonderful moon.

Sunday November 22
Went to early communion, also morning service. Went swimming and then to Number 9. Had a grand time for tea. I invited to tea a coloured gentleman from US boat that was sunk. He kept Alan, Wilf, Frank, Ken V, Dick B, spellbound for two hours with his chatter. Before eating his tea he said Grace. It made a very strong impression on Frank and I.

Monday November 23
Another death today from the camp making a total of fourteen since we've been here. I go on WP but return early in time for a swim. Lovely moonlit night makes one think of home.

Tuesday November 24
We are going to do a panto. Alan, Wilf, Frank and myself are taking part. It sounds good but Alan has bad toe and for the first time for many moons does not come over for our usual morning chat.

Wednesday November 25
Went on WP. Have quite enjoyable day. I am having a little trouble with my toe. Had usual evening chat - Wilf and Frank going to bed about 1am.

Thursday November 26
Weather becoming very warm. We seem to be able to stand up to any heat. We have potatoes nearly every day and have quite a lot of fun in the evening making up a meal.

Friday November 27
I do not go on WP or swim because of my bad toe. We play Camp 6. Win rather easily. I do not play because of my bad toe. I'm not allowed to go on WP because of tomorrow's parade. I'm very annoyed.

Saturday November 28
The parade and inspection was not quite such a success as the last one. We hear rumours of a move. I am hoping that we will spend xmas in this camp. I wonder how they are at home and whether they know that I'm a POW. I am certain that we will be here after the European war is over.

Sunday November 29
I went to early communion and to church and listened to a jolly good sermon. I was rather impressed. Wilf and I weighed and found that we were still gaining. Me 86kg 13st 10lbs. Wilf 90kg 14st 2lbs. Have Alan, Wilf and Griff in for evening.

Monday November 30
Went on WP. Very quiet, not much doing. The library was opened officially today. I think [it] will be a success. We have about 30 books. I wonder if we will move.

Tuesday December 1
The time does go quickly, it's really amazing that it is nearly 12 months since we started on our ill-fated trip. We shall soon be celebrating our first anniversary as POW.

Wednesday December 2
Went on WP, had quite a good time. My toes are becoming sore. I suspect that I've got a touch of Singapore foot. The weekly concert was not so good. Frank did not perform.

Thursday December 3
A small storm has broken out over next week's concert. It appears that HRH wants to organise his own. The library is extending and have now nearly 60 books. I have a touch of Singapore foot so will not be able to go on any WP.

Friday December 4
A year ago to the day of the week was our last at home. I have a small row with Alan but soon make it up. I was probably at fault. We had a grand meal in the evening. Alan, Griff and Wilf bring in some food and make stunning meal. It was grand.

Saturday December 5
All WP cancelled and we have a Nip roll call during the morning. Rumour states that two men have escaped. Next five days will be practice raid warnings. Roll call is now 7.30 instead of 8. Light went out at 8.30 and made the night very long. Wilf for first time for many weeks was absent from this evening's chat. He played bridge with HRH. I shall tell Alan and Griff in the morning and we'll pull his leg unmercifully.

Sunday December 6
Went to early communion also to church service. I do not think all is well with the panto. My toe is very sore. I will not be able to go on WP for some time. A year ago to the date we embarked on the Warwick Castle. As soon as my foot is better I will start on my little garden.

Monday December 7
Wilf has a really big row with HRH and tells him pretty straight that he dislikes his shouting at officers. HRH threatens to take away his commission. Doc Lloyd arouses Wilf's ire over WP. I must say I think Wilf is correct in his attitude.

Tuesday December 8
Doc Lloyd went out on WP and ordered Wilf to go tomorrow much to Wilf's annoyance. I simply cannot understand why Doc behaves in such a manner. He is certainly becoming very unpopular.

Wednesday December 9
HRH again butts in on my friendship with Wilf and Griff by telling them they must not visit me daily and must confine themselves to occasional visits. That man will certainly have something to answer for when we return home. Concert fair but HRH is pleased.

Thursday December 10
I am very annoyed with HRH and will at the first opportunity tell him what I think of him. I see MO re my toe and get excused duty for seven days. Also Wilf, who damaged his toe last night.

Friday December 11
My toe is rather painful so am taking things easy. Am not doing rehearsal for panto which I hope will be a success but I have my doubts.

Saturday December 12
Got paid today but have heard that I'm not in future being paid for orderly officers' duties. Will see the colonel about it. Frank Fryett seems to have lost his

job with the concert party and was on guard today. I am still taking things very quiet. Am playing more chess and improving my play. I wonder how they are at home and when shall I see them again.

Sunday December 13*
I did not go to communion because of rain and my bad toe. The morning service was cancelled but big parade was held for men to learn Nip orders. It was farcical. I see HRH in the evening and point out to him that I've no money and that I should do OO in order to collect 25 cents.

Monday December 14
Did not start OO today because of Doc Lloyd but will do tomorrow. HRH again speaks to Griff re his calling on me also Alan.

Tuesday December 15
Orderly Officer today for the first time. Brought good news in the evening. 50% in camp allowed to send broadcast message home. I was lucky, managed to send one. I do hope that they will receive it before Xmas.

Wednesday December 16
I handed in all the messages this morning and wondered how many if any would arrive at their destination. I had a big shock today but I suppose I deserved it because I take everything for granted amongst friends.

Thursday December 17
Camp inspection by the Nip commandant. HRH excels himself in saluting the Nips. Am afraid the boys do not respond. Result of inspection Camp 9 best in saluting. No rehearsal today but full rehearsal tomorrow. Did not do OO because of inspection. Long argument with Wilf and Frank.

Friday December 18
Last rehearsal before full dress. I don't think it will be such a good show. Camp 5 plays 4 and wins but are very lucky. My toes are bad and I'm given another seven days excused duties.

Saturday December 19
We had another "do" today. Griff and Alan coming to tea, also Wilf. It was very good. Had to finish tea quickly because of full dress rehearsal which was very poor. Nips have not made any concessions for Xmas day except no working parties. No rice Xmas day.

Sunday December 20
Another day when service is cancelled because of Nippon parade. I go to early communion and just managed to get to the guardroom in time with figures. Went to church in the evening, addressed by Aussie padre.

Monday December 21
Caught [illegible] last night when he fell into a trap set by Fryett and myself. I felt sorry afterwards and have let the matter drop. In doing orderly officer daily I find the job quite agreeable.

Tuesday December 22
Nip general inspects camp. HRH gets frightened over roll call. Aussies receive Xmas messages from home. Lucky devils. Maybe we hear some news from home before next Xmas.

Wednesday December 23
Not much doing. We are going to be allowed to write home for Xmas. I'm not looking forward to Xmas. Concert was good. I wonder where we will be for next Xmas. Hear that Col Lane is leaving us. Not so good.

Thursday December 24*
Christmas Eve. We are being allowed to write a pc and sentence of our own of 20 words. The Nips are giving us soap, sweets, cakes and some clothes for Xmas. Unfortunately not sufficient to go all around. Camp open til 10 o'clock and carols were sung. Felt very depressed and wished that we would not celebrate Xmas. Alan, Wilf and I went to the cookhouse to stir pudding. Wilf was pushed in head first much to our amusement.

Friday December 25
Christmas Day, 1942. The day started badly, the Nips taking a roll call at 8.15 without any warning. I was at communion with many others and we had to chase back to camp. I went to morning service after breakfast which consisted of eggs, jam and rice. After the service we had grand sports meeting and the morning was very enjoyable. Then came the Xmas dinner, officers serving, sergeants collecting from cookhouse. What a meal. Stew, rice with vitamins (A, B etc), Xmas pudding, sauce, coffee with sugar. It was grand. There was much joking and fun serving it out. The Xmas dinner was better than last year. In the afternoon went swimming and most of the officers got ducked in [by] their own camps. I did not escape, it was all good fun. Tea was another excellent meal, followed by football match. Brit v Dutch, result 1-1. Went visiting in the evening, saw Alan, Griff and the rest of the boys from no9. It was excellent day and everybody enjoyed themselves including the Nips who must have thought we were mad.

Saturday December 26

Boxing Day. Yesterday was a red letter day and everybody happy. HRH is down with damaged ankle through showing off during yesterday's festivities. The panto was put on this evening but was not a great success which was not surprising. However it will be something for the boys to talk about. Frank Fryett has collected nearly 150 Gilders for the hospital which is a splendid effort on his part. So ended Xmas 1942 and a much happier Xmas than 1941. I hope that 43 will be even better than any previous Xmases and that we will be free.

Sunday December 27

Went to communion. No church service because of Nip parade. Went swimming, do not feel so good. Aussies leaving end of the week. It looks as if we will soon follow. I hope not. Went to bed earlier than usual after writing my pc home. Feel a little out of sorts.

Monday December 28

All pcs in Jap hands. Hope they will get home safely. Panto in our camp this evening was not so bad. Most of the boys enjoyed it. Am not feeling so good. Maybe it's the weather which is b- warm. Col Lane left today and it appears that we all will soon move. Worse luck.

Tuesday December 29

Last night of the panto, not too bad. Alan sick in bed with septic ankle. The three ducks that we have are looking very eatable. Most of the boys are feeling despondent over the impending [move] which must mean that we will be POWs much longer than if we stay in Java.

Wednesday December 30

Very warm. Did a little gardening. Tomatoes are coming along nicely. The ducks seem to be enjoying themselves in the water. It seems a pity to have to kill them. Weighed today. Me 86½kg. 13st 11lbs. Wilf 91kg. 14st 4lbs.
Another death today from No2 camp and we now have three men in our camp who have lost the sight of one eye.

Thursday December 31

Strong rumours of moving, maybe in two weeks. Tomatoes are coming up and planted another 14 this evening, thanks to Wilf. I now come to the end of my diary for 1942, am not sorry. It's been a terrible year and by far the worst I've yet experienced. I hope that '43 will see our release and perhaps our return to our homes. I wonder how they are at home and what they are doing. Poor mother, she must be very worried.

1943

Friday January 1
This is the 1st entry. I wonder where I will be at the end of the book.
I wonder how they are at home. I went to bed early but Wilf came and woke me up to wish me Happy New Year. Went to communion. This first day of the New Year is very miserable. I feel rather depressed. It's raining and when it rains here you feel very homesick. Nip holiday and they certainly celebrate same. They became very drunk in the evening.

Saturday January 2
Meals are very poor. No meat. Played football in the evening for Camp 5 against 8, we won 2-0. First time for me to play in league game for two months. Alan is laid up with septic foot it does not look so good. The library is growing and have now nearly 100 books. The Aussies are leaving on Monday and are being issued with nets, boots and clothes. Do not think they are going to Japan.

*Sunday January 3**
Went to early communion. Missed kiri parade. Went for a swim. Made my daily call on Alan who is improving. 80 chickens came in today and we had chicken soup. I had two feathers.

Monday January 4
Aussies left this morning. 600 more coming on Wednesday. Wonder when we shall move. We do not seem to be making any headway in this area, it looks as if we will be here for years. Feeling fed up.

Tuesday January 5
It's rained all day making life very miserable. I should imagine we shall soon be having more and more rain. The library is being disbanded after getting over 100 books.

Wednesday January 6
What a night last night.
It simply rained and rained and still is raining. 700 Dutch arrived from Tjilatjap. Concert fairly good. Frank making money with cigs, helps Wilf and me. I wonder if it's ok with [illegible].

Thursday January 7
Another 200 Dutch to arrive on Sunday from Malang. We are getting rid of 20 men from this camp but receiving another 50 from 8. We shall be terribly overcrowded. Wilf, Frank and I try to learn a poem but we're not very successful.

Friday January 8
Floods have come on the sea coming right into the camp. No 9 flooded out. Water all over football pitch. Many fish caught by enterprising and faster men. Wind terrific, also rain.

Saturday January 9
Floods continue and the boys get quite a lot of fun trying to fish. I think we are going to be POWs for some considerable time and as the time passes without any action to retake these islands then our position seems to be hopeless and we will be POW for another two years.

Sunday January 10
Went to communion, also morning church. Nips have started taking roll call in the morning which means we have to get up at 7.30. 70 men arrive in our camp, we lose 20. HRH suggests I have one or two in my room. I shall do my best to avoid it.

Monday January 11
200 men arrived from Malang last night. No British. Alan is down with dengue, his first illness since a POW. We play Camp 12 and win by 1-0. Not a very bright game spoilt by rain. Another very wet night.

Tuesday January 12
700 Dutch leaving tomorrow, destination unknown. I go sick with my toe and am excused duty for five days. Alan appears to be better. Griff has a wart removed.

Wednesday January 13
Another wet day. Swimming is still off on account of the bad weather. No concert, weather too bad. Dutch leave in morning.

Thursday January 14
Dutch left this morning in terrible weather.
I think we will be leaving before the end of the month. Alan much better. Frank
still making money. We intend F and I to give the sick a lot of special stew on
Sunday.

Friday January 15
Another party of Dutch leave on Sunday. Weather still bad, and still no
swimming. HRH buys a gramophone for the officers' mess. The flies are
becoming more prevalent.

Saturday January 16
Still rains. A few Dutch arrive and 500 tomorrow. Alan much better. The
English lose to the Dutch for the first time 1-0. I think we shall soon move.
I hope we all go together. I think it must be Japan which means another two
years POW.

Sunday January 17
Missed early communion but went later on in the morning. Splendid sermon
by Aussie padre. We lose 70 men of the 6th to Number 1 Camp which makes
our camp not so crowded. The officers swap their billets. We're due to move
now.

Monday January 18
Well it's come at last. 400 from the 77th will make up next party after much
speculation and arguing. Wilf, Alan, Griff, Frank and myself are not going as
yet. HRH goes. No regrets. Sorry had to leave the battery.

Tuesday January 19
It now appears that 400 will leave on the 24th or 25th. 320 are actually leaving
with 4 officers including HRH. Feel rather sad losing many friends but would
prefer to stay with those that are left.

Wednesday January 20
Everything points out to the fact that this party will be going to Japan because
they have to take warm clothing and no mosie nets.

Thursday January 21
Rumour that Camp 9 will move over to Camp 5 which will be ok. I fancy that
we will be pushed into some other camp. Concert that evening was not so good.
Farewell concert tonight.

Friday January 22
I am sorry to see Ken T, Dicky B, Ken V and the Major leaving. I hope that a few of them might still not go. England played the Dutch and won 4-3. Quite a good game. The rain continues.

Saturday January 23
A farewell concert this evening to the 77th was the best show ever. Fryett was on top of his form. Had a smashing tea and supper with Wilf, Dicky B, Ken Taylor. We had pork, onions and roast potatoes. It was delicious. All officers are going but only 290 men. It's definitely Japan and I should think we will soon follow.

Sunday January 24
Went to early communion also to church in the morning.
HRH and most officers from the 77th there. We had a musical recital in the evening, which was very good. I cannot understand the Major is not allowing some of the boys to change places on the draft.

Monday January 25
We are now on the last day of the draft. I feel sorry to see some of the boys go, am very miserable. 77th play Dutch and win easily 4-1. The draft leaves tomorrow morning 6 o'clock. I wonder when we shall see them again.

Tuesday January 26
Sensation, draft cancelled, 3am. I say it's divine providence. Dutch go. All Dutch and Aussies leave Thursday. Americans and English arrive same day. What a day.

Wednesday January 27
Many rumours but decide to go on with canteen. Draft still may go tomorrow. I think they will go as previously stated between 6 and 10.

Thursday January 28
Another day of rumours. Dutch and Aussies leave. RAF and Americans arrive. Canteen opens. Gee what a day. Take over 50G in the canteen. Profit is rather vague. I do hope that the draft do not go. Very tired.

Friday January 29
Another heavy day. Intended to play soccer, rugger and table-tennis but only played rugger. Played RAF and won 3-0.
Sorry missed concert. Rumour that draft will leave Sunday or Monday. Have a rotten cold.

Saturday January 30
Weighed today and I was amazed at the weight I am now 88kg, 13st 12 lbs. I must have some exercise.[Illegible] played sapper row and won easily.
My cold is making me feel rather depressed. This has been a memorable week, meet many friends from the jail and we still have our old ones with us.

Sunday January 31
Went to early communion and morning service. Played football in the afternoon and quite enjoyed. Church in the evening. We miss the Aussie padre. My cold is still bad. I wonder how long.

Monday February 1
The canteen still makes a good profit. Wood is going to be a big problem. I play HRH at table tennis and win much to my satisfaction.

Tuesday February 2
52 weeks today we arrived on this wretched island and for four weeks we had freedom. I wonder how many weeks we shall be prisoners. Not less than 100 and I hope not more than 200 weeks.

Wednesday February 3
Great surprise today. The people injured in train smash arrived with exception of Fitzpatrick who has gone to Surabaya.

Thursday February 4*
We had sad news last night when we heard from the train party that Pat Cox died last March. It came as a great shock All the boys look very fit in fact they look much fitter than our fellows. Great rugger match tomorrow.

Friday February 5
We played RAF this evening in rugger and won a most enjoyable game. HRH was most pleased. I must say that I enjoyed it. Boys are still hoping that draft will be cancelled.

Saturday February 6
Have told the boys they will be gone by the 10th. I hope not but I fear that by this time next week they will be a long way off. I am now certain that our stay will be 1000 days. I have altered my counting up.

Sunday February 7
Went to early communion and to church in the morning. The draft is now leaving Tuesday morning 6am. I think they will go this time. Played TT in the evening against RAF and lost. Feel low.

Monday February 8
Went on a WP not much doing. Fairly easy day. Soccer match. Last night with the draft I feel rather miserable at losing so many friends. Am rather hurt with the attitude of some of the officers.

Tuesday February 9*
The draft left this morning just after 6am. I wonder if we shall see them again. I think we shall soon be moving. Frank and Wilf have slight rift. Wilf was right but rather hasty.

Wednesday February 10*
Number 9 camp moved in today. Also Dai Grandon's party. We now have 145 [of] 240 men left in the camp. Wonderful concert this evening and best show ever.

Thursday February 11
What a grand show last night. The RAF certainly have some good talent. We are now settling down to the usual camp routine and should by the end of the week be back to normal. I miss the usual faces but will soon get accustomed to the new.

Friday February 12
I have now a septic toe and it's stopping me going on WP. I have been to the concert this week three times and have thoroughly enjoyed it. My days are still full up and have very little time for slacking.

Saturday February 13
I wonder what Cherry is doing, whether Mum and Dad are keeping fit. It's now 14 months since I last heard from them. I hope to receive letters soon. We are definitely out here for another two years of that I'm certain.

Sunday February 14
Went to early communion, also to church. Old Nip commandant left today. My birthday and my first as a POW. I had a good tea with Dai Grandon, [illegible] and Harry Hardacre. It was excellent meal. Chatted with Alan, Griff, Wilf and Frankie, til after midnight. A very pleasant day.

Monday February 15
I celebrated my birthday properly today when Alan got a magnificent supper consisting of three ducks, potatoes and also custard and bananas followed by cigars and coffee. I certainly had a better birthday than last year.

Tuesday February 16
I did enjoy last night's meal thanks to Alan. It was a nice little party of six. Wilf, Griff, Frank, John, Alan and myself. Concert tonight was not so good.

Wednesday February 17
The new Nip commandant seems to be a decent chap. He gave cigs and chocs to the artists in the concert. Promised nets etc to the camp.

Thursday February 18
We are having a lot of rain. Have now started on a flower garden or a path. It should look good when completed. My toe is still bad and stops me from swimming. Alan's leg very bad. He has to lay up with it.

Friday February 19
Rains have come again making life most unpleasant. Every man issued with mosie nets by new commandant. He's certainly getting things done.

Saturday February 20
Poor old Frankie is feeling fed up because of the cig market going bust. He's now going to concentrate on a book but knowing Frankie I should say it will go for a few days then finish. The commandant took all musical instruments from the boys because they could not play Jap national anthem.

Sunday February 21
Went to early communion also to church in the morning. Missed the piano and organ at the services. Played table tennis in the evening and won only game. Very heavy rain.

Monday February 22
Did not go on kiri parade because of my Singapore toe which is becoming better. Much talk about Nip commandant confiscating music from band.

Tuesday February 23
Play quite a lot of chess these days with Alan, Wilf and Frankie. Also do a spot of gardening and reading. Have laid a lawn outside my little home.

Wednesday February 24
We had the instruments returned today and had concert. Feeling sick, have a temp of 100. Will stay in bed tomorrow. Blood test taken for malaria.

Thursday February 25
Stayed in bed, feeling better. Temp down to normal. Negative slide. Have still a headache. Alan's legs are still bad. I think they will take a few weeks before they become healed. Rain, rain and more rain.

Friday February 26
Nip commandant visit to camp cancelled until tomorrow. Went swimming and surf riding for first time this month. Much enjoyment.

Saturday February 27
Rain and more rain. The whole camp is very pessimistic. The popular view is that we will be here til '45. I think that date may be optimistic.

Sunday February 28
Went to early communion but before leaving camp was violently sick. Felt ok rest of the day. Went to service in the evening and listened to organ recital. Rain, rain, rain.

Monday March 1
Played rugger in the evening and lost one of my front teeth in the last couple of seconds of the game. Rotten game army won 6-0.

Tuesday March 2
Went on WP, nothing interesting. Played soccer in the evening. Camp 5 winning by four goals. Still more rain. My foot is becoming bad again.

Wednesday March 3
I have another dose of Singapore foot but manage to go to concert which was very good.

Thursday March 4
Promised to write article on rugger for the JJ. Our little gardens are looking very pretty. It's really amazing the way the camp has changed since [illegible] left. It would do him good to return and see improvements.

Friday March 5
We are going to have a cinema show. Hinchley will be blowing Nip call on his bugle. All camps were vaccinated late this evening. It was exactly 2 years since I was last done.

Saturday March 6
My garden has been a huge success and have had many tomatoes. Will soon start a second crop. Have also got a couple of banana trees, am told will fruit in six months.

Sunday March 7
Went to early communion also morning and evening service. Rather good musical evening after service. Still rains. Officer from Number 1 Camp broadcast a message for 18 mins to Britain. Hope it gets through.

Monday March 8
Went on kiri parade though I had a bad foot. Griff and I have a few words over it. Am rather surprised at his attitude. Frankie in the show this week and he is rehearsing very hard.

Tuesday March 9
Rather long argument last night over communion with Wilf, Alan, Griff and Frankie. It's a year today we packed up and now we seem to be as far away from release as ever.

Wednesday March 10
Rain and more rain. My toe is still sore. Concert off til tomorrow. This new commandant seems to be very good. Has made a lot of changes.

Thursday March 11
A really excellent show. I think it was the best ever. Frank was very good. These concerts do help you to forget your prison life. If we lost them it would be a sad day for the camp. The girls were again the hit.

Friday March 12
The big day arrived and it was fine. The Nip commandant played up well and gave prizes for all winners of the spoils. He and the Nips took part in the races. Fishing and swimming in the afternoon. Good Day.

Saturday March 13
Rumour that we may soon get some letters. Do hope it's true. Camp 5 played 10 and rather luckily win 3-1.

Sunday March 14
Went to early communion also church in the morning. Very hot. Playing in chess tournament limited to 10 seconds a move. Won 6 of 9 games. Letters arrived today. One only for 77th. Great disappointment. Hope that tomorrow may bring more.

Monday March 15
I promise to referee rugby match with RAF and Army tomorrow night but want to go to tennis talk. Do not go on kiri parade. Nip commandant pays camp a visit and seems to be pleased.

Tuesday March 16/Wednesday March 17
Referee rugby game against my better judgement, missed tennis talk. Very few watching game. My tomatoes are nearly all gone. Good crop. Another good concert but not up to usual high standard. The girls are still good. Frank and Joe were also very good. Rumour of a move. Hope it's not true.

Thursday March 18
Wilf and Alan both sick. Alan with squitters and Wilf with a temp. A few more letters arrive but none for our camp. We had our first cinema show last night, all Nip propaganda. I was fed up and did not see it all. I thought it was poor propaganda.

Friday March 19
Alan and Wilf both better. My toe is now fit. Letters are coming very slow. Don't suppose we have had more than 50 for the whole camp of 2,500.

Saturday March 20
Camp 5 which is our camp is certainly looking very good. I think it's the best of the whole camp. We played Camp 1 in the evening and after a very hectic game we lost 2-1. Wilf got badly fouled several times and when he retaliated he was most unpopular. A good game spoilt by fouls and bad referee.

Sunday March 21
Went to early communion and also to church. Do not agree with [illegible] as he has attitude towards certain sergeant. A sign of weakness by Ted. Went fishing in the afternoon. Had a most enjoyable day.

Monday March 22
Hear that 239 fellow passed away in Batavia. It's now becoming very warm. Wales played the rest in rugger and after a splendid game Wales won. I thoroughly enjoyed the game and was agreeably surprised at the result.

Tuesday March 23
Went on a WP today and had a very easy day. Feel rather stiff after yesterday's game. Still no news of letters. I don't think we will get any more.

Wednesday March 24
Went swimming and fishing today and really enjoyed it. Went to concert in the evening quite good and well dressed show. Rumours of a move.

Thursday March 25
Went swimming and fishing this afternoon and had great fun in the water. Have got slight pain in my tummy, also John Rutter. Played TT in the evening against CH and won rather easily.

Friday March 26
Went on WP today and had another easy day. Wilf and Griff sick. Griff dengue and Wilf tummy. A long argument in the evening with Wilf and Frankie re religion.

Saturday March 27
Strong rumours of a move. I would not be surprised. Probably be 15th of next month. I think it will spilt up the camp.

Sunday March 28
Went to early communion also morning service. It's now becoming quite warm. The boys are getting busy on their gardens. I think our camp will possibly get in first [illegible].

Monday March 29
Rugger match. Army played RAF and won. I did not play. It was not a very good game. We still do a bit of fishing but the catch is becoming small.

Tuesday March 30
We are having a bridge and crib tournament but I have not been very successful and am out of both events.

Wednesday March 31
Another good show with the concert. One big fault, too much [illegible] who is the producer. Heavy rain in the evening.

Thursday April 1
Very quiet day. Spent most of the time in the garden. What an experience this evening! We were talking outside my little shack about 11.15pm when we had an earthquake shock. It lasted only 30 seconds but was really alarming.

Friday April 2
Much talk of earthquake last night. It is very amusing to hear people talk of their bed moving. Alan, Wilf, Frankie and I were talking and did not actually feel the beds moving.

Saturday April 3
Last night Wilf, Alan, Frankie staged another quake by moving my chair and pretending to move. I certainly thought it was another quake. Wales played England at soccer and won.

Sunday April 4
Went to early communion, also to church which was interrupted by Nip parade. Rumour of move. Had row with Wilf over some tomato plants. Maybe I was wrong but took exception to his attitude.

Monday April 5
Went on WP today, a very easy day. Our camp came second in the camp competition. Played rugger against officers at night and lost. Very hard game. I feel a trifle sore.

Tuesday April 6
Feeling lousy after last night's match. Hardest game we've played in. Nine Aussies played, they certainly are tough. No concert this week. Big one next week.

Wednesday April 7
Went again on WP. Nip states we all go to Japan before end of next month. Went to concert. A very long and heated argument with Wilf and Frank in the evening re surrender.

Thursday April 8
Supposed to go on WP once again but refused just a bit too much. Camp 5 played Camp 12 but game was abandoned at halftime owing to rain. Strange uneasiness today. This date 8 and 9th are 2 fateful days.

Friday April 9

It's come again. Another draft. 1,000 men, 110 from this camp. Frank, nor I go, nor Wilf, Alan or Griff. Many rumours of draft. It appears to be a good thing. But I have my doubts.

Saturday April 10

This draft will make a big difference in the camp. It appears that they are staying on the island and that we will follow them. All concert party going and band which seems a shame.

Sunday April 11

Went to early communion, also church in the morning. Much speculating over move – seems to be a good one. Rumour states near Badong. I do not think it will be off island. Commandant going.

Monday April 12

Sports held today, quite good. Many cigs given away for prizes. I got 5 packets for doing orderly officer. Les Spence goes on draft. Very surprised.

Tuesday April 13

Many people trying to go on this draft. Wonderful game last night. Played Aussie rugger and won. A really hard game. A night of musical play, an astounding success.

Wednesday April 14

A smashing show in our new theatre. What a pity that the concert party are leaving.

Thursday April 15

Played last rugger match this evening. Draft leaving tomorrow and the whole camp moving on Saturday to some place in Batavia. Very sorry to leave Priok and my little "cabin" where I saw many pleasant hours. More letters today. Wilf was lucky and got one. I had nothing.

Friday April 16

The boys left today for ? [sic]. Sorry to see Ted Sumption leave. Busy today moving camp stuff. We all leave tomorrow and Sunday. Splendid supper tonight with Alan and co.

Saturday April 17*

A very sad day. Leaving Priok. Arrive at new camp in Batavia called Cycle Camp. First impression not so good. Commandant has a bad reputation for slashing people. What chaos. Tired and very sleepy.

Sunday April 18
Another Palm Sunday and another move to a new prison. This camp is similar to the prison. No football, no church, no entertainment. Run by Dutch who are very much afraid of Nips.

Monday April 19
After a very long rest I become once again a very busy man. Now in same billet as seven colonels and 27 officers with 300 men and am in charge of same.

Tuesday April 20
Have had very little time to see Wilf, Alan and Griff because of my new duties. Managed to see them during the evening.

Wednesday April 21
The general opinion is that this place is putrid - only one good thing and that is the food. Had supper with Alan, Wilf, Griff – very tasty.

Thursday April 22
I am having a very busy time – have had no time to stop and have a chat with any of the boys. Have found that the men here are very poorly disciplined. The canteen has now been closed. This will make a big difference.

Friday April 23
Good Friday. What a day. No church service. Everybody on parade in the afternoon. Quite a number thought somebody was going to be shot, however it was a roll call. I'm afraid it was a miserable day.

Saturday April 24*
I wonder how many more Easters in prison. I think at least 2. I think we will be here for a few weeks. The Nips keep us very busy with roll call and working parties. Nobody allowed to cook and everybody must work morning and afternoon. What a life!

Sunday April 25
Went to service in the morning and communion. Not a very good service. We miss our little church at Priok. Service in the evening interrupted by roll call. Dysentery on the increase, situation becoming alarming.

Monday April 26
The dysentery is becoming very serious. Rumours of more letters. Dutch send in many sweets, sweet biscuits etc help us to enjoy Easter Monday. Quite a good day.

Tuesday April 27
We are being continually moved around in our billets much to the annoyance of the boys. Cigars and cigs and sweets were very good.

Wednesday April 28
The people who were removed arrived from Surabaya with news about last party. Have left the island and were packed in a ship.

Thursday April 29
Today Emperor's birthday – a whole holiday. Many rumours of a move. The 77th are now all in one camp with no officers only myself.

Friday April 30
Another bad day. Nips had everyone working. No rest. The boys all browned off. More rumours of a move.

Saturday May 1
A very hot day to add to our many discomforts. A man died in his sleep yesterday. Much fun in bathing. Water luke warm. I'm in a billet with the Dutch. It's noticeable the different attitude between Dutch and English. Dutch are morbid, the English jocular. Concert not so good.

Sunday May 2*
A very quiet day. Service in the morning and communion. Communion held with Nip sentry on guard. Chickens all over the place. Men working in same building. Good service in the evening. Alan dressed my feet and put some MB on.

Monday May 3
Visit by Nip general. Quick. Rumours of move. I think it will be soon. I wonder how they all are at home. I sometimes feel very uneasy.

Tuesday May 4
Quiet day. My feet are much better. I'm feeling hungry. We are all feeling the lack of food owing to closing of canteen. I think the food position will become worse.

Wednesday May 5
Canteen open today. Got sugar, eggs and fruit. Food much better. Started playing chess once again.

Thursday May 6
Hear more news. We move to the jail over the weekend. Most of the 77th are going including Wilf, Alan, Griff, etc. I do not think it will be so bad. Most of the boys prefer the change.

Friday May 7
We move on Sunday. It's almost a year since we left the jail. Wilf and I interviewed by the Nips re AA. It looks as if they have found some of our guns.

Saturday May 8*
Had a great shock today. Wilf and I were taken by the Nips to a place called Serang presumably to fire a 3.7 gun. We left Bat 6pm by lorry arriving Serang 9pm thoroughly soaked by rain and very tired. We were treated very well by the Nips who gave us plenty of food and cigs. Feeling tired. We wonder what is in store for us tomorrow.

Sunday May 9
What a day! We had plenty of food but was not very palatable. At 11am we had to show the Nips how to fire a brand new 3.7 gun. It was not a very nice position to be in. We did not fire the guns and the gun will never be fired. The Nips returned us to our camp at 10pm. Very tired.

Monday May 10*
I feel very miserable. Everybody gone to the jail. I get a lucky break and manage to get to the jail leaving Wilf at the Cycle Camp. Meet all the boys again. Joy.

Tuesday May 11
Am now in a factory with Alan, Griff, Frank, Noel. All work in the administration office. The jail has not altered much but I think it's clean.

Wednesday May 12
We start work at 9 and finish at 5 with half day on Sunday. I wonder how long we will be here. Nobody knows.

Thursday May 13
I don't think much chance of Wilf arriving here. All his kit been returned. I feel very tired after finishing work. Food not too bad but feel hungry. I still have much pain in my stomach. Rumour of a move.

Friday May 14
Many men are becoming bored with this prison but I think it's not so bad. A year ago today we are out of the jail. I am certainly losing weight. Must be lack of food.

Saturday May 15
I weighed today, am 81kg without boots so am probably 83kg with. Means that I've lost 5kg which means about 12lbs. I have many pains in my stomach and am very worried. I wonder how much longer?

Sunday May 16
I went to early communion this morning, only three attended. We have our first half day and was very acceptable. Still rumours of a move. Am still suffering from stomach ache. Service interrupted by Nips this evening due to fire alarm.

Monday May 17
We could do with more food. Feel very hungry. I am losing weight. Have now been here a week. I wonder how Wilf is getting on at the Cycle Camp. I should imagine he is fed up.

Tuesday May 18*
Good news. North Africa is ours according to Nip news. Hope. We are to have another half day Thursday and perhaps a cinema show. See Alan, Griff every evening and swap news.

Wednesday May 19
I do wish I could get a letter from home, would feel very relieved.

Thursday May 20
A nasty incident today resulting in one of the seamen having three stitches in his head and solitary confinement. He certainly asked for it and got it. We got our half day. Was very acceptable. Had a chat with Alan, Griff and Frank.

Friday May 21
Got weighed with boots etc and only touched 84kg. We are settling down in the factory and are becoming automations. Frankie is not well complaining about his tummy.

Saturday May 22
All the boys got paid today and are feeling very happy. I wonder how long this factory racket will last. I would not be surprised if they closed it down tomorrow. I feel that I am lacking exercise.

Sunday May 23
Went to Holy Communion this morning. Worked all day but was officially half day. We all received another inoculation against malaria, dysentery etc. I feel very tired and missing my exercise. These days are becoming more irksome.

Monday May 24
Many rumours of the war through Nippon news which rather depressed the men. Am not feeling so good here as I did at Priok but do not feel unhappy. We had our first rain today.

Tuesday May 25
The more I think of it the more certain I am that we will be POW for another 500 days making 1000 all told. Harry Hardacre and Syd [illegible] and a few old-timers help to pass an enjoyable evening.

Wednesday May 26
I am not half as fit here as Priok.

Thursday May 27
Factories are increasing their output but [not] yet enough to please the Nips. Half day today slept most of the afternoon. Enjoy chat in the evening with Alan, Griff and John.

Friday May 28
We talk today of the possibility of letters from home. Griff thinks no but I'm more hopeful. Have a most enjoyable fruit salad made by Alan.

Saturday May 29
Very busy in the factory. Nips are pressing us for production.

Sunday May 30
Went to early communion, not many present. Went to the factory in the morning also the afternoon because we were below Nip output. Another inoculation. Went to service not so good. No piano. Padre preached rather a good sermon.

Monday May 31
Some of the boys feeling sick after inoculation. Boys have been promised prizes for best output.

Tuesday June 1
Great surprise today. Wilf arrived with nine officers. He is looking fit. The boys are working hard in the factory but do not think it will last.

Wednesday June 2
Derby Day but I'm afraid we will hear nothing of it and there will be many more Derbys we will miss.

Thursday June 3
Had half-day today. I did some gardening. Gee it was hot. I certainly perspired. Strained my back. Have now to do PT probably tomorrow or the next day.

Friday June 4
We do PT in the morning before going to the factory. It's rather a bore but will not do us any harm.

Saturday June 5
Some of the boys left for the Cycle Camp today. I'm told that they might perform in some show. The Nips gave prizes today for the best results in the factory.

Sunday June 6
Went to early communion, only six of us there. I am reading a very good book called Fame is the Spur. Have gained a lot of knowledge by its contents. Many many rumours but still no letters from home. Food getting worse.

Monday June 7
Working in the factory is becoming very monotonous but it is giving the boys something to do. Have bought a few chickens.

Tuesday June 8
Have started PT, rather a nuisance as we have to rush our rice down for breakfast.

Wednesday June 9
We lose four chickens through some disease. A dead loss.

Thursday June 10
Rain this morning much cooler. Rumours of letters but have nearly given up hope of ever receiving one. Half day in the factory. But I had to finish a job for the Nips. Went to a bible class in the evening.

Friday June 11
Had my half day but did not sleep. Did a spot of gardening. Nips are becoming excited over visit of some big noise.

Saturday June 12
We are now being rushed and bothered about by the Nips. Supposed to come tomorrow but postponed til Tuesday. Saluting becoming more acute.

Sunday June 13
Went to early communion, started one of our worst days. Nip commandant on the war path to make camp clean. Everyone works, meals late and everybody becoming irritable.

Monday June 14
Only one more before visit of big noise thank goodness. Today King's birthday but no celebration like last year. Everybody browned off.

Tuesday June 15
The big day has arrived. Everything went off ok much to our relief. We get the afternoon off which came as a surprise. Lose more chickens must be disease.

Wednesday June 16
Production is still the main topic. Wilf falls foul of Mr Johnson who is an English civilian with a Nip outlook on production. He seems to forget that he's working for the enemy.

Thursday June 17
Another conference today re food, recreation and production. More food, more work is our motto. Another half day I do a bit of gardening. Tomatoes are coming up should pick within a few weeks.

Friday June 18
It does not appear as if much good will come from conference. I am afraid I'm rather cynical about the whole affair.

Saturday June 19
From the news we get from Nips the war seems to be a stalemate. Everybody feeling fed up. Am trying to get a few banana trees planted in our garden.

Sunday June 20
Went to early communion but no service in the evening owing to rain. The padre did not make any attempt to hold service later in the day. Band arrived from Cycle Camp. Very good. I see no hope of early release.

Monday June 21
We are given opportunity to write home. Unfortunately only 20 words are allowed. I wonder if they will eventually reach their destination.

Tuesday June 22
The weather is much cooler and is easily the best time of the year. The days pass very quickly but if we only knew how long, they would go even quicker.

Wednesday June 23
Output dropped. Rumour that our half day tomorrow may be cancelled. 30 men arrive from Cycle Camp.

Thursday June 24
Half day today. Did a spot of gardening and also played table tennis with Alan. Killed a duck and eat [sic] it for tea. It not much but what I had was very tasty. Upset Griff over ridicule of Wales and Welsh. Surprised to hear he had taken me seriously.

Friday June 25
A day that began badly and ended disastrously. Two officers put in cells because missing from factory. Officers [illegible] were then put in for giving them food. All were badly beaten up. We were all paraded with 13 machine guns trained on us.

Saturday June 26
Everybody talking about yesterday's nasty incident. The officer who passed the food got 20 days solitary. Two of them look badly knocked about. The Nips certainly lost their heads. It makes one think what will happen to us if we should be here when we are relieved. Played netball this evening first exercise I've had.

Sunday June 27
Went to early communion and played table tennis in the afternoon with Alan, afterwards playing netball with Alan, Wilf and Griff, finishing the game in time for me to go to evening service. I feel very tired but think exercise will do good.

Monday June 28
Slapping incidents are now becoming too frequent. I think a strong protest should be made to Nip commandant as it will become worse.

Tuesday June 29
I feel stiff after exercise but think it will do no harm. Played TT with Alan and enjoyed game very much. Very enjoyable evening with Alan, Wilf, Griff and Frank.

Wednesday June 30
Last day of June and still nothing happens. It seems as if we will be here for years. Tomatoes are now coming along. Should be ok in three weeks.

Thursday July 1
Big sensation. Another draft of 350 men leaving. 300 English and 50 Dutch. No officers. The 77th send 53 out of 106. Frank nor I go but will certainly go on next draft as it leaves only 40 men, most of these are sick. Boys are very disappointed as they thought there would be no more moves.

Friday July 2
Another 50 required makes our total 60. Many rumours of destination. I think it must be off the island. Many friends are parted. It makes one feel very fed up. We lose two of our sergeants.

Saturday July 3
No further news of draft. A general depression exists in the jail and I feel very depressed. I have given up any hope of early release and can see years of captivity in front of me. What a shocking waste of our life, in fact the best years are slipping past. Rained all afternoon, made one think of Sat afternoon at home.

Sunday July 4
Went to early communion. Usual rumours of draft's destination but nothing official. The nights are becoming much colder and the days also. Played TT in the afternoon. Went to evening service. Not many at the services, average of 20, which is very poor.

Monday July 5
Noel James arrives back from Cycle with many funny stories. No news of draft. I will not feel contented til I see draft so I'm certain it's off the island.

Tuesday July 6
Played table tennis, basket ball, won the crib tournament, had quite a full day. Damaged my foot by playing in bare feet. No further news of draft.

Wednesday July 7
Another sensation today. Only essential men to stay in the factory. Frank, Wilf, Alan, Griff, John and myself decided we were not essential. Later all 77th officers put on draft. Frank, Dai and myself also put our name down.

Thursday July 8
Well, I'm on the draft this time for better or worse. The sea journey will be the worse. Much speculation where we will eventually go. I am rather sorry to leave this jail as I have had a very comfortable time. Not many of the 77th left. I wonder if I have done the right thing.

Friday July 9
Lists are now being made up for this draft. I'm with John Rutter and Griff, Dai and Frank. I think we shall move before the 15th but goodness knows where.

Saturday July 10*
Have just finished reading Gone With The Wind. Excellent book. Had the glass rod this afternoon which makes our destination overseas. Played crib against Noel and won 15 cents. I think we will move next Tuesday. I hope it's not Japan.

Sunday July 11*
Went to early communion and I don't know when and where the next time will be. We left the jail this evening for Cycle Camp by lorries. This is the first stage of our journey. Very sorry to leave, leaving so many friends behind.

Monday July 12
Slept well last night. Many rumours of our destination. Sooner we start the better. The sea journey will be the worst.

Tuesday July 13
The food is bad here. No news of our next move. Many parades. Two RAF officers have arrived from Glodok. No pay yet from Glodok. I think we will leave within two or three days.

Wednesday July 14
Another glass rod today. More parades today. Time of our departure is drawing nigh. Japan I think.

Thursday July 15
More Dutch put on the draft which appears to be getting bigger every day. Total blackout this evening causes friction between John Rutter and myself. I feel very annoyed and keep away from him.

Friday July 16
We have wool blankets etc issued to us and now we are waiting for the next move which will be tomorrow. I think we will go from Priok and board a boat from there.

Saturday July 17*
We left Batavia today eventually arriving at Tjimahi near Bandoeng where we appear to wait for another draft. I don't think we'll be here very long. However a change is as good as a rest. Much cooler here.

Sunday July 18
No communion or church service. This is the first that I have missed since POW. Rumour says that we are here for some time. I am feeling fit and would not mind this food and climate for a few weeks although very cold in the evening.

Monday July 19
Food not so good, have started cooking our own. Canteen opened and we are going to get paid every day. Have started playing volleyball and find it good fun.

Tuesday July 20
Food still very bad. Have now started PT. Blackout a big nuisance, makes evening very long. Canteen stuff comes in and helps to make the rice go down. No news of moving.

Wednesday July 21
So this is 500 days as a POW and we are no nearer to release than the first day. We again moved today to another camp. Many rumours of a move at the end of the week.

Thursday July 22
Many more people arrive in this camp and the draft is beginning to look big. We are still being kept on our own, not being allowed to talk to other POWs. The food is fair but nothing to rave over. This is the best camp we've been in.

Friday July 23
Another batch comes in today and we see some of the old boys. [Illegible] Tudor Owens and we hear news of the boys we left 14 months ago.

Saturday July 24
We hear today that Surabaya was bombed on the 21st, 500 days after capitulation. We should move from here very soon. I am feeling fair but having several attacks of rheumatism in my legs due no doubt to sleeping on stone slabs.

Sunday July 25
Went to service in the morning and pleased that we will have a padre with us. Played basket ball in the afternoon. Quite good. Played chess in the evening with Wilf. Frank, Dai and I had a chicken for tea. Lovely.

Monday July 26
I am rather disappointed over cooking of chicken. Owing to some mishap the chicken innards went bad. I have made up my mind to keep away from officers' quarters when the food is scarce.

Tuesday July 27
Still no news of departure. Many complaints re food. Last night of blackout.

Wednesday July 28*
Sensation. Old Musso drops out. Italy should soon pack up. I think we shall move in 10 days.

Thursday July 29
Am feeling groggy but manage to play baseball. Got a nasty crack on my arm from Wilf. Rumours of a WP. 600 go from camp.

Friday July 30
Have now started making mats. Shake Wilf and John Rutter into looking into the question of food.

Saturday July 31
Feeling really lousy today and see the doc who gives me two days rest.

Sunday August 1
Went to early communion and then went to bed with rather bad cold. It's amazing how easily one catches cold. I feel really groggy, have a very sore throat but no temp. Boys still making sacks.

Monday August 2
Still in bed but throat much better. All the boys seem quite happy here. I wonder how they are at home. Had to go on Nip parade in the evening.

Tuesday August 3
Got up today and am feeling much better. Think we will be moving very soon. Sack making suspended.

Wednesday August 4
Many rumours floating around the camp. Dutch are always spreading rumours. Go to Wilf and Alan and join in quiz.

Thursday August 5
We celebrate the Dutch Princess' birthday causing a lot of argument among the British. I think it was a poor show to stand to attention for the Dutch Royal family when we ignored our Queen's birthday.

Friday August 6
My rheumatism is still bad. I'm getting old and not so sprightly as I used to be. Rain and more rain.

Saturday August 7
Played handball and had quite a good game. I have now got a really bad toe. Am feeling rather depressed and sometimes wonder if I will get home before am 40. Received 2G from Wilf for Frank and I.

Sunday August 8
Went to communion at 8 o'clock also to morning and evening service. Very good. Toe is very painful. Now rains every evening. Still no news of move. I think we will move very soon.

Monday August 9
Received 20 cents. Money position is desperate, have got nothing except some of the money Wilf gave me. Last bit of tobacco went today.

Tuesday August 10
Shaving is now becoming very difficult. Many men growing beards. I think I will soon be doing the same. Food better, no soap to wash.

Wednesday August 11
Many are becoming optimistic but their optimism does not bring our release before '45.

Thursday August 12
Hear from the Nips that we will move in a few days. Destination unknown but all of us will die, not a very pleasant thought. The climate here is very good. Enjoy the nightly quiz with Wilf.

Friday August 13
Slept very bad. My toe is getting better. Went out with big party for recreation. Played football in the evening and lost 6-2. Very wet!

Saturday August 14
Still no news of any move although rumour states we will move within five days. I wonder how much longer. Received money that had been left by Major Gaskell, it amounted to 30 cents per man.

Sunday August 15
Went to early communion also to morning and evening service. Have a spot of bother with Wilf over football. He makes himself very unpopular which is stupid. My toe has become very sore.

Monday August 16
Many of the boys are becoming communists. I hope they will stick to their views when they return to England. We must all stand together.

Tuesday August 17
We signed for pay today which we did not receive. All wrong. Went out for exercise today and enjoyed it. Concert in the evening – good.

Wednesday August 18
Received 40 cents today. Rice cut to a quarter. Very serious. It looks as if it has come to stay. We shall certainly become hungry.

Thursday August 19
We still do sacks but the food is becoming scarce. One meal of rice per day, one piece of bread for breakfast and one piece for tea. The fat ones will become thin. The thin ones will just fade away.

Friday August 20
The climate here is very good, much better than Batavia which was so darned hot. Spend most of the evening doing a quiz. Have good fun.

Saturday August 21
Nips got nearly everybody out on sports fields then searched billets for torches, candles etc. Blackout until further notice. It appears that Nips are beginning to worry over air raids. Hear that Sicily has fallen. Good. Sack making finished, no more money and less food.

Sunday August 22
Went to early communion also to morning service. Many rumours of our move now that sack-making is finished. Meet 2 more fellows from Cardiff, Ken Evans' cousin, Ben Thomas' son. Went to evening service.

Monday August 23
Very cold in the morning and evening. We have lice in our billets which makes it very bad for the boys.

Tuesday August 24
The food is very scarce and what we do eat is bad. I suffer much from indigestion through bread not being done. Feel very sick.

Wednesday August 25
Another Nip parade today. I think we shall move in a few days.

Thursday August 26
Definite news of move today when Nips asked for retinue of men unable to stand 10 days rail journey. Many rumours of likely destination. Played handball and got bumped by Wilf. Damaged my toe.

Friday August 27
Many rumours of move. Think unable to travel, have been examined by Nip MO. By this time next week we will have moved from the camp.

Saturday August 28
Food is very scarce. There is no doubt we are now having the worst food we've ever had and no money with which to buy any extras. Canteen is now closed which makes our departure more certain. The boys will lose weight on this food. Weighed today, 82kg without boots.

Sunday August 29
Went to early communion. No morning service, Nip parade. We hear that we move on Wednesday. Many rumours of destination. I will not be sorry to move. Went to evening service.

Monday August 30
It's taking two days to move. I think we will go to Priok and to north of the island. Draft cancelled. Food has been very bad here. Played soccer and won.

Tuesday August 31
First party left today for Batavia. Rumoured that we stay in a camp for three days and then off the island. I feel certain that we are now bound for Nippon.

Wednesday September 1*
We arrived back at the Cycle Camp much to my disgust. Will be glad to leave. See many old friends.

Thursday September 2
Had the glass rod today also blood test which makes the boys think we will go to Nippon. We are very crowded and the Dutch are treating us very shabbily regarding food.

Friday September 3
Four years today war commenced. How much longer before we are freed? No hope for another two years. I think we will move in two or three days time.

Saturday September 4
Still no news of moving, many rumours. Nothing definite. Am sharing a room with [illegible] and I find he's good company. Nippon news seems good and I think Italy has had it. I give her two months. Frank says 18 months.

Sunday September 5
Went to early communion which had to be held in secret. No other church service. Forbidden by Nips. I think we will move next Sunday. Food is better.

Monday September 6
Am sorry to see Griff and Alan gradually drifting apart. Griff feels it very much. I will not be sorry to leave this camp.

Tuesday September 7
Another big surprise today. One officer to each 50 instead of two. Alan, Griff and Noel are now off the draft. A great pity. I would not be surprised if Wilf and John came off, leaving no officers.

Wednesday September 8
Wilf, John R and myself are going, leaving Alan, Griff and Noel behind. It's getting messy. Many rumours. I think Nippon.

Thursday September 9
Glass rod today once again and also cellophane and we move tomorrow 5am. Just 500 of us. Big draft cancelled. I don't think we see the remainder of camp after we leave. I think it will be Sumatra.

Friday September 10*
We sailed today from Java at 9.25. Sea fairly rough conditions, much better than what we thought they would be. Many of the boys sick. We are all on deck. Everybody seems happy.

Saturday September 11
Sea much smoother. Have now settled down to our voyage which is Singapore. Everybody delighted with food and accommodation. The only smog is coal dust which covers us when the wind changes. John Rutter, Dai and myself sleep together.

Sunday September 12*
For the first time for many months no church service. We anchor at 6 o'clock in Sunda Straits. Wilf and other officers have now got a cabin and are very comfortable.

Monday September 13
Thought we would get in Singa [sic] today but seem to be a good way off. Should be in tomorrow. 2 men down with dysentery. I wonder where we go from Singa.

Tuesday September 14*
We arrived Singapore at 4pm. Very little damage to be seen. Red pillar boxes. Went to a transit camp and saw some of Burma draft that were too ill to move.

Wednesday September 15
Seems to be a very good camp. Food is fair. Prices are very high. Eggs 25 cents, sugar 80 cents.

Thursday September 16*
Many 240 boys in other camp including Sgt Davies. Burma left a very bad impression on him. See very few Nips and have a large area in which to roam about.

Friday September 17
We cause a lot of trouble by one of our men, a sailor, being out of camp. He's put in jug. I think we will move very soon and my guess is Japan. Allowed to play rugger.

Saturday September 18
The climate here is not too bad. I could enjoy staying here a few months. We are getting 3 cents for a sheet of paper. I sold 500 sheets. We have glass rod today so expect to move very soon.

Sunday September 19
Went to early communion today, also evening service. We move tomorrow and I'm certain it will be Nippon. Played basket ball and tear my skin. Blisters. Sorry to leave Singapore.

Monday September 20*
A day of many shocks. We go on board a large ship. Very cramped quarters. All officers leave us except two MOs and two English. Wilf and I are parted for first time.

Tuesday September 21
We are terribly crowded and the heat terrific. Not many sleep. Hope we will be able to go on deck. Have got over yesterday's shock.

Wednesday September 22*
We left Singa 10.30 this morning. I think we will go to Nippon. Meals very poor but could be worse.

Thursday September 23
It could be much worse. We are allowed on deck from 8 til 8 and we can wash frequently. Night-time is the worst. Heat terrific. It will go hard with us if any disease breaks out.

Friday September 24*
Still am going East N.E. Our destination must be Nippon. I should think we should arrive in six days time. DV.

Saturday September 25*
What a day! I was down below at 2pm when I heard an explosion and all the boys ordered below deck. The ship alongside us was torpedoed and sank in 5 mins. No survivors. The boys behaved very well. No panic. I have grave foreboding over this trip.

Sunday September 26
We are now below deck all the time and one cannot help but think it maybe our turn next. We are now alone, the convoy having spilt up. I will say a thankful prayer when we get on land.

Monday September 27
We sight land today, much to our surprise. We find it's the Philippines. We anchor in Manilla Bay. I don't think this is our destination.

Tuesday September 28
Still not allowed on deck. Very hot in the holds. Many boys unable to wash because of Nips. May be here for three days.

Wednesday September 29
We left Philippines this morning 10 o'clock in a very slow convoy escorted by a destroyer. Still not allowed on deck.

Thursday September 30
We are doing only 6 knots an hour and will take us to Monday to get to Formosa. That's our destination. A heavy swell today and we are allowed on deck once again. Starting to blow in the evening.

Friday October 1
Very rough night. Did not sleep. Heavy seas. Many boys sick. We are going dead slow. Much cooler.

Saturday October 2
Sea still very rough, did not sleep. Most of the boys seasick, I have still to be. I feel very depressed today and wonder what the future has for me.

Sunday October 3
We arrived Formosa today at 10 o'clock. I should think it must be the south part of the island. We are not getting off here so we'll be aboard for a few more days.

Monday October 4
We are still at Formosa. Many Nip troops and ships. Surprised to see such activity. Very cold in the evenings. We have glass rod again. I hope it's the last.

Tuesday October 5
We left 10 o'clock this morning and immediately ran into heavy seas. Hatch battened down, gale blowing. I lose my bed – probably the best one in our small space.

Wednesday October 6
All hatches closed and portholes. Heavy seas. Much colder in the night. I have slept very badly last three nights.

Thursday October 7
We see land once again and find out it's coast of China. Everything still closed down. We have no escort. I find Wilf's coat – a godsend. I would be very cold without it.

Friday October 8
I sleep very badly and feel rather tired during the day. We still hug coast. Sea becomes calmer. I think we should arrive on Monday if no accidents.

Saturday October 9
We still have showers on deck but not many use them. The latrines are not so good. Only three for 500 men which means you have to queue every time you want to use the lats. The food is now bad, only rice and watery soup. The Nips food is also bad.

Sunday October 10
We leave coast of China go more into the open sea. We have a plane as escort. I get my bed back. Sea much calmer. Food getting worse. A couple of nasty incidents today.

Monday October 11
We are getting nearer Nippon. Will be pleased to get off boat. Have not slept well for over a week. I wonder if we will see other boys.

Tuesday October 12*
We arrive at Nippon at 10 o'clock, leaving boat 2 o'clock. We are spilt up once again. Capt Williams and I with 250 men go to one camp. I sleep in transit camp and take first party, 125 into camp.

Wednesday October 13*
I get up 4am and arrive in new camp 9 o'clock. Searched thoroughly. We will work in coal mines, not so good.

Thursday October 14
First impression. Many Nips in new camp, only Capt W and I in charge. Will have to work very hard. Slept like a log. Receive four blankets, still cold. Very cold in evenings. Lovely hot bath. Definite work in pits.

Friday October 15
Have a very bad throat, pity no doctor. I find that we are Inatsukimachi, Kyushu, southern island of Japan. Not so cold in the evening.

Saturday October 16
I think the food is much better here than in Java. Feel very depressed at times. Hair cut and photo taken. Not much chance of any sport. Feel the loss of our books. My tongue and lips are swollen now making eating very painful.

Sunday October 17
No communion and no church service today. Hope to arrange some for the future. A very quiet day til the evening when we get issued with miners' clothes and are told that we will all go to work in the morning.

Monday October 18*
A very bad night. Everybody goes to work with exception of 10 cooks. We go to work and I with 70 others have to go down the mine. Remainder on the surface.

Tuesday October 19
Work is very hard. We have many parades and kiri which make life unbearable. I think this is our worst period and is going to last.

Wednesday October 20*
Second day at work much better. Still too much bull-s. I do not relish the idea of going down the mine.

Thursday October 21
I go sick after a very bad night. I go to the lats about 16 times. I see Nip doctor, am off all food. We get issued with warmer clothes but conditions here are far from ideal. I think we are in for a rough time.

Friday October 22
Have still got diarrhoea, still no food. 30 boys go down pit and are agreeably surprised. I'm afraid they have not seen the worst of it.

Saturday October 23
Still no food but diarrhoea much better. The boys work very hard from 7 til 5pm and with so little good food am afraid there will be much sickness.

Sunday October 24
No church service. Everybody working. Rest day is Tuesday. I have some little rice. Have become very weak and thin. Frank went down mine, not so good. Very dangerous, expect many accidents.

Monday October 25
Am now having pap three times a day. Not very filling. Boys do not go down the mine but start shift work on Wed. I am put in charge of miners. I shall soon be going down.

Tuesday October 26
Rest day and I am off sick but told I am fit for work. Feel very weak. Lost weight. I go down mine first shift Thursday.

Wednesday October 27
I feel very nervy about going down mine. Will be glad to get down and get over this tension. I have a feeling that something will happen when I'm down there.

Thursday October 28*

Owing to some error in Nip admin I do not go down mine today but have made certain that same error will not occur tomorrow. Hot bath went phut today. Great disappointment I hope it will soon be repaired. The boys working in the shaft find it very dangerous. I do hope and pray that we won't have any serious accidents. Cigs issued this evening.

Friday October 29

I do not go down mine again owing to Nip error. I will not go now until they call me in the morning. My mouth is very sore and my tongue is raw due to lack of vitamins.

Saturday October 30

Do not present myself on work parade so do not go down mine. Nearly lost 11 men yesterday when fall in the shaft. I tell them it was God's providence that saved them. They all should go on their knees and thank God for deliverance. I am told to go down mine tomorrow. I go sick.

Sunday October 31*

Another Sunday, no service of any kind. Nips allow us to have service on Yasme days. Issue of sweets and biscuits. I do not go down today but will definitely go down tomorrow. I hope I come back safe.

Monday November 1

Went down mine for first time and returned safely thank God! No fear at all, if fall does come well you've had it. I do no work. Long hours til three.

Tuesday November 2

What a night. I could not stop my teeth chattering. Went sick. Terrible throat. Temp 100. Put into sickbay once again and I do feel ill. Lack of good food.

Wednesday November 3

Yasme day and I am feeling worse. Temp still high. Being treated for malaria. What a farce. Missed church service.

Thursday November 4

Saw Nip doctor today. Have my throat painted twice a day. Tongue, lips and mouth very swollen. Unable to eat. Sheer agony even to speak.

Friday November 5

A little better today. Am using Capt Williams' Vaseline. Frank has crystal for gargling. Had beef tea, a piece of meat. What joy!

Saturday November 6
Saw Nip commandant. Told him we need meat, also saw doc who said I was better. Am still in sickbay. Another issue of meat today. Not enough to go to each man. My lips and tongue are now nearly normal. I do hope and pray that we all will soon be able to go home. At the moment it looks like two years.

Sunday November 7
Boys went to work as usual. Got paid today. Was able to buy cigs and biscuits. I bought 30 cents of biscuits. Meat in stew again. I am feeling much better. Should be working in a few days time.

Monday November 8
Eleven men refused to work seven hours down shaft. Are put in jug. Ugly situation. Rain all day. Feeling better but miserable. Boys get soaking. No dry clothes.

Tuesday November 9
More rain. Very miserable. Men out of jug but still have to do seven hours down shaft. Still in sick bay, feeling better. I wish it was all over.

Wednesday November 10
I see MO and am discharged. Much better. Expected to go down mine on nightshift but did not go.

Thursday November 11
Yasme day. Not much of a rest for the boys who had to work doing gardens etc. Had a church service in the afternoon. Observed two-minute silence. I wonder where I will be next Armistice Day. Concert in the evening. Good. I go down mine tomorrow.

Friday November 12
Went down mine afternoon shift. Saw number 1 who seemed very pleased to see me. Did no work but feel tired. Still no news. More meat, food better.

Saturday November 13
I did not relish the idea of going down today and was very lucky as I went down with managers and came up at 6 instead of 11. I was in camp by eight. Had quite a good day. Have been told that I will lead gang of 11. May be ok. Frank has the worst job in the mine.

Sunday November 14
No church service but down mine. Start new job tomorrow. Feel very fed up today. Everybody feels browned off. No bath made matters worse. Another sale of biscuits and tobacco.

Monday November 15
Did not start on new job today. Will start on 19th. Rained all day. Was very sick last night. Better today. Very easy, read a book.

Tuesday November 16
Another easy day. I can't understand why Nips refuse us papers. It must be because we are doing something big. Another cold.

Wednesday November 17*
Very cold and very wet. Frank and Norman get reported for not working but I smooth it over. Everything OK.

Thursday November 18
Still cold and wet. I wonder how much longer. I hope it will be next year. I am feeling older and I will marry as soon as I get home.

Friday November 19
Yasme day. Had church service and concert. Very cold, sleet fell. I start on new job tomorrow, keeping on afternoon shift for better or worse.

Saturday November 20
Have a good day. Started on new job, afternoon shift. Had conference with Nips and managers of mine and get about a dozen oranges. They were delicious. I gave a few to some of the boys and Capt Williams.

Sunday November 21
No church, everybody working. I start my work today with three other chaps. Rumour of 150 Dutch arriving.

Monday November 22
150 men arrive soon and what poor devils, they do not know what is waiting for them. Still very cold but not wet. New job seems OK.

Tuesday November 23
I have been feeling OK for last few days but am not feeling as good today. Tomorrow will be my 13th day down mine and not like it. Very cold.

Wednesday November 24*
Still no word of 150 men. Receive some Red+ stuff, Bully beef, M&Bs and sugar. I think this is answer to our prayers for more food.

Thursday November 25
Yesterday was 13th day down mine and I'm glad it's over. I have lost my voice, bad cold. I feel very fed up at times. Frank Fryett feeling sick and has got the squitters. No news of fresh men.

Friday November 26
Go down another part of mine, very cold. I have another interview with manager, satisfactory. Oranges, cigs and a drink similar to cider.

Saturday November 27
Yasme day, visit by Nip major, satisfactory. Went to church service also concert. Good meals, fish and meat. Also cup of sweetened cocoa at night. Part of Red+ fund. Library opened and get a book by LAG Strong. Seems good.

Sunday November 28
Another Sunday down the mine. Fairly easy today. Weather very cold. Have still got a cold. Rumours of hot water bottles seem a farce. We still get meat and fish but no oil to fry anything.

Monday November 29
Hardest day yet down the mine. I still fear going down the mine every day and always thank God when I arrive safely on top.

Tuesday November 30
Still no news of new arrivals. New guard arrived and seem rather decent. I must say that the days pass very quickly.

Wednesday December 1
I was thinking today how little leisure I get. Ten hours work, 10 hours sleep, two hours for roll call, bath and meal. Two hours for roll call, wash and meal.

Thursday December 2
I am feeling very hungry these days. Could eat a lot more. I have a row with cookhouse over food. Capt Williams and I are not having same as men. We must stop being foolish.

Friday December 3
Biscuits and cigs today. Newcomers arrive tomorrow. It seems that they are Dutch. Pity.

Saturday December 4
A very busy day. Glorious news. We received our Red+ supplies and are being issued tomorrow. Boys are very happy. Half tin bully, half tin [illegible], a little tea, sugar, cheese, jam and biscuits. It probably means only a couple of spoonfuls of each but it will be grand. Dutch arrive tomorrow.

Sunday December 5
Yasme day and we have a church service. Memorable day. We get some of our Red+ supplies. Delicious. 151 Dutch arriving, bringing good news. I think they are rather optimistic. Very cold for them. I don't think they will stand up to this weather.

Monday December 6
Two years to the date we embarked. What a fateful day. I think we are on the second half of our POW. Working harder in the mine. Feeling fairly well.

Tuesday December 7
The Red+ rations helped but our rice ration has been cut. Capt W and I have been given a pair of leather boots. Mine are being changed.

Wednesday December 8
Nips celebrate anniversary of war. I work very hard in mine. Rice very short. We may have Yasme on Christmas Day.

Thursday December 9
I wish I had a letter from home to say they are all well. Sometimes I feel very anxious. I wonder how much longer we will have to endure this life. I am certain we shall have greater hardships.

Friday December 10
A very easy day. Frank has a hard day working in 2ft seams. Refuse to work tomorrow in same place. Paid today. Cigs and sweets. I think I have scabies.

Saturday December 11
Frank did not go to same place. Everything OK. Yasme day Xmas Day. Capt W and I draw up a programme. If the Nips play up it should be a fair day. I think the Nips are becoming fed up with the war. I hope that we will get cracking soon.

Sunday December 12
Down the pit as usual. No service. Just like any other day. Many of the men are suffering from the wet. Swollen limbs etc. Snowed today.

Monday December 13
Went down mine and had a very lazy day. I do not like the 13th. Feel very nervous. Cigs and biscuits for sale.

Tuesday December 14
Yasme Day. I have a terrible cold and feel very depressed. Very busy with meals. Am glad when it's all over to get to service.

Wednesday December 15
Am getting fed up with hearing Nip orders. Feel lousy. Many Nip changes.

Thursday December 16
Nips cannot change boots so have got a brand new pair of boots, unable to wear. Started having pap today. Boys seem to like it. Dutch have started on their week's training. Do not like it.

Friday December 17
A quiet day. Have a bad cold. Feel very depressed. I see no hope for the future. Our freedom seems further away than ever.

Saturday December 18
A serious outbreak of dysentery in the camp. All Dutch. I feel very miserable. I do hope and pray that I will receive a letter from home saying they are all OK. Capt W and I spent the morning talking about our childhood days.

Sunday December 19
Went down mine as usual. Do not notice when it's Sunday. All days are now the same. Work, work and more work. I feel very embittered.

Monday December 20
Dutchman died today. Dysentery. The first death. I wonder how many more. I bruised my ribs when I slipped rather badly in the mine.

Tuesday December 21
Dutchman cremated today. His ashes handed to Dutch officer to take home. We have inoculation against dysentery. More likely to die.

Wednesday December 22
Another Dutchman died today. Dysentery. Still no news of Xmas. I think we will have three dead before Xmas.

Thursday December23
A day I shall not forget. Worked down the mine in terrific heat. Wore only a short pair of pants. Came back filthy. Worst day yet. Not looking forward to this Xmas.

Friday December 24
Xmas Eve. Yesterday was worst day down mine but today was worse still. Soaked to the skin for eight hours. Terrible. Worse Xmas Eve of my life. Third Dutchman dies. I went down mine as usual having spent morning talking with Capt W of previous Xmas Eves. Had worst job yet in mine. Was soaked to the skin by 3 o'clock then had to stay in clothes til midnight shivering with cold. I felt really miserable and no doubt it was the worst time I've yet spent. I have very little hope of a good show with all decorations and Xmas trees.

Saturday December 25
Xmas Day. Worst Xmas Day I've ever spent. Men had a fairly good Xmas, beer, cigs, oranges, rice pudding, and sauce. Service in the morning. Pap with sugar and rice. Concert in the evening. Capt W and I work hard all day. I was up today at 6.30 arranging breakfast for the boys. Pap and sugar and soup. Parade at 10 for prizes for good work. 85 receiving oranges, cigs, pepper. Church service at 11am. Nip wanted to take photo but I told them it was not honourable to break service. Xmas dinner was good. Rice, meat, pudding, sauce, beer and oranges. I suppose it was a good effort by the Nips to make us happy but I was very miserable. Had no breakfast. Christmas dinner at 3 then was busy til teatime while the boys were sleeping their dinner off. Concert in the evening finished off with hot cocoa, sugar and cake. So ended Xmas Day 1943 and I pray it is the last as POW.

Sunday December 26
Not much to be said because we all were working. I went down the mine and slept for four hours. A much easier day for me than Xmas day. We have been told we can write home. I do hope that we will soon get some letters. It would be grand.

Monday December 27
Had fairly easy day. Am afraid that the boys will not be able to stand up to this hard work.

Tuesday December 28
Worked in [illegible]. Do not feel so good. Rice cut. Fred Woods seriously ill. I think he will be OK.

Wednesday December 29
Bad night last night. Squitters. Not feeling so good. Fairly easy day. Slept in the mine.

Thursday December 30
Shock today. Two of my gang went working on coalface and I pushed wagons. I don't like the look of it. It seems that I'll be made to work on the coalface. Not so good. We'll see what tomorrow brings. Not much hope.

Friday December 31
Worked on top. Very monotonous. Two of men worked at coalface. Squitters. Very fed up.

1944

Saturday January 1
Yasme day. Another hard day. What a start for New Year. I wonder what this one will have for us. Peace I hope. I feel that we will be lucky if we are free by Xmas 1945. I honestly think it's not a very bright future.

Sunday January 2
Am feeling very depressed. Wondered today if it was worth carrying on. Terrible thoughts. I must not feel so down – there are many worse.

Monday January 3
Bad day down mine. Worked very hard and late. It looks as if we have had all the good times. I will carry on despite fed up.

Tuesday January 4
Write postcard home. I wonder if we will ever receive any from home. Bad day in mine. Get soaking. Started new job with Nips.

Wednesday January 5
New job fairly harsh. Not used to such heavy work. Have got a decent Nip with us.

Thursday January 6
We appear to be learning a spot of mining. Very cold. Snowing. We get no news now of any sort.

Friday January 7
Went without dinner down mine owing to some mistake on cook's part. This job we are doing is very dangerous and I will be glad to see it finished.

Saturday January 8
A big shock today. Roof came in and we were saved only by a Nip miner. It makes one think. Am now working very hard. Only hope I will be able to keep it up and that my health will hold out.

Sunday January 9
Another Sunday down the mine. You cannot tell one day from another. We now work 10 days and then one rest day.

Monday January 10
Had conference with number 1 of the mines. It appears that I must work with the others. I shall have to keep fit.

Tuesday January 11
Yasme Day. Usual bustle. Now in fire brigade. A very short but impressive church service. A very busy day.

Wednesday January 12
On sand job but no Nip, had a fairly good day. Food is still the main hope. One can't get enough rice.

Thursday January 13
Unlucky day and was glad to get out of mine safely. Our job is dangerous and I will be glad when it's finished. Some more Red+ arrives. Food I hope.

Friday January 14
Feeling depressed. No news of any kind. The longer we are POWs the further away appears our release.

Saturday January 15
Got right down to the mine and was taken ill. Went back to camp. Feel better. I wonder how long my health will last under this strain. I am not able to do all the heavy work. How much longer?

Sunday January 16
Another Sunday, no service. I still have bad stomach. Many boys sick with squitters. Mine work is now very hard.

Monday January 17
I narrowly escape death today when I was carrying a girder, struck by trucks and all came off line just in front of me. Severely shaken. I thank God for being still alive.

Tuesday January 18
I worked very hard. Hear some good news from one of the Nips. I tell all the boys and they are very bucked. I must say I feel much better after hearing the news. Inspection was good. Free issue of cigs and biscuits.

Wednesday January 19
I vomit blood after my meal. Very worried, do not go to work. I feel very sick after each meal.

Thursday January 20
The boys are now going down the road rapidly. Most of them losing weight and there are now 40 in hospital. I do not go to work and have cut some of the barley down.

Friday January 21
Yasme Day. Another nightmare of a day. 70 men had to work. Rations cut. Small issue of rice and veg. Church service, only 13 present. No concert. Everybody depressed.

Saturday January 22*
Sad news today. Number 22 Corporal Gibson dies in his sleep after heart attack. Young Woolley also crushes his leg. Rice still short. There will be many more deaths unless we get change of food. I work. I am feeling very weak. Lost another kilo.

Sunday January 23
Another Sunday and no service. Cpl Gibson buried today. Fit of depression in the camp. I am feeling the strain of working. I wonder how long I will be able to carry on.

Monday January 24
Good news of rations. Supplies increase. Hard day in mine. Many men feeling weak. Two more likely to die. Keep on thinking that many will die in this camp.

Tuesday January 25
Feeling lousy, becoming weaker. Have now got the squitters. Surprised at my lack of strength. Must be the food. Will go sick tomorrow.

Wednesday January 26
Went sick today. I have got a day off from work. Issue of five of Red+ parcels. One tin corned beef between 10 men. Prunes, sugar, tea, milk, butter etc.

Thursday January 27
The Red+ parcels would have been smashing if we could have had one whole parcel between two men. However we must be satisfied with small mercies. Another day off. Still got squitters and I feel weak.

Friday January 28
Rice cut today because many men have got squitters. No more pap. Serious food shortage. I am only eating a bowl full of pap each meal.

Saturday January 29
Started baking today for the sick and Yasme men. Roll each meal. No rice, one bowl of soup. I fainted in the bath this morning and messed my pants. I feel disgusted with myself. No news. I wonder how they are at home.

Sunday January 30
Another Sunday and no service. Still off work. Many complaints over food. I think we are here til we are released or die.

Monday January 31
Still another day off. Feeling much better. Am feeling hungry. So are all the boys. Yasme Day tomorrow.

Tuesday February 1
Yasme Day. Another cut in the rice. We have prunes and a small meat pasty. A very hard day. Nip doctor examined men who are not fit.

Wednesday February 2
Start work today and go with Fryett. Nasty shock when Nip wants to change shifts every week. Food better.

Thursday February 3
Shock today. Spilt up railway gang and put them all in shaft leaving me with Frank. I am very thankful as I want to keep out of the shaft if possible.

Friday February 4
Still with Frank. A quiet day. No news. Many rumours of a peace talk. I wonder if we will be released sooner than we expect. I pray to God it's so.

Saturday February 5
Saturday once again and we talk down the mine of what we would be doing if we were at home. We often do this and it's interesting to hear what others do when at home.

Sunday February 6
Another Sunday and it passes by as just another day. Work is fair. I do not feel so weak. I hope I get stronger.

Monday February 7
Another issue Red+, double last time. Very acceptable. I try to get day off to help Capt W but fail. Went on jackhammer today. Not so bad.

Tuesday February 8
Feel OK and enjoy a little cheese from the Red+. Boys are happy. Rice still short and veg. Rather deaf through jackhammer.

Wednesday February 9
Many grumble re food and clothing of ill. I think we need a change in the cookhouse.

Thursday February 10
Capt W has a temp. I hope it's nothing serious. Am very busy in the camp helping Capt W with Dutch. Feeling tired.

Friday February 11
Yasme Day. Terrific day. Not a moment's rest. Received soap, razor blades, cigs and toilet paper from Nips. Played Dutch in table tennis and won prize given by Nip commandant. Church service very impressive only a few present. I have toothache. No rice all day. Just three bread rolls all day.

Saturday February 12
Another Saturday and we talk of what we would be doing if at home.

*Monday February 14**
Continuation of my diary of 1944 commencing on my birthday 14 February, Monday, 708th day of captivity.
Today I look back on my past life and wonder will I ever go back, not to the same life but more solid and sedate, also to become married. Now I'm in the mood for reminiscing I feel I must quote part of Rupert Brooke's delightful poem The Great Lover:
"These I have loved:
White plates and cups, clean-gleaming,
Ringed with blue lines; and feathery, faery dust;
Wet roofs, beneath the lamp-light; the strong crust
Of friendly bread; and many-tasting food;
Rainbows; and the blue bitter smoke of wood;
And radiant raindrops couching in cool flowers;
And flowers themselves, that sway through sunny hours,
Dreaming of moths that drink them under the moon;
Then, the cool kindliness of sheets, that soon

Smooth away trouble; and the rough male kiss
Of blankets; grainy wood; live hair that is
Shining and free; blue-massing clouds; the keen
Unpassioned beauty of a great machine;
The benison of hot water; furs to touch;
The good smell of old clothes; and other such --
The comfortable smell of friendly fingers,
Hair's fragrance, and the musty reek that lingers
About dead leaves and last year's ferns. . . .
Dear names,
And thousand other throng to me! Royal flames;
Sweet water's dimpling laugh from tap or spring;
Holes in the ground; and voices that do sing;
Voices in laughter, too; and body's pain,
Soon turned to peace; and the deep-panting train;
Firm sands; the little dulling edge of foam
That browns and dwindles as the wave goes home;
And washen stones, gay for an hour; the cold
Graveness of iron; moist black earthen mould;
Sleep; and high places; footprints in the dew;
And oaks; and brown horse-chestnuts, glossy-new;
And new-peeled sticks; and shining pools on grass; --
All these have been my loves."

Beautiful lines and they fall in with my mood today. I look back on my home life and thank God for such a wonderful and devoted mother and father. Mother, by her fine example showed me how to be kind and generous and Pa how to play the game and take a defeat with a smile. I am proud of them and today when I think of them I hope and pray we will soon be reunited back home in Cardiff. This is my most miserable birthday I've ever spent. My thoughts go back over past birthdays when I received many Valentine's cards etc. What fun I had in those days. Dear old Joe read most of them before I got a chance to see them. I wonder how he is and his wife Joyce and the baby. How I envied their little home and how it made me determined to get married and settle down. How many more years of this terrible bondage must we suffer before we are released? I only hope it will be soon because I feel myself becoming weaker. I do not think I will be able to stand up to this hellish existence.

Tuesday February 15
Woods has been told that he's dying poor fellow. No news or rumours though I'm sure that some good news is about. Capt W not so good. All looking forward to tomorrow's Red+ issue.

Wednesday February 16
Saw the Nip commandant today and got remainder of Red+ supply. Everything OK. Capt W still sick but will be up tomorrow. My abscess has burst. Do not feel so hungry. I am losing my appetite.

Thursday February 17*
Poor Woods passed away today. Very sad. I will go to the funeral tomorrow in place of Capt W.

Friday February 18
Had a terrible night last night and am now sick in bed with temp 102. I feel really lousy and do not feel I want anything to eat.

Saturday February 19
Still in bed, not eating. Temp still up and have now got squitters.

Sunday February 20
A very bad night last night. Went to lats about 20 times. Feeling weaker. Nasty incident in mine. Seven men got hit with iron bar by under-manager.

Monday February 21
Yasme Day. I get a great shock today. I am weighed. 73kg. Have lost 6kg in a month. Am very worried. Snowing heavily. Still feeling ill. Temp down slightly.

Tuesday February 22
Temp over 100, feeling groggy. Terrible pain in stomach.

Wednesday February 23
Feeling better. Red+ clothing arrived today. Many rumours of moving.

Thursday February 24*
Great shock today. Sgt Burrluck Number 5 passed away at midday. Pneumonia. No treatment. In hospital only two days. It makes one think who will be the next. Red+ clothing issued today. Good stuff but not enough to go around. Feeling better but still weak.

Friday February 25
Poor Burrluck buried today. Three English have died within the last three weeks. I think there will be many more before we leave here. I still feel very weak but not so much pain in tummy.

Saturday February 26
Another Saturday, how many more? I get a pull-over, pyjama trousers, gloves and a hat from Red+. Feeling better. Many boys have got squitters.

Sunday February 27
I am feeling better. Will get up tomorrow. Hear that Yasme Day are on the 5th and 18th next month. One of the boys in hospital is losing his reason – very sad.

Monday February 28
Feeling very depressed. Got up today for a couple of hours. Felt very weak. Capt W has a bad foot. We are lacking food. I am feeling hungry.

Tuesday February 29
Got up again today feeling weak. Nip MO visits camp. Nothing special. Another Englishman seriously ill. Not much hope of recovery.

Wednesday March 1
We hear today that we may move next month. It's only a rumour at the moment but I hope it's true. It will make a big difference to the health of this camp. I feel that I must have a change otherwise I'm afraid that I will never be able to stand up to this life. A year ago today I lost my front tooth playing rugger at Priok – the time has certainly flown.

Thursday March 2
Still feeling groggy but will probably be out working in a few days. Rumours of move still strong. I do hope it will come off.

Friday March 3
Saw Nip MO and was told work tomorrow. I feel better but am very weak on my pins. I hope I will be able to manage the work and regain some of my strength and weight.

Saturday March 4
Started work today and was very thankful it was not very tedious. I still feel weak in the legs. No news of moving. I am very doubtful about it. It rained all day, feel very miserable. Letters arrived in camp but not one for anyone in the camp. They were sent here in error.

Sunday March 5
Yasme Day. Another rush day. New clothing issued and prizes for good workers. Capt W and I received 12 oranges. We kept one and gave rest to sickbay. I had a straight talk to one of the boys over bread roll for good work and was surprised

at the result. Had church service which was very sparsely attended. Only 12 present. The sick look better.

Monday March 6*
Another terrible shock today. Joe Smead (135) passed away at midday. The deaths in this camp are becoming alarming. One a week. Something must be done. He was only ill five days. Pneumonia. No stamina to fight. Went down the mine working with new shift. Not so good. Wanted to be with Fryett.

Tuesday March 7
J Smead buried today. Who next? Terrible weather. Bitterly cold and snowing. Hard work in mine. My job not so bad. Very wet.

Wednesday March 8
Very cold. Snowing, miserable. Work very hard in mine. Two years today we packed up.

Thursday March 9*
One o'clock this morning another man died - O Hara. He just packed in. Two in three days. We will have very few men going back if the death rate continues like this.
I wonder where I will be this time next year if I'm still living. I hope that I will be free.
Snowing and very cold. Practice air raid makes life more miserable.

Friday March 10
O Hara buried today. Very cold much snow. More air raid precautions. Work very hard. Rations cut, no rice. One small piece of bread. Bill the Dutch boy gets a Yasme from the commandant after Capt W has failed. Nice work. Bill is a West Indian and speaks perfect English. Has got a very bad record for pinching.

Saturday March 11
Still very cold. No news. I wish I could hear news from home and know that they are all safe and well. I put our stay in Japan for two years and we have another 18 months to do.

Sunday March 12
Not so cold today. Bread for three meals per day, not so good. Feel very hungry. Worked very hard today. My back feels like snapping in two.

Monday March 13
Unlucky day but passed off without incident. Rumours again of a move which I suspect originated from cookhouse.

Tuesday March 14
A general feeling of depression in the camp. Lack of news. Worked very hard.

Wednesday March 15
Am very sick in mine. Feeling lousy. Suspect appendicitis. Worked so terribly hard.

Thursday March 16
Have lost my appetite and am feeling sick. Many of the boys are sick and looking very ill. All are complaining of general weakness. We can never last on this food and the hard work, long hours, and no rest. Many will die.

Friday March 17
St Patrick's Day. Three years today I was at Llandough feeling lousy after vaccination. I could not go on leave. I wish I was there now. Feeling a bit better and easier day at work which was a blessing. Another man is about to die, made a grand fight but odds against him.

Saturday March 18
Yasme Day. It rained all day and very quiet. Church service, only 14 there. Big shock when I got weighed, found I was 80kg and had gained 7kg since last weigh in. I was amazed because I have not been feeling so good. And have been sick several times. Everybody seemed to have gained.

Sunday March 19*
Brandon died this morning. Poor lad. He was in a terrible state. I go down in new shift and go to another working [area], easier but dangerous. Lovely day, saw first butterfly.

Monday March 20
Brandon buried today. Much colder. Job still dangerous. Very low roof, about four foot, making it very difficult to work. Still no news.

Tuesday March 21
First day of spring in England. Weather much warmer. News of two Americans arriving in camp for medical purposes.

Wednesday March 22
I gave all my MB tablets today to a chap with pneumonia. I hope they will save him.

Thursday March 23
My MB tablets have done the trick and the fellow is much better today. Many rumours of the war but no real news. Rations today very short, I feel very hungry. When oh when will we get some news from home.

Friday March 24
Capt W and I worked out the date of Easter Sunday and agree on April 9th. Much colder today. Arrival of American doctor and medical orderly. Very little news, a little disappointing. I was hoping for something new and good.

Saturday March 25
Nothing that we do not know. Lovely weather. Home is much in my thoughts today especially Mother. I wonder if there is anything in telepathy because I had a feeling that Mother was very near to me. Rations still short.

Sunday March 26
Another Sunday, no service. Terrible weather. Food in shocking condition. Men are very depressed. Work fair.

Monday March 27
Very easy day down mine. Surprise to hear boys talking of not living to see the day of peace. Lack of news makes us feel depressed.

Tuesday March 28
The weather becoming milder. Civvies take over duties of guards etc next Yasme Day. Not so good.

Wednesday March 29
Still feeling OK. Hope I can keep fit and well til the day of peace.

Thursday March 30
I dreamt that I was escaping just for the night to see Mother and had then to return in the morning. It was so realistic that I was tremendously disappointed when I woke up. Poor Frank Fryett is really depressed and was actually weeping when I saw him at the mine. It certainly shook me.

Friday March 31
One more day for Yasme then Red+ issue. This has been a good shift and I have been feeling much better. Have been graded as one of the fit men in camp. Fryett will probably get a job in the camp. Rumour of many changes which may or may not be true.

Saturday April 1
Yasme Day. April Fool's Day started very bad by Commandant too busy to issue Red+. Had a sumptuous meal last night, best since Christmas. Eyes tested today, fairly good. Church service and only six attended. Very disappointing. Rations cut today after last night's extra.

Sunday April 2
Guard still with us. Down working in mine with a very low roof. I find it very difficult and have to go on my hands and knees most of the time. Weather fair, news none.

Monday April 3
Terrible issue of rice. I feel very hungry. Capt W generally leaves me some of his rice but now he hardly gets sufficient for himself.

Tuesday April 4
Worked pushing truck. Lovely day. Some of the men stayed on top. Red+ promised next Yasme Day.

Wednesday April 5
Started new coal face today. Not too bad. No water.

Thursday April 6
A lovely day. No news of a move. The work in the mine is not so hard but the boys are very weak. Food is improving and if we can get over this month without any more deaths we might improve health of camp.

Friday April 7*
Good Friday. Another Good Friday as a POW. I wonder how many more. We all got a bread roll with a cross on it. Another death. Musson died at 12.20am this morning. It's terrible this pneumonia. Only ill for two days. Weather very wet.

Saturday April 8
Poor Musson buried today I hope and pray that Cpl Sutcliffe will pull through. More rain makes life very miserable. My thoughts are home today and I feel very despondent. I do hope and pray that I will be spared to go home.

Sunday April 9*
Easter Sunday. Poor Sutcliffe passed away 12.20am this morning. I found him dead when I went to see him. Very sad. Paid today, everybody got an increase of five cents. No church service, just another day. Very wet. Feeling very miserable and depressed. This is the third Easter as POW. Surely we will be only one more.

Monday April 10
Easter Monday. Lovely day. Beautiful sunshine and I had to go down the pit
in such weather. It's a tragedy. I have just read a book called This Above All by
Knight. The finest book I've ever read. I must try and get a copy when I'm free!
Sutcliffe buried today. Who next!

Tuesday April 11
Still wet, miserable day. Work fairly easy but feel fed up. Number 1 of the mine
leaves. I wonder if this will make a difference to me. I hope not.

Wednesday April 12
Yasme Day. A very tiring day, also a memorable one. Red+ issue and was really
good. Bully beef, butter, cheese, cigs, and pipe tobacco. Boy o boy was the pipe
good. It made me feel very happy. About 30 of the boys received letters from
England dated 1942 or 1943. Capt W had 14 out of a total of 58. I was greatly
disappointed at not receiving any, better luck next time. Church service was
good and a few more attended. Felt very tired after busy day.

Thursday April 13
Unlucky day. Felt more homesick today than I've ever been. Capt W gave me
his mother's letters to read. I was very much moved by his gesture. Working
with Fryett F not too bad. Have bad day with guards.

Friday April 14
Feeling lousy, have got squitters, go sick and get a Yasme. Good news for Fryett,
last day down mine – lucky dog! I wish I was not going down again.

Saturday April 15
Another day off. Still running. Fryett started to work in camp today. I feel
very miserable and low spirited. Lovely day. I just cannot see any hope of
freedom for years. The longer we are POW the further away seems to be the
day of our release.

Sunday April 16
Another Sunday and I do not go down the mine. Beautiful day. Another death,
a Dutch man making a grand total of 12. Eight English, four Dutch. Capt W
and I have some delightful talks and we spend many happy hours ruminating
on our plans for the future when we are free. I enjoy these talks very much. It
helps one to forget his troubles.

Monday April 17
Another beautiful day. Dutchman buried. I still do not go to work but now feel OK. I spend afternoon looking over my photos and showing them to a few of the boys. I'm a bit worried whether I will be put on a permanent shift to take Fryett's place. I do hope and pray that it will not happen.

Tuesday April 18
Wretched day. Rain, rain, more rain. Another day off but work tomorrow. Spent most of day reading. Nip commandant came to visit our room, stayed for an hour looking at snaps etc. We could have worse.

Wednesday April 19
Work today fair. I am afraid I might be kept on this shift. It would break my heart.

*Thursday April 20**
Lovely day. Capt W got around the commandant to agree for him to have a clerk.
Sgt Missen has taken over. He has just come out of hospital with injury to his hand and is unable to do any work. Lucky fellow. I certainly envy him. I wonder if he will 'dig' with us or that I will lose my billet. I hope that will never happen.

Friday April 21
Yasme Day. A very busy day. Glorious weather. I get weighed and find that I am 81kg. Have gained another one. It seems incredible especially with the food we have here. Church service was impressive. Very few present. Concert in evening was fair.

*Saturday April 22**
Five years today I was at Twickenham. I feel very depressed. Rice very small. If we don't move soon there will be many deaths in this camp. The men are looking ghastly.

Sunday April 23
Another Sunday and just another day. The boys are very depressed and many think they will not live to go back home. I am doubtful and put my chances at 25/1 of getting back home alive!

Monday April 24
Rice, rice, rice is sole topic of conversation. Actually three bowls of rice a day keep us from dying of starvation!

Tuesday April 25
Went sick and Capt W got me a day off. Temp 37.8. Have got the flu. Capt W read a wonderful poem which Churchill quoted in '41. Gives one hope.

Wednesday April 26
Still got a temp but was sent to work down mine. Felt lousy. Work fairly easy thank God.

Thursday April 27
I feel better today but feel very weak but I am not alone in that respect. I suppose 95% of the camp feel the same. More Red+ arrive today. Food and boots. I do hope it will soon be issued.

Friday April 28
Lovely day. I suppose we can hope now for some better weather. I do hope and pray that we will get some news from home next month. The last two nights I have dreamt of home. Both Mother and Dad were dead.

Saturday April 29
Last day for football and first day of cricket. Oh I wish I were home. Nip commandant leaving. I will miss him as I was fortunate to be one of his favourites. Surprise issue of some of the Red+. Very good but I do not feel so good in myself.

Sunday April 30
New commandant arrived. Very young and nervous. Old commandant still here. More Red+ tomorrow. I feel sick and am off my food. I hope I feel better tomorrow.

Monday May 1
Yasme Day. I feel lousy. Have got squitters and sickness. Unable to eat. Went to church service, only seven present. Very poor attendance. Commandant said goodbye. Got a pair of boots and all Red+ issued. I feel better towards evening and went to a very good concert.

Tuesday May 2
A lovely day. No greatcoats now. A fair day down the mine. More coal more coal is the motto by the Nips.

Wednesday May 3
Another fine day. Still no news. Very depressed.

Thursday May 4
The weather is certainly becoming much warmer. The old commandant left today. I was sorry to see him go. We were issued today with gas capes for rain. The Nips shout "speedo speedo" and bash the boys at every opportunity.

Friday May 5*
We did not receive any biscuits or cigs as promised by the Nips every Friday. I was not surprised. A few more go into doc with pneumonia including Stanton who has never had a day's illness. More than ever a case of survival of the fittest.

Saturday May 6
Got some good gen today. Makes one feel very optimistic regarding European war. The sooner that is finished the sooner we get free.

Sunday May 7
Another Sunday and my thoughts go back home and think of the Sunday school anniversary held on this date. I have still got the squitters and feel lousy.

Monday May 8
I wear shorts today and feel much cooler. Accident down the mine, one of the men breaks his leg. I take him to hospital to get it set. Poor view of so-called hospital.

Tuesday May 9
Rain, rain and more rain. It seems as if rainy season has started. Hear a rumour that I might be put on shift work. I do hope it will not be so.

Wednesday May 10*
Terrible tragedy this evening. Rabinovitch fell down shaft, instantly killed. Very popular fellow. Cast gloom over camp.

Thursday May 11
Yasme Day. Poor Rabinovitch was buried today. A very impressive service. Concert cancelled. We will now miss his cheery personality and his acting on the stage. Issue of biscuits and cigs. I get weighed today and have lost 3 kg. I am now 78kg. Worried re shifts, whether I will go on permanent shift. Only four in church service so we had a prayer meeting.

Friday May 12
I heave a sigh of relief and count my blessings when I find I am still on the same shift. I work with Norman Welsford and have a fair day although I dislike the Nips with them.

Les Spence (sitting, second from left) poses with other rugby playing members of the 77th. They played a number of games in South Wales before going to war. Wilf Wooller is sitting between the two uniformed officers. Standing third from the left is Ken Street who would be killed in a train crash in Java in February 1942. (Courtesy: Jeremy Spence)

A group photograph from the 77th. Les Spence is sitting front row, fourth from the left. (Courtesy: Jeremy Spence)

Four members of the 77th. Les Spence is on the left. (Courtesy: Jeremy Spence)

The sergeants of 240 Battery. Les Spence noted that the photograph was taken on December 1, 1941, presumably in Mary Hill Barracks, Glasgow. Les Spence is in the third row, eighth from the left. Ken Street is in the front row, fifth from the left. (Courtesy: Jeremy Spence)

A good luck message from his brother Ken which Les Spence received in Glasgow on December 4, 1941, days before he left for the Far East. (Courtesy: Jeremy Spence)

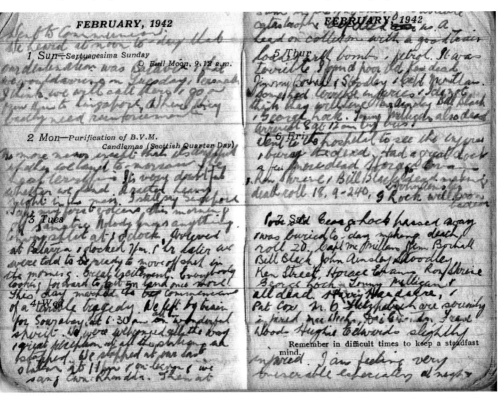

A page from Les Spence's diary from February 1942 in which he describes members of the 77th taking a fateful journey through Java. The men sing 'Cwm Rhondda' as they leave one station. Soon after, in the early hours of February 6, 1942, the train is involved in a horrific crash.

Around 30 members of the 77th were killed and a further 100 were injured in the crash, which happened just outside Surabaya. The track was littered with overturned and damaged wagons.

Sergeant Hugh Edwards officiates over a service in a hut at Camp 8, Inatsukimachi, Japan, at Christmas 1943. (Courtesy Peter Edwards/Rev Hugh Edwards)

A parade at Camp 8, Inatsukimachi, Japan. (Courtesy Peter Edwards/Rev Hugh Edwards)

Propaganda photographs taken by the Japanese at Camp 8 at Christmas 1944. (Courtesy Peter Edwards/Rev Hugh Edwards)

レンゴウグンノホリョヘ
ALLIED PRISONERS

The JAPANESE Government has surrendered. You will be evacuated by ALLIED NA-
TIONS forces as soon as possible.

Until that time your present supplies will be augmented by air-drop of U.S.
food, clothing and medicines. The first drop of these items will arrive within one
(1) or two (2) hours.

Clothing will be dropped in standard packs for units of 50 or 500 men. Bundle
markings, contents and allowances per man are as follows:

BUNDLE MARKINGS				BUNDLE MARKINGS			
50 MAN PACK	500 MAN PACK	CONTENTS	ALLOWANCES PER MAN	50 MAN PACK	500 MAN PACK	CONTENTS	ALLOWANCES PER MAN
A	3	Drawers	2	B	10	Laces, shoe	1
A	1-2	Undershirt	2	A	11	Kit, sewing	1
B	22	Socks (pr)	2	C	31	Soap, toilet	1
A	4-6	Shirt	1	C	4-6	Razor	1
A	7-9	Trousers	1	C	4-6	Blades, razor	10
C	23-30	Jacket, field	1	C	10	Brush, tooth	1
A	10	Belt, web, waist	1	B	31	Paste, tooth	1
A	11	Capt, H.B.T.	1	C	10	Comb	1
B	12-21	Shoes (pr)	1	B	32	Shaving cream	1
A	1-2	Handkerchiefs	3	C	12-21	Powder(insecticide)	1
C	32-34	Towel	1				

There will be instructions with the food and medicine for their use and distribution.

C A U T I O N

DO NOT OVEREAT OR OVERMEDICATE   FOLLOW DIRECTIONS

INSTRUCTIONS FOR FEEDING 100 MEN

To feed 100 men for the first three (3) days, the following blocks (individual
bundles dropped) will be assembled:

3 Blocks No. 1
(Each Contains)

2 Cases, Soup, Can
1 Cases Fruit Juice
1 Case Accessory Pack

1 Block No. 5
(Each Contains)

1 Case Soup, Dehd
1 Case Veg Puree
1 Case Bouillon
1 Case Hosp Supplies
1 Case Vitamin Tablets

1 Block No. 3
(Each Contains)

1 Case Candy
1 Case Gum
1 Case Cigarettes
1 Case Matches

3 Blocks No. 2
(Each Contains)

3 Cases "C" Rations
1 Case Hosp Supplies
2 Cases Fruit

1 Block No. 7
(Each Contains)

1 Case Nescafe
1 Sack Sugar
1 Case Milk
1 Case Cocoa

1 Block No. 10
(Each Contains)

3 Cases Fruit
2 Cases Juice

One of the leaflets dropped from a United States airforce plane to
inform the prisoners of the Japanese surrender. It also informs them
of upcoming supply drops of clothes, food and medicine.

Two photographs taken in Nagasaki in the days after the detonation of the plutonium bomb on August 9, 1945. They were taken by Lt RC Nomsen, USCG, who had been waiting for freed prisoners of war, and given to Captain AA Duncan. The pictures were first published in 'AA Duncan is OK' by Meg Parkes. The second photograph was taken three miles from the centre of the explosion. (Courtesy: Duncan Archive)

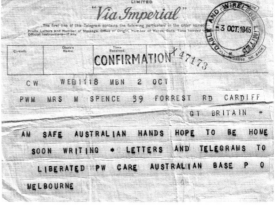

An October 1945 telegram from Les Spence to tell his parents he is coming home. It was probably sent from Manila. The operator has mistakenly taken it down as being from Len – but that would not have spoilt his family's joy. (Courtesy: Jeremy Spence)

Sergeant Major Les Spence and Captain Peter Williams photographed at Camp 3 after the liberation in August 1945.

Les Spence married his sweetheart Babs in 1947. His best man was
fellow former POW Wilf Wooller. (Courtesy: Jeremy Spence)

Members of the Java Club, formerly the Java FEPOW 1942 Club, at a reunion in
August 2011 at Stratford-upon-Avon. Set up by Java POWs, the club is now open
to people interested in all Far East prisoners of war. (Photo Greg Lewis)

Saturday May 13
Am feeling sick again and have got squitters very bad. Feel very homesick in this glorious weather.

Sunday May 14
Feeling rotten and have difficulty in keeping my food down. The number of miners decreases every day as larger number go sick.

Monday May 15
Got the squitters very bad today. Work very hard. Strong rumour that we go down the shaft after Yasme Day. All miners. I do not like the idea because it will mean I will be on shift work and may have to move.

Tuesday May 16
Red+ arrived today. I am very worried about move to shaft. It may mean that I will be moved from Capt W which would be a calamity.

Wednesday May 17
Red+ promised for Yasme Day. Good.

Thursday May 18
My squitters are very bad. I think I shall try and go on bread. I am becoming weaker because my little food is doing me no good.

Friday May 19
I reckon it's 50/1 that we move into the shaft after Yasme Day. Most of the miners are pleased but I'm withholding my judgement til I have seen the actual conditions we are to work in.

Saturday May 20
Well I think this will be last day down the mine and I'm not sorry except that it may mean an end to my constant shift and I will go on shift work and may have to transfer my billet. I am very worried about this and do hope and pray that it will not happen.

Sunday May 21
Yasme Day. No official news of move and it appears that we go down the mine tomorrow as usual. Red+ issue today very good. Church service in morning, not many present. Good concert in the evening. I think my squitters have stopped.

Monday May 22
Go down the mine once again. Now stated we change next Yasme Day. Worked very hard today. Do not like new Nip boy.

Tuesday May 23
My squitters really cured. What a blessing. I think our days in the mine are numbered.

Wednesday May 24
Five cooks and few of factory people change for shaft next Yasme Day.

Thursday May 25
Still many rumours of transfer to shaft, nothing definite. Capt W promised by Nip Commandant office a new living and sleeping quarters. It will be grand if I can go with him. I do hope that it will be so, otherwise I will have to mess it with any Tom, Dick or Harry.

Friday May 26
Still no definite news. Able to buy salt, and nine biscuits today. Very close work down the mine, very hard. I feel myself becoming weaker. Have got the squitters once again. Serious accident down mine – Dutchman breaks his back.

Saturday May 27
Told today that shall go down the mine. New lists made out and find myself on permanent shift and maybe have to move from Capt W. Very serious and I will do everything in my power to keep as I am. I think billets will be OK for present, not optimistic re shifts.

Sunday May 28
Whitsun. I wonder where I shall be next Whitsun. Capt W reads a wonderful poem, Ulysees. I am very worried about the change and can see no good can come out of it. Have still got the squitters and very worried re the work.

Monday May 29
Have decided to do it and will have a go tomorrow. I hope I'll be successful. It's my only chance. Red+ issue Yasme Day. I do hope that this mine work will soon finish and we will all get easier work to do.

Tuesday May 30
Well I did it. I am now in hospital with suspected fracture of left foot. It's very painful but I think I slipped up. X ray tomorrow.

Wednesday May 31
X ray discloses no fracture. Out of hospital. Cannot walk. I've messed it up.

Thursday June 1
Yasme Day. Big change round with billets. I stay put. Red+ issued, very small.
Kept in bed by my badly swollen foot. Will try and make it last for a few days.
What a pity it was not broken.

Friday June 2
Weather frightfully hot. Shaft people say they prefer working down the mine.
Well they can have it. My foot is still very painful. I cannot put it on the ground.

Saturday June 3
Another Saturday and I think of them at home, wondering how they are and
what they are doing. The years are going by and we are still POW. No hope of
early release.

Sunday June 4
Many rumours of peace talks. If they are true then we should be free this year.
But I have yet to be convinced that they are true. I have told many of the boys
that I feel we are much nearer the end than we anticipate in order that they will
be happier in mind and spirit.

Monday June 5
My foot is still painful and I am still in bed. There is a great deal of optimism in
the camp and everybody is silently hoping that we will be free this year.

Tuesday June 6
Capt W receives two letters out of three that arrive in camp. I do hope and pray
that we might all receive letters very soon.

Wednesday June 7
Derby Day. Feel miserable. Nip MO examining my foot tomorrow.

Thursday June 8*
Foot examined by Nip MO who twists my foot and ankle back to front.
Very painful. Not satisfied it's not broken. I have to go and get x rayed again
tomorrow. Rumours of invasion of France. I hope it's true. Waiting for further
confirmation.

Friday June 9
Rumours confirmed. We are told that invasion commenced on the 6th, that we are now fighting in France. Glorious news. Great excitement in camp. I wait all day to be taken to hospital for x ray but I wait in vain. Had nasty shock when I hear that Capt W and two doctors are having a room together. Capt W is trying to get me in with them but I don't think he will be successful. This is a big blow to me.

Saturday June 10
More good news re invasion. I pray that it may mean the beginning of the end and that the war in Europe will be finished this year.

Sunday June 11
Yasme Day. I am still in bed but foot is better, not so swollen. No more news of invasion. Receive biscuits and cigs for being good ? [sic] worker. Went to concert on crutches. Very good. Did not go to church service, hope to make it next Yasme Day.

Monday June 12
I am still waiting for a further x ray. Have now got Singapore toe on my injured foot. Rumours are still very good, hear that Goering has passed out. I am hoping that Germany will finish before the autumn. Then we may be free next year.

Tuesday June 13
My foot is becoming better. I don't think I will have another x ray. Rumours still good. Boys are becoming optimistic.

Wednesday June 14
I have got rid of my squitters and am feeling OK. My foot is better.

Thursday June 15*
Am now eating better and can manage my bowl of rice each meal. The meals are very small with occasional fish. Rumours still very good. Air raid alarm went at 6.30pm and is still on at 9 o'clock. All lights are out. I'm writing this by light outside hut. I think it's the real thing. No smoking, miners' food may be taken down the mine.

Friday June 16*
Phew. What a night! Alarm went again at 1am, kept on til 6am. I was put in hospital at 3am and have now to stay there. All the camp went to air raid shelter. The shift went out til 8.30am. All smoking in billets prohibited. Three or four planes came over and gun-fire was heard and many search lights seen. No doubt it's the real thing! We are told that it was a real pucker raid. Am now in hospital.

Saturday June 17
No raid last night but we have strict blackout. Nips claim to have brought down five planes and we did very little damage. Ten persons killed. I get my foot massaged today by Dutch MO and it shows great improvement. I think I will be out in a few days. Then what! Once again down the wretched mine. I wonder how much longer! Are we nearing the end!

Sunday June 18*
Still ban on smoking in billets. Hospital allowed to smoke. Dutch doctor massaged my foot and is improving rapidly. Frank Watson visited me and read chapter from bible and we had a simple prayer meeting. I appreciated it very much. No more rumours.

Monday June 19
Had best meal in this camp, only hospital patients. Baked potatoes, boiled onions, rice and gravy, lump of meat for tea. I have my first bath for three weeks and feel much cleaner. Rumours are good but vague. Everybody extremely optimistic but I am afraid they are going to be very disappointed.

Tuesday June 20
I have now been laid up for three weeks and have Singapore foot. I am still unable to walk. I am not trying very hard. Food is still very good and the boys are looking very fit and well.

Wednesday June 21
Yasme Day. Longest day. Nips had a hut inspection and took a lot of clothing from the boys. I did not go to concert or church. Feel rather seedy. I tell Capt W do not agree with his policy re ice-cream. I think Number 2 is taking advantage of Capt W's good nature and generosity.

Thursday June 22
It's very warm and the heat is very similar to Java. My foot is much better but have not commenced walking on it. I've got a touch of diarrhoea. Food still continues to be good.

Friday June 23
Phew it's hot. MO tried to take fluid from my foot but got nothing and swelling still remains. Nip tells me that I must walk so must have a go tomorrow. Rumours still going strong. Had a bath today and played chess.

Saturday June 24*
Still very warm. All men in camp work without shirts. I still have the squitters. Rumours still are good but vague. I look at some of my old papers pass the day in dreaming of days gone by. My foot about the same but I now walk on my heel. I dreamt last night of dear old Stan.

Sunday June 25
Wonderful news! 360 letters arrive in camp. I have four. 90 men receive letters. Will be issued tomorrow. Our prayers have been answered. I am certain they are from Mother, Dad, Ken. I feel sorry for those who have none. I can hardly wait for tomorrow. Foot better but am sick and diarrhoea.

Monday June 26
Prayers have been answered and today I received letters from my dear Mother and Dad, Ken and Babs! I could hardly read them because my eyes were dimmed by the tears that came to them and I'm not ashamed to say it. I have already read them over a dozen times. It's the best tonic I've had since I have been a POW. How those who I loved must have suffered in those 17 months of anxiety, not knowing whether I was alive or not. Our captors have something to answer for. I am now an uncle and am looking forward to seeing my niece Wendy. Babs' letter was a gem and I hope that if I am spared to return home that Babs will be my wife. I must try and let her know next time I write a postcard home. O I do feel happy! Mere words cannot express my feelings. The weather today is miserable, it has rained all day, but nothing can dampen my spirits today. I am now more than ever waiting for the day that I shall be free and see once again those whom I love. May God bless them all and keep them and me safe and well til that day.
Summary of letters. Mother and Dad: Wendy married, Peg still alive, Marjorie married, fit and well both of them.
Babs: Mother and Dad going to Bateman's once a week. Dunbar still in Cardiff. Wendy marries a widow [sic]. Pop Bateman sick selling cars. Mrs B will cycle. Babs not married.
Jo: his daughter Wendy, his visits to Mrs Lindop and letters to Mrs B at Nottingham, I wonder if we will play together again. Mother and Dad go to B at least once a week. Wilf not mentioning me in the broadcast.

Tuesday June 27
I give my letters to some of the boys to read who did not receive any. Rumours very good and if true the European war should be finished this year. My foot is much better and I think I will soon be out of hospital. Then what! Unable to eat, sick and diarrhoea.

Wednesday June 28

Feeling pretty groggy today. Still very sick and squitters. Do not eat anything all day. Rumours very vague. I think we are becoming too optimistic. The reaction will be great if Germany does not fall in three months.

Thursday June 29

My foot is much better. I anticipate being out of hospital very soon. I went and had a bath today and a cold shower. Very warm and did a spot of sunbathing. Rumours still coming in and if true then the Huns must be near the end. In fact it should be finished before the winter arrives.

Friday June 30

A very rough day, terrific wind. I am feeling better, no sickness or squitters. The new hospital is nearing completion and I think will be ready in a week's time. The camp is also being extended. I do hope I will be able to keep with Capt W.

Saturday July 1

A year ago today lists were made out for this draft. The year has simply flown. Very warm but showery, a typical English Saturday afternoon. Had half an egg today, the first since I have been in Japan. It was choice.

Sunday July 2

Yasme Day. A very quiet day and much rain. Capt W gave a lecture on motor-racing. Very good. Concert very good. I stayed in hospital all day. Dai Grandon gets first Yasme. Food not so good. On bread tomorrow. Foot improving but still painful.

Monday July 3

Very heavy rain. No gen. Feel miserable. My toes are bad again. New hospital nearly finished. Will move in a few days time. I do hope I will be able to stay with Cap W.

Tuesday July 4

Independence Day. Rained all day. Air raid warning. Rumoured peace talks. If true it must be nearly over. Thank God! My foot is better.

Wednesday July 5

Hear that the hospital moves tomorrow. News still good. I wonder how much is true.

Thursday July 6
Have got a chap in with me who is very weak. He does not eat anything and Alan Cox (the other patient with me) [and I] have to look after him. Had a bad night. Serious accident down mine. "Joe", one of the 77th, had bad head injuries through a fall of the roof. Lucky to be alive. Got paid today and received full pay. Another 90 letters arrived but I did not receive any. Rumours of peace conference.

Friday July 7*
A very sad day. Reg King, the fellow who was so weak, passed away at 9 o'clock this evening. He was taken worse about 4 o'clock and I called American doctor but it was hopeless. Poor lad, married with four children. We were supposed to move to new hospital but lighting not yet fitted. Toes are very sore but foot is much better. I move to another room.

Saturday July 8
Poor old King was buried today so we have now lost 14 in the camp. Ten English, four Dutch. My foot is much better and am able to walk on my heel. A year ago today I volunteered to go on draft. This month is my worst of the year and I shall be glad when it's past. Rumours still good. I wonder if it's true about peace conference. I do hope and pray that it's true.

Sunday July 9
I leave hospital today and become Capt W's assistant temporarily. I hope it will become permanent. New hospital opens tomorrow. Listen to Welsh choir practising and went to prayer meeting. I feel rather weak. Still worried over work in mine and where I will sleep when Capt W moves.

Monday July 10
New hospital opened today. No visiting allowed. A really good building, plenty of fresh air. I feel very sick and cannot eat my breakfast. News still coming in of peace conference but I'm still rather dubious. My foot still sore.

Tuesday July 11
Capt W and 2 doctors are to have the old MO room and will move tomorrow. I do not know where I shall go. I hope I may stay in same billet with Nick, Capt W's batman. My foot is still sore. Frank is very optimistic re war. I go every evening to epilogue.

Wednesday July 12
Yasme Day. A very busy day. A big Nip medical inspection. I am classed grade B and now weigh 79kg. Went to service, 16 present. Also went to concert, very good. Welsh choir excellent. My foot is still swollen.

Thursday July 13
My unlucky day. My foot and leg badly swollen, must take it easy. Capt W moved into his new quarters today leaving Nick and I sharing one room. Nine months ago we arrived here. No news.

Friday July 14
My foot is very painful and my Singapore toe is much worse. I slept very well but was sick during the day. No news except commandant leaving tomorrow.

Saturday July 15
My foot is still painful and swollen. I am still optimistic after hearing the gen which confirms peace talks. Why not this month – it's got to be some time.

Sunday July 16
Another Sunday and the boys go to work down the mine, factory and shaft. I do not think I will keep this camp job when my foot becomes better. Am afraid I will [not get] support from the right quarter. Find great comfort in evening epilogue.

Monday July 17
My foot becoming better. Nip making inquiries if it is OK. Looks like work down that lousy mine. I feel very miserable today and am losing my optimism. Dare not show it to the boys as I have been so optimistic lately. Commandant still with us.

Tuesday July 18
The Nips are getting nasty – big change in their attitude. I am very depressed again these days. Hoping and praying that I do not go down the mine.

Wednesday July 19
Weather still very hot. Had half a peach today for tea.

Thursday July 20
No gen for some days, the boys are becoming depressed and optimism is declining. My toes are still sore and my leg is now swelling. I am able to walk with difficulty. The guards are very annoyed and are doing a lot of bashing.

Friday July 21*
Hear that Tojo has been pushed out, good gen if true. Moving billets tomorrow and have arranged to be opposite Capt W's room and office with Nick and Sgt Missen. We were up to midnight making out new accommodation chart. I hope Nips will agree. No concert tomorrow because of ban on rehearsals.

Saturday July 22
Yasme Day. What chaos. Our accommodation chart scrapped and Nips arranged move. I am agreeably surprised. I am put in with Capt W and two medical officers and fall in on parade with same. My prayers have been answered and I thank God. We held our first communion today when we had 10 communicants. I do not know whether I am permanent camp staff or not. I pray that I am.

Sunday July 23
The Nips are treating us better. My leg and foot is badly swollen. I'm worried. No gen today but am hoping it will be good when we get some. Slept very badly in my new quarters.

Monday July 24*
Received terrible blow today when I heard that dear Norman Welsford was instantly killed down the mine. Norman was one of my greatest friends in this camp and I had made many plans with him for the future when we got released. Thank God he was killed instantly and suffered no pain. It happened at one o'clock, one hour before he was due to come up. Next to Fryett and Dai Grandon he was my nearest friend. He had such a loveable disposition and we always had a daily chat together. Oh why did it have to be Norman. I feel that I should never have allowed him to come on this draft. I think he suffered more mentally than any other man in this camp. He was very popular with everybody. A guard of honour has been arranged to keep watch over the coffin throughout the night and he will be buried tomorrow. Letters have been received in the camp "234" but will not be issued until the receipt book arrives. I hear a whisper that I may be put on permanent camp staff but will not believe it til I see it in black and white.

Tuesday July 25
Poor old Norman was buried today. I was unable to go to the funeral but I went to the short impressive service that was held in the camp. It still seems hard to realise that Norman is dead. We have not yet been able to locate his watch. Capt W and I went through his belongings today and gave Frank Fryett and Jack Wood what they required. I have been thinking of Joe today as it's his birthday. I wonder how they are at home and how is my little niece Wendy. I do hope and pray that I will have a letter in this bunch that have arrived. News of a Red+ delegate coming to camp.

Wednesday July 26
I am feeling very miserable. Did not receive any letters but was pleased that many received letters that had not received any previously. Poor Norman received two from his father. Very sad. Camp being cleaned today for visit of delegates from the Pope. Issue of soap, razor blades, towels and loincloths. I am still awaiting news whether I go down the mine.

Thursday July 27
It was certainly a big day today. We first had a visit from an RC minister who was just shown around and on leaving the camp gave us 500 Yen. The next visitor was a Swede who saw for himself state of men and camp. Dutch MO did some good work when speaking to the Swede and pointed out poor condition of men. I hope it will do some good. He told us to keep our chins up.

Friday July 28
We found Norman's watch yesterday and Capt W is going to hand it back to his father on his return to England. From letters received by the boys, dated this Jan, it appears that they know we are in Japan. My feet are still sore and my left foot and leg is still badly swollen. The guards have still got their wooden rifles.

Saturday July 29
I have got the commandant's bed to sleep on – not so bad. I am feeling much better than yesterday and do not feel so pessimistic. I wonder if this war will be over before the European one. It's certainly got possibilities. I feel very weak and can still only hobble along.

Sunday July 30
We had an air raid alarm yesterday from 1 til 3. Rumour says 10 planes. My foot is still very sore and I find great difficulty in walking. Am still waiting for news of my permanent working in the camp. Went to epilogue. Another Sunday and work just the same.

Monday July 31
No gen for some time. Boys are becoming very pessimistic. Fryett thinks we will be free by Nov. I'm afraid I think it will be next year now. That peace conference seems to have failed.

Tuesday August 1
Frank Fryett gets place in the permanent camp hut. He seems to be OK. I am very comfortable in my new quarters. Cigs are very scarce. Small increase in rice ration.

Wednesday August 2
Yasme Day. A quiet day spoilt by practice air-raid alarm. Commandant notices my bad foot and says I must go to hospital. I will try and get out of it. Had communion service and church, also concert. Received another 50 Red+ books. My foot is very painful and sore.

Thursday August 3
Well I'm in hospital once again. I suppose I'm the only chap in camp who does not want to go in. I am afraid I may be sent down the mine when it becomes better.

Friday August 4
My foot is very painful but the swelling has gone down. Gen is very good. Turkey has now come in on our side. Peace conference finished. Had a warning this evening but did go in shelter. 30 years ago first European war started.

Saturday August 5
August Bank Holiday Saturday. I wonder if I will be free for next Bank Holiday. I am rather disappointed at our progress in France. It's now two months since we started invasion and we have not yet got Paris. My foot is better but am still in hospital.

Sunday August 6
Five years today I left home for a month's training with the Terriers but am still waiting to return home. The commandant has taken his bed back but I am to take this bed in hospital when I go out. Got paid today. We had a short prayer in the evening by Watson in the hospital.

Monday August 7
Another Bank Holiday spent in captivity. I wonder if it's the last. I am thinking of them at home today. Am wondering whether they are all well and happy. It's very hot today and the temp for the last few days has been around 100 in the shade. The meals are very poor today. I had one piece of bread and a bowl of pepper water for soup.

Tuesday August 8
Terrific rain this afternoon. Much cooler. No gen. My toes and foot much better. I am feeling rather depressed once again. Tea was worse than last night.

Wednesday August 9
Terrible night last night. Rain came down in torrents flooding the hospital. Much finer today. Feeling in camp pessimistic.

Thursday August 10

I am afraid I may be going down the mine very soon. Big changes are being done today. 15 men taken off camp work to work day work on shaft. Capt W fails to get me on camp staff, a big blow to me because it will mean that I will go down mine when my foot is better. I feel very fed up, all my troubles seem to be starting again. My foot is nearly normal. Gen is bad. We have lost Paris.

Friday August 11

We had air-raid warning last night from 12 til 3. I think it was practice. Heard yesterday that they were making inquiries for me down the mine. It looks bad. I also hear that I have been transferred to Number 1 hut for roll call purposes but will still sleep in Capt W billet. Weather still very warm. My foot and toes are nearly better. I should be out of hospital in a few days.

Saturday August 12

Three years ago today we left Cardiff for Frome on our mobile training. I feel fairly fit but weak through being in bed. Also our food is very small. One bowl of rice and four thin slices of cucumber for tea. It amazes me how we ever work on such food, let alone live. About eight of the boys had 50 ccs of blood taken from them today.

Sunday August 13

Yasme Day. I did not go to church service but communion service held in hospital. Blood test today, also weigh-in. I weigh 77kg, losing two on last month. Frank Fryett gains six. Heard a very good talk on Russia. Went to concert in the evening. Very good. Welsh choir good. Frank goes out to work after four months in camp. Work is said to be easy.

Monday August 14

Frank went out to work on top of shaft and found it fairly easy. Rumoured that factory men were going down mine and sick men in camp going to factory. My leg and foot is now fit. I will be out of hospital soon and then what? Down the mine?

Tuesday August 15

A very interesting day. I go out of hospital for two hours and then am ordered back by commandant. It does not make sense. Ten of the factory go down the mine tomorrow. I am sorry to see it.

Wednesday August 16

No gen. Very warm. I am opposite to Dutchman with broken back. He is very ill and in great pain. I feel very sorry for him.

Thursday August 17
Eight rabbits arrive today and we start another garden outside. Also five pigs are due to arrive tomorrow. The food may get better now that a complaint has been made. The soup has been just plain water. No more tea, only hot water. It's about time we had some more letters. I am still in hospital but do not feel at all secure. I'm afraid the commandant might say out of hospital down mine.

Friday August 18
Weather still very warm. Two pigs arrive. One collapses in the camp and is killed. Hospital patients receive a small piece of liver and we have pork soup tomorrow. I make mistake in speaking to hospital orderly and telling him something in confidence. Wise tongue keeps a still head. Am still worried re my ultimate position in camp.

Saturday August 19
Young Woolley and Dutch boy who broke their legs last Jan are put to work in Bamboo factory but still stay in hospital. Heavy rain in the afternoon. I do not think Dutchman will live very long. The mosies are a nuisance and bite very much during the evenings. I have been graded A in blood group and have had to sew it on my shirt.

Sunday August 20
We had air raid warning at 4.30 this afternoon til 7.15pm. Many planes were heard, also AA fire and machine gun. The biggest raid yet. And the sirens went again at 11.30pm til 2.30. No planes heard but bombs were heard to drop so we've had two raids within the last 12hrs – good going. I hear rumour of more men working down [illegible] supposed to be light work. Work commencing on the 23rd. I wonder if I'm on the party.

Monday August 21
Nips say 60 planes over and from 2 up to 30 shot down. It appears that more changes are taking place. Frank afraid that he might be going down shaft. I feel that I'm sitting on the edge of a volcano, waiting for something to happen. I speak to the doctor about my foot but get no satisfaction except that I should have another x ray.

Tuesday August 22
Yasme Day. Another change round in billets and work. I am still with Capt W. Frank still on his own job. One shift of miners go down shaft, not so good. I go to church service and communion afterwards. We have a practice alarm in the afternoon. No concert in the evening and the Welsh choir have disbanded, owing to Nip restrictions on rehearsing.

Wednesday August 23
A lot of activity in the camp. It appears that a big inspection will take place on the 25th. No gen but most of the boys think it will be over by Christmas this year. I wonder!

Thursday August 24
This is the 900th day of captivity. I was hoping that we would be free by the 1000th day but it does not seem so. The war in Europe is still undecided and we do not seem to be making any progress. Great sensation. Shaft caught fire. Blacksmith's shop and changing rooms all burnt down. Boys lose all their clothing and great pity it did not burn down the machine house. It would stop all work down shaft for months.

Friday August 25
Boys still go down shaft and have lost all their clothes. Nips have provided new. Able to buy half a bottle of vitamin tablets. Gen seems to be the same.

Saturday August 26
The Dutchman with broken back sleeping opposite me died this morning – a happy release. He was in a terrible condition. The funeral took place this afternoon. I'm afraid the other Dutchman will soon be dead. The camp is in a turmoil over this coming inspection. Nobody seems to know exact date of inspection. The weather is now changing, becoming cold in the morning and evening. Had a shock today when I hear that the men in the camp think that Welshmen get preference in camp jobs.

Sunday August 27
The Dutchman with TB died this morning 5am and was buried at 2pm. Two deaths in two days but they were expected. We have now lost 11 English and six Dutch. It was very cold last night and I had to put another blanket on my bed. This morning reminded me of our first morning in Japan and I feel extremely miserable. My foot and toes are practically normal. I anticipate an early discharge from hospital. The number 1 and number 2 from mine visited hospital. Bad omen for me I think! I think of home today and imagine how they are spending their Sunday.

Monday August 28
Big inspection tomorrow 8.30am. Camp is looking very clean, very few in hospital. 12 in one building and three in TB ward. I wonder what will be the reaction of the Nips after inspection.

Tuesday August 29
Inspection took place 8.30 this morning by Nip Colonel and Number 1 and Number 2 of the mine. It looks as if it's something to do with the work. They went down the shaft. We had excellent breakfast. Significant fact guards had wooden rifles. My foot examined by Nip orderly who said something about a splint.

Wednesday August 30
We are issued with apple and two bars of soap. Guards have got their rifles back. Three cases in hospital of some peculiar epidemic.

Thursday August 31*
We get some more gen about conference but have very little faith in it. I have a talk every afternoon with American doctor which I find very edifying. Nip doctor examined everybody in hospital and took down all particulars. Gosney, the other lad who broke his leg, starts work in the basket-making [factory] tomorrow.

Friday September 1
Gosney started in basket factory today and like the other two did nothing. I had a terrible night last night. Sick and squitters all night. Temp 38.2. Could not eat during the day, had two puddings of flour and water. Nick, Capt W's batman, comes in hospital today with boils and a bad back. His temp 39.3. Am a bit worried about Dai Grandon. He is not looking at all well. Stanton had a providential escape from death today.

Saturday September 2
Yasme Day. A most quiet day and the best restful day we've had. Went to church service in the morning, also communion. It's still very hot temp in hospital 98 degrees. I played chess with Frank and have some very good games. We talk of old times. Five years ago I played against Bridgend and was made a Bombardier.

Sunday September 3
Another Sunday and the fifth anniversary of the war. Five years today war commenced and we are still at war and peace still a long way off. I wonder where I will be this time next year. I do hope and pray that I will be safely home. I wish some more letters would arrive. I was very sick during the night.

Monday September 4
Gen seems to be very vague. I am still off my food, have got the squitters once again. Nip doctors examine my foot and I have to go for x ray tomorrow.

Tuesday September 5
Went for x ray today and had only one plate taken, exactly same as before. Another apple today. I feel very sick. Am worried about the mine.

Wednesday September 6
Still in hospital. Very wet today. Much rain. We were issued with apple. I am still feeling sick.

Thursday September 7
All men kept in camp. Many speculations for reason. We soon found out. A most thorough search was made of all the billets and men for matches, maps etc. It was the most thorough search we've had. It seems that the fire at the shaft has caused all the bother. Nine men are kept in custody pending investigation of shaft fire. I hear result of x ray and find that I did break a bone in my foot. Now what! My foot is still painful but I don't know what my position is in the camp.

Friday September 8
The nine men who were kept in custody re the fire were dismissed today. I start working in the office from 9 til 11.30, 1 til 4.30. Fairly busy as we are starting a savings bank because men are not allowed to keep money in billets. I see Nip MO and try to get out of hospital but fail.

Saturday September 9
Four men in clink for stealing. They only get a small bowl of rice and water, also a blanket. It's now becoming colder and I am afraid winter is fast approaching. We have not had any gen for a few days. Had raid alarm this afternoon but it appears to have been false.

Sunday September 10
The weather becoming colder. I think of home a great deal these days and long for a letter. The boys in the camp are looking better but I fear the winter. The food is going to become scarcer.

Monday September 11
We hear today that 300 men are due to come to this camp at the end of the month. I think it's true and maybe we will see some friends and get some real gen. My foot very painful today. Raining and cold.

Tuesday September 12
Yasme Day. Very wet. Nips busy making plans for alteration in huts. Capt W's room and office are being altered. I wonder where I will go when I am out of hospital. I promise to give a talk on sport this afternoon but cried off rather late much to Capt W's indignation. I am afraid I was at fault. Went to church service and communion. Good news – 125 letters received. I wonder if I have one.

Wednesday September 13
Letters issued today. I receive one from Babs, dated July 1943. Hear that Ken Williams is married. I now wish that I had married Babs before leaving England. I do hope that I will be able to do so if I return safely. It's grand to get a letter. It makes you feel nearer home. Some of the boys get letters dated April 1944, only five months. About 50 men get letters.

Thursday September 14
No real gen coming in. Commandant leaves camp for three days, presumably to get dope on newcomers. I am feeling very hungry these days.

Friday September 15
We get our usual two packets of cigs for 46 cents. Since my accident I smoke very heavy. Very heavy rain today. Nip workmen in camp start making new building for hospital.

Saturday September 16
We are finding some of the thieves in the camp. Capt W has put them in the guardroom for seven days. We have issue of half an apple. We hear that the rations are to be cut for all who are in hospital and working in camp to be cut by half. If this happens it will mean the death of many. They might as well shoot the lot. Terrible day. Rain, rain and more rain. We had to return 50 Red+ books.

Sunday September 17
What a day! Terrific gale, all the walls of the camp blown down. Many huts have the rain coming in. The hospital floor is like a lake. The storm abated about tea-time. It was the worst storm we have yet had. Dai Grandon comes back to camp to help repair fence and huts. My foot is becoming much better.

Monday September 18
I read my letters very often. They give me much comfort and joy. Workmen come in and repair roofs but as yet no new buildings have been put up for the newcomers. I go to evening epilogue. Rumour of change in cooks.

Tuesday September 19
Issued one pear. I gave mine to Capt W's batman Nick who is looking very ill. The Nips are making our rest room into a billet so we will have no place for any church meetings. Will ask Nips to build one. I go to epilogue.

Wednesday September 20
We hear today that four officers are coming with 300 men. I think one MO, 3 2nd Lt.

Thursday September 21
We get some good gen. One of the boys finds a Nip map and we are able to see that our line is in Holland and along German, French border. Russians about the same as three months ago. As I see it we are further advanced towards Germany than we were in Nov 1918. Nips very busy on alterations to camp.

Friday September 22
Yasme Day. Not a very good day. Boys had to work cleaning their billets all the morning. I was supposed to give a talk in the afternoon but it was cancelled. Went to service and communion in the afternoon, also concert in the evening. Boys have to work in the garden for half hour before going to work.

Saturday September 23
We hear of more good gen. I am optimistic enough to hope that the European war may be over within a month. A Nip got killed down the shaft today. Frank had the hardest day yet down the mine. I took for the first time the epilogue service. I felt very nervous but was very pleased that I did the service.

Sunday September 24
Capt W was told by commandant that we will soon be allowed to write a letter home – 100 words. Splendid news. I will write three letters in one. Mother, Joe and Babs. We also get a number of Nips in the camp from HQ making preparations for new draft. Another Sunday and we have to work. Nip killed down the mine.

Monday September 25
I write letter to home, also Babs asking her to marry me. I hope that it will be OK. More changes in camp. Four cooks go out to work and four of the sick go in cookhouse. We hear that [we] may soon buy cocoa, butter and coffee. I believe it when I see it. News good I still feel optimistic. Nips ask for men for building purposes.

Tuesday September 26
No news of draft coming in. Help Capt W to censor letters. Capt W goes to dentist for filling in tooth. More good gen. I hope it's true.

Wednesday September 27
It's becoming much colder especially in the morning and evening.

Thursday September 28
Five years today we had concert at the docks, brings back happy memories. Capt W has toothache goes to dentist but finds him absent. Some more good gen. Paratroops invade Nederlands. The war in Europe should be over this year. Still censoring letters which are very optimistic. Nip doctor saw my foot today and I thought I would be put out of hospital. Still swollen at night.

Friday September 29
John, Dutch boy with broken leg and Tony, also broken leg, left hospital today after eight months. Capt W kept to his bed feeling seedy. I take over and kept fairly busy listening to complaints, charges etc. I collect cigs from Nips and issue same. I'm afraid Nick has got TB. Temp this afternoon 103. No news of new draft except rumour that they will not be coming til December.

Saturday September 30*
Wretched day. Rained all day and cold. Many doubling up on meals. Four men put on charge. Doctors say that Nick has got TB. Very sad. I am afraid he will not go home. He coughs very often and he's getting much weaker. I'm trying to get him to eat but he's got no appetite. Hugh Edwards volunteered to go down mine in place of Fryett's cousin Frank. I'm afraid I would only do it for my own brother.

Sunday October 1
Yasme Day. Another bad day for the boys. Everybody had to work in the morning making a fish pond. Church service and communion in the afternoon. My talk was again cancelled. Nick is still very ill and a sputum test was made today. Went to concert in the evening, not so bad. Dutch were very good. New working list made out. I find myself still down the mine.

Monday October 2
The doctor finds a spot on Nick's lung which makes it very bad for Nick. It's becoming colder and we start issuing two extra blankets. Capt W is much better, went again to the dentist. We have alarm at 9 in the evening.

Tuesday October 3
Rained all day. My foot very painful and swollen. I gave Nick all my soup powders I had saved, also a little bit of tea. He seems to be eating more but still not enough. I feel very tired.

Wednesday October 4
100 Red+ books came in today. Not a very good selection. Stayed up til 10pm listing same. Feel very tired.

Thursday October 5
Very busy day. Issued library books. Got paid. Many men on charges for doubling. Men pay all their money into bank. I was unable to take service this evening but will do it tomorrow. We had to close down on unofficials for today because we thought a rat was smelt by our host.

Friday October 6
Accident down mine. Alf Owen lucky he was not killed. Thought leg was broken but x ray showed no bone broken. My foot is still painful. More gen but not verified that we are in or around Koln. Was unable to do the service this evening. Will do it on Sunday. Have been very ill-tempered all day. Wrong spirit.

Saturday October 7
Very stormy and wet. I dreamt of home last night and that we were at peace. I feel sick and could not eat my mid-day meal of pap. As I was checking the meal through at lunchtime I could smell the mine and I think that's what made me sick. The boys are very depressed over cigs. We should have had our issue of 20 yesterday but have been promised them on the 11th.

Sunday October 8
By gum it's getting colder. Started work again on extension of office. Rumours that the draft will come in December. We seem to have got the food racket in hand. My foot is still swollen. I think we can thank the Soya beans for keeping us with sufficient protein etc.

Monday October 9
Much warmer during the day but still cold in the evening. Issue of five cigs. Capt W and I do not have sufficient to go around. Issue of two blocks of soap which were badly wanted. I eat no rice these days. I swap rice for three quarters of a bread roll. So my meals consist of dry bread and coloured water.

Tuesday October 10
A very busy day. Did not get to bed til midnight. Had to prepare new working sheet as men are transferred from shaft to mine. They have to work for 10 hours. We had a daylight raid. Heard the planes but could not see them. Blackout in the evening.

Wednesday October 11
Yasme Day. A very busy day. Issue of winter clothing. It was our old clothes returned to us all torn and battered and very dirty. I go to service in the morning and communion, about 14 present. We get weighed. I gained 1kg, my weight being 78kgs. Concert in the evening was not so bad.

Thursday October 12
We receive another 30 books, a very poor selection. We hear that the draft may come next month. Working on Capt W's office. Our letters home are still in Nip office. Boys find the 12hr shift very hard, something must be done about it.

Friday October 13*
Friday the 13th. A year ago today we arrived in this camp. Day started badly. A man loses his "bento" and commandant threatens to stop a meal if nobody owns up. Nobody took it so man was put in jug. Capt W's office knocked down. Very cold.

Saturday October 14
New office should be ready in few days time. My foot still swollen. Doctor says must rest. I now have a sore mouth.

Sunday October 15
Another Sunday and the day passes by just like an ordinary day. We were able to buy for 10 cents a small piece of bread about six inches long, two inches wide, one inch thick, exactly about a third of what we get issued for a meal when we are on bread. Not so cold. I'm feeling fairly good. But still worry about my future work in the camp.

Monday October 16
Not so cold. Good news. The 12hr shift has been cancelled. Our prayers have been answered. I am thankful for it was too much for the boys. Progress is being made in building new huts for draft who I think will be coming from another camp.

Tuesday October 17
A very bad day. I felt as if I was sitting on a volcano all day. The Nips found out that the boys were taking unofficial Yasme. 26 men were caught but nothing done officially. Nips are afraid they might lose their jobs. Boys had a bashing but not too hard.

Wednesday October 18
The unofficial Yasme are finished. We have been very lucky not to have been found out. All's well that ends well. Issue of orange today. Very wet and miserable. Gen smashing, if true then it must be all over soon in Europe. Foot better, not so much swelling. Blitz on camp workers.

Thursday October 19
Issue another orange and a quarter pound of tea between three men. Tea costs 1.50. Very mild. Capt W looking very seedy. The soup is not so good, just digons (white turnips), makes one very sick.

Friday October 20
The camp is in a turmoil. We have a spy in our midst who is reporting men to the Nips. We don't know for certain who he is. Suspect Dutch half-cast. Closed up everything.

Saturday October 21
Yasme Day. A very quiet day. Good news. 182 letters received. I was not fortunate this time, pleased that some of the boys got their first. No service, only communion which I attended, also went to concert.

Sunday October 22
Another quiet day but still cold. News of men coming in but feel certain that they will be coming from mainland. The American and Dutch boy are very much in love with one another and I think they are both homosexual. The gen still continues to be good. We are being watched by several half-casts.

Monday October 23
I was disappointed at not receiving a letter from home. I do hope and pray that they are safe and well. We hear official news that 300 English are coming in next month. Very cold in the evening but warm during the day. I am still sleeping in hospital. My leg and foot are still swollen.

Tuesday October 24
A large spot of bother over gas capes. They are our own gas capes but we are not allowed to keep them. I took evening epilogue about 10pm.

Wednesday October 25
Had fish for breakfast. The first for six weeks – only for hospital. Another raid today. We were 2hrs in the shelter. Many planes and heard a few bombs. Gen very good. Rumoured that war in Europe was over. I hope and pray it is true. I have a very bad cold, feeling rough.

Thursday October 26
A most alarming day. Nips went mad over gas capes. Kept men who had lost them standing to attention all day. A big sort out of camp workers. 20 men sent down mine and shaft. I was sent for by commandant and was asked if I was OK for the mine. I showed my foot and was dismissed. It certainly shook me because I thought I was through with the mine. I am feeling lousy and have a temp of 100. Go to bed early. So ends a bad day.

Friday October 27
A year ago today we started work down the mine. I feel a little better today but still have a rotten cold. Able to buy 2ozs of cooking fat and egg cup full of pepper. Very busy day but very wet. I wonder how much longer. Hospital had a small piece of fish.

Saturday October 28
Not so cold today. My cold is better. Able to buy some seaweed, more tea and mustard. Shop is being enlarged. I still feel that I am sitting on edge of volcano and may be sent down mine any day. I hope and pray that I never go down again.

Sunday October 29
Another Sunday. How many more? 72 letters received. I was unlucky once again. I do hope and pray that they are all well at home. Big change in billets on Yasme Day. All camp being moved to make room for new draft. Rumours that 10 officers are coming. I am rather worried about my position and whether I will be shifted from Capt W's room.

Monday October 30
Terrible accident down mine. Hampson breaks his back, similar place as Dutchman who died. This is the fourth accident in the last five days. Woods got caught taking a day off, also Fryett for taking a bath when he should be in bed. Woods gets away with it but Fryett goes working down the shaft tomorrow. The Nips have been waiting to catch Fryett.

Tuesday October 31
Fryett went down the hole today. Nips presented officers and myself with a pipe and a packet of tea. A big change in the billets tomorrow.

Wednesday November 1
Yasme Day. A fine day and on the whole rather quiet. Nips allowed us to do the changing of billets. Issue of soap, orange, mustard powder, tea. We also had a bit of sugar in our tea. I don't know what's coming over the Nips. They are certainly bashing out the stuff. Held church service and communion in the hospital, now that the restroom has become a billet. No concert in the evening. Rumour says that 300 yanks will arrive on the fourth.

Thursday November 2
Rumoured that Americans are arriving. Frank says that the shaft is worse than the mine and he would rather work 12hrs down the mine. Very wet day and miserable. I wonder if I will go down the mine very soon.

Friday November 3
We received our weekly issue of cigs – 20 each. We pay 46 cents for two packets. Nips have now roped off empty billets in readiness for new draft. Only another 29 days for 1000 – I wonder?

Saturday November 4
A lovely day and quite warm. Feel very depressed, also very jumpy. Capt W and I talk of old times and also read some of the poems that we like. The guards are becoming very nasty again doing a lot of slapping. The first case of pneumonia comes in hospital, not very serious. I take the evening epilogue service.

Sunday November 5
Another Sunday. I wonder how many more. I wish I had some more letters from home saying they were OK. I have not received any dated later than July '43. No gen coming at all, everything seems to be quiet. I am thinking that my 1000 days will have to be lengthened to another 100 at least. Went to epilogue in the evening.

Monday November 6
Air raid alarm but no planes. Becoming colder in the day. Now started on barley and rice, beans having finished. I am still changing my rice for bread. Still no gen.

Tuesday November 7
A fairly busy day. Boys got paid. I think that the war in Europe must be over. Can get no real gen on it.

Wednesday November 8
We hear that war in Europe finished on 23rd Oct. Hope it's true.

Thursday November 9
We are still unable to be certain that war is over in Europe though everything points that way. Some of the Nips are treating us much better. I think they can see which way the wind is blowing. We now get music in the dining hall from 11.30 til 1 and from 6 til 7. Frank is feeling rather depressed over working down the shaft.

Friday November 10
We hear today that the commandant is leaving. I will be sorry to see him go, it will probably make a big difference to me as he is keeping me in hospital. Had a very busy day balancing camp funds and it was satisfactory.

Saturday November 11
Yasme Day. Another Armistice Day. Started well. We had air raid and was in shelter for 3hrs. Held thanksgiving and memorial service in the afternoon, also observed 2 mins silence. Had communion service. Frank and I opened the tin of condensed milk which we'd brought from Java. It was wonderful on the rice. I weighed today and have gained 1kg, now weigh 79kg.

Sunday November 12
Still yet another Sunday. How many more? Poor Fryett is down in the dumps. No doubt the shaft is a nightmare. Bitterly cold today. We hear that a peace conference is in progress. I do hope and pray that it's true. I now say that this war will not last more than six or eight months if Japan refuses peace terms.

Monday November 13
We have sweet potatoes with our rice – very tasty. Unlucky day but passes off without any incident. My foot is better and not so swollen. I fear Nip MO may say work down the mine when commandant leaves. Went to epilogue.

Tuesday November 14
New Nip commandant arrives. Old one leaves on the 16th. A pity, I seemed to get on very well with the old one. Fantastic rumour today that it was all over. The Nips are feverishly building air raid shelters. Frank gets a Yasme. I take epilogue service in the evening.

Wednesday November 15
New Nip commandant takes over. He looks very military. I am walking much better.

Thursday November 16
Very cold today. I put on Nip trousers and woollen stockings made by Mother. Old commandant said goodbye to Capt W, doctors and myself. My foot is much better and I am able to walk easier. We get issue of new cigs, a real dead loss, 40 a month. Frank gets a Yasme with cement feet. He is very despondent these days. No new gen come in.

Friday November 17
New Nip commandant seems to be OK. He gave Capt W and doctors a packet of cigs and actually took his hat off when he came into room. We had short alarm this morning but did not go down shelter. The communist in the camp (who went to Russia) was caught red-handed pinching another man's rice – the worst offence possible in this camp.

Saturday November 18
We get further news of European war being finished. It appears that we are taking over Germany without any resistance. The Nips appear to be going to fight on, as I thought. I think we should finish the war in six or eight months time.

Sunday November 19
Another Sunday. Everybody works. It is hard to see a difference in the days of the week. We are having lovely weather but cold. Coal shortage in the camp. We had to burn a lot of wood. I do the epilogue service in the evening and have a very heated argument later on with Capt W, Frank and the doctors. Subject being forgiveness. I want to forgive Nips and Gerries [sic] because they are not to blame for our conditions.

Monday November 20
A very fine day but cold. I make £10 wager with Fryett that this war will not be over in six months. My foot is not so swollen but I cannot walk properly.

Tuesday November 21
Yasme Day. A very bad day. Practise air raid alarm for 2hrs in the morning. Rain and very cold. Nips made another search and did a lot of bashing with sticks, made my blood boil. Went to communion, also concert. Very few present owing to cold.

Wednesday November 22
Very very cold in the night and morning but the sun came out and then very warm. The temp was 39 inside the hospital, heavy white frost outside. We hear Red+ ship in Moji plenty of food and letters. I hope and pray that it's true because we need food, clothes and medical supplies to keep us alive in these hard months in front of us.

Thursday November 23
A lovely day but cold in the shade. New commandant checks up on sick, lame etc and creates a good impression. No cigs til the 25th. Boys very fed up. No news of newcomers.

Friday November 24
Not so cold. We were asked by Nip commandant if we could make up a list for Xmas Day. We are hoping it will bring forth good fruit. Red+ arrived today. Nine boxes very acceptable.

Saturday November 25
Fryett is still in camp with badly swollen cement feet. He's still very optimistic, he thinks the war will be over by Xmas. I still say next May. We had meat in today for the first time for many months. We should have a bit, about one third of a bar of chocolate.

Sunday November 26*
Very mild but wet. We had our small bit of meat, it was very nice. The Nips are becoming nasty again and there is much slapping. We had a very nice dinner, having some nasi goreng. Very tasty. I went to evening epilogue, only four present. I think of them at home and pray that they are well.

Monday November 27
Very wet and miserable day. No gen but the Nips attitude has definitely altered these last few days for the worse. Capt W had a long conference with the commandant. Hope it will make some difference. Took evening epilogue, seven present.

Tuesday November 28
21 in hospital, most since new hospital started – three pneumonia. We get a couple of oranges. American doctor makes a bet with me that the war will be over by Jan 20. We have a prayer meeting for peace.

Wednesday November 29
We hear that 42 men leaving the camp three days time. 42 new men will take their place. Two American papers arrive from Red+.

Thursday November 30
Accident down the shaft last night, not very serious. The goat dies and is put into the stew for tomorrow. Most of my friends are staying, only two or three of 240 Battery moving on this draft. The boys who are working down the shaft and mine will be much better off.

I think it's a real blessing to them. We hear very little gen and what we do hear is very contradictory. Frank is still on Yasme but very depressed. I am very sorry to see him so down. Some of the boys are very down.

Friday December 1
Yasme Day. Very wet, very cold, very miserable. 42 men who are going away had a medical. They are very lucky to be leaving this camp for I am certain that the working conditions cannot be worse. A big comb out of men to go down mine or shaft. I was sorry to see some sent to work who had been off for four to five months. I went to service in the morning and saw some of the concert in the evening. I have a chat with Frank and he tells me the shaft is hellish and he's scared stiff every moment he's down. He also gets pushed around by the Nips who think he's slacking.

Saturday December 2
1000 days POW. The day has arrived when I thought we might have been free. It's been a long time but I think we are on the last lap though it's going to be the hardest. The men in the camp are feeling rather downhearted as the general opinion was that it might be all over this month. Some of the boys are already looking ill. The lack of meat, fish and fat is the cause of our weakness. It seems impossible that we live on 3 small bowls of rice and 3 bowls of soup (made up of green leaves) per day but that is our staple diet. We must have more food if we are to survive this winter. Many men are already at their last gasp. I predict at least 60 deaths before the end of the year. I am afraid to tell the boys but I think the war is still on in Europe. From information received I am sure that we have suffered a reverse and that Germany has pushed us back. I have a chat with Capt W and tell him what I think and show him how I formed that opinion. We'll not tell the boys because I think it will do a lot of harm. I do feel very unhappy over the situation.

Sunday December 3
42 of our men left today and we had 42 to take their place. They brought very little gen. Heard that J Lewis was dead and that Major Street tried to commit suicide but failed. Many of the boys who left Java on the first draft died on the way. Conditions on the boat must have been terrible.

Monday December 4
The new men start work tomorrow. They think this is a better camp than their last but have not seen the work yet.

Tuesday December 5
The new men think the working conditions are terrible. They do not like the mine or shaft.

Wednesday December 6
From what we have gathered from newcomers the death-rate of Nip POWs will be very high. I should say roughly 25%.

Thursday December 7
Gee it's cold. I use hot water bottle for first time this winter and was I pleased to have it. No gen but I do not feel too despondent about it. We get issue of cigs and pipe tobacco. Small fall of snow which helps to make life more unbearable. Once more we changed billets and have now gone back to our original billets.

Friday December 8
Very very cold, more sleet fell. We had a real mixture of weather today. Rain, hail, sleet and snow and sunshine all in one hour. Three years today we set sail from England and Nippon started this war. We hear today that Russia and America are at war. What rubbish the Nips tell us.

Saturday December 9
Sensation. One of the Dutch boys walked out of the mine and returned to the camp without being challenged. He said that he left the mine because the Nip in charge of him let him. He is now in the clink. I do not think his punishment will be too great. It's very cold, the temp being down to 3 degrees.

Sunday December 10
Still very cold, temp down to 1 degree. I am afraid the men are going to crack up with this cold weather. I have to keep my greatcoat on all day and only feel warm when I have a bath in the afternoon.

Monday December 11
The sun shone today and it was a little warmer. I use my hot water bottle every night and find it a blessing. I do hope and pray that the war will soon be finished.

Tuesday December 12
A Dutchman died today, only in hospital four hours. He died of starvation. I am afraid there are at least another 12 who must be very near death.

Wednesday December 13
Very wet and miserable. Dutchman was cremated today. Capt W and I go into cookhouse racket re bread.

Thursday December 14
Very cold in the evening. Capt W speaks to Nip commandant re lack of fat, meat and fish. The Nip appeared to be very sympathetic and promised to do what he could to help us. It's now two months since we had meat or fish. Then it was very small.

Friday December 15
Good news! The commandant handed over the Red+ to us intact. All packages and tins were unopened. We will issue it out tomorrow. It means six men to every parcel which contains tea, sugar, milk, butter, cheese, shoes etc.

Saturday December 16
Yasme Day. The best Yasme we've had, undisturbed by any Nips. We issued Red+ packages and did it in one hour. We also had Nip issue of clothing, pants and shorts. I get thrown out of hospital having been in for four months. Went to service in the afternoon, very few present. Weighed today, 80kg.

Sunday December 17
We get issued another blanket. It was from stores that had been kept for new draft of 300 men which never arrived. Fryett and Watson both get out of shift down mine. I'm very pleased. Answer to prayer. Watson loses butter. Capt W gives some of his ration away.

Monday December 18
Big inspection today by Nip Colonel went off very satisfactory. Meat comes in today. It looks as if Capt W's talk has done a bit of good. Av weight of Dutch down below English. The Dutch are cracking up very quickly.

Tuesday December 19
Still very cold. We get air raid alarm in the morning lasting for 2 hrs. It was quite warm in the shelter. Receive 30kg of meat. Very good.

Wednesday December 20
Another Dutchman died this evening. He was one of those who we thought would not make it.

Thursday December 21
387 cartons of Red+ came in late last night, part of it will be issued on Jan 1. American this time. We find that the Nip commandant improves every day and he is doing his best to make our existence better. Another Dutchman not expected to live. My foot is still badly swollen and I have great difficulty in walking.

Friday December 22
Dutchman died today, making third in 10 days. I hope the others will now pull through. The Nips are trying to make our Christmas a bit brighter. It looks much better one than last year. Twenty letters come in but I am not one of the lucky ones. I should have liked to have one for Christmas.

Saturday December 23
Very busy today decorating dining hall and putting up a stage. We have been promised much meat and fish for Xmas Day. Much warmer today. I hope it will keep like this over Xmas. I think of home a lot today and hope and pray that this is my last Xmas as a POW. I get a Xmas card done for Capt W and all the boys sign same.

Sunday December 24
Christmas Eve. A very busy day. Nips fail with the meat but get most of the other stuff which they promise us. We will kill the pig so it should be good day tomorrow. Twenty letters come in but I do not get one. The gen appears to be good with another conference on.

Monday December 25
Christmas Day. I was up very early, put Capt W's Xmas card on his chair so that he would get it as soon as he got up. Weather quite mild. Nip commandant wishes us all a merry Xmas. Breakfast was very good. Piece of fish, bowl of pap, 3 spoonfuls of fried veg and 1 loaf. We had quite a good church service in the morning from the dining hall. This was relayed to the hospital, the Nips having fixed a mic in the dining room for that purpose. Christmas dinner was a huge success. Pork, sweet potatoes, nasi goreng and veg with onion sauce, a piece of [illegible] with sauce, oranges and a cap of wine. We toasted the King and also sang national anthem. The English had dinner first, then the Dutch with English sergeants, Capt W and myself. The Nip commandant and Sgt Major also sat with us. We had another 170 letters in the afternoon and I received one from Joe (good old Joe) with a snap of Mother and Wendy. It was all that was needed to finish off the best day we've had in Japan. The tea was good with bread, cake, fish in batter. Then we had a concert in the evening attended by some of the Number 1 mine, factory and shaft. To end the day we all had a pint of milk taken from issue of Red+. Altogether it was the best Christmas since leaving home and all the boys were in good spirits. I had a very busy day and was completely worn out by the time the milk was served but it was worth it to see the boys so happy. I do hope and pray that this is the last Christmas as a POW and that next Christmas I will be with those that I love.

Tuesday December 26
Boxing Day. Feel very tired. Nips issue us with sweat towel and soap. Boys very pleased with yesterday's effort. I am very pleased with my snap of Mother and Wendy. I think Mother looks much older but she still looks very fit.

Wednesday December 27
We hear today that conference is over. Personally I don't believe there ever was one. We are allowed to write home a letter containing 40 words. I also doubt whether it will ever reach there. We are having a lot of thieving in the camp. It seems impossible to catch these people. It's certainly a big problem.

Thursday December 28
Not so cold but mountains are covered with snow. We receive 100 new books in exchange for 100 which we sent back. I was pleased to see Larwood's book on leg theory and his Aussie tour. I think this is a good selection of books. Cold in the evening.

Friday December 29
Boys are very pessimistic and the dates for war ending are becoming further and further away.

Saturday December 30
Still cold but I do not think so cold as last year. We talk and think of what they are doing at home at the present time. Hope and pray that all is well.

Sunday December 31
New Year's Eve. I feel very homesick today and feel rather pessimistic. Very busy making list for Red+. I took epilogue service in the evening, only seven present. I feel very tired and do not stay up to see the New Year in.

1945

Monday January 1
Is this peace year? Capt W and doctors woke me up to wish me happy New Year. We had first fall of snow in the early morning. Did not last long. At 9 o'clock we issued the Red+ parcels, one between four men. It was wonderful. Everybody in excellent spirits. I think it was a better day than Xmas Day because we had no Nips to interfere. A parcel contained one tin corned beef, two tins spam, one tin paste, one packet raisins, one packet sugar, four tins butter, jam, salmon, cheese, chocolate, seven packs cigs. Two doctors, Capt W and I shared one parcel. These parcels I hope will help us over the winter. Capt W and two doctors had dinner with Nip commandant. I had a very tiring day being kept very busy checking Red+ meals. Had a lovely cup of coffee about 9pm with Capt W. Smoked a few American cigarettes ending an enjoyable day. I now feel that this year must see the end of this ghastly war. Maybe it will come sooner than what we expect but we are all feeling the worse for wear, some more than others, and the next two months will make a big difference to the health of the camp.

Tuesday January 2*
A very beautiful day. Big sensation last night when Billy the Kid, a West Indian, was caught stealing man's Red+ [illegible]. He was caught but stabbed two Dutchmen who caught him. Nip commandant sentenced him to 21 days confinement. He was very lucky to get off so light.

Wednesday January 3
My foot is very badly swollen and I still find great difficulty in walking. I am now certain that the war is not over in Europe and that we are still fighting.

Thursday January 4
A glorious day of sunshine, very mild. I hope we will have many similar days. We have nearly finished our Red+, only left one tin of meat and salmon. I have a small bit of choc. We have many meat bones in the cookhouse making the soup very thick in fat. We also get a little piece of whale-meat, very delicious. The food has improved these last few weeks.

Friday January 5
I am busy with a sweepstake on naming the correct day on which we finish work through cessation of hostilities. Most of the days are in the months March, April, May. I am becoming very pessimistic once again but do not allow my thoughts to come to the front.

Saturday January 6
Heavy fall of snow this morning. The heaviest since we've been in Japan and while it was snowing we had an air raid alarm which lasted from 9 til 11.30. We heard many planes but no bombs. Very cold in the shelter. Sunshine in the afternoon melted a lot of the snow but still very cold. Temp in the evening 0 degrees centigrade.

Sunday January 7
It's very cold and we have many falls of snow. The temp this evening was 4 below freezing centigrade. We are having quite a lot of bones in our soup. I think we are all feeling the benefit of same. I am afraid to tell the boys that I feel sure the war in Europe is not finished. Went to service in the evening.

Monday January 8
From information brought in by the boys I firmly believe that we are still fighting Germany and that we have been pushed back. I will not tell the camp this because I'm afraid many of the boys will throw in the towel. I have a feeling that something is going to happen today, was sorry to see Fryett going out to work this evening.

Tuesday January 9*
An Englishman came in from work this morning, collapsed and died. All the shift thought he was shamming, a pretty bad show. I was disgusted to hear how he was treated. I am very upset with Frank. It makes one think when fellows drop dead like this one, Henry Owens.

Wednesday January 10
A lovely day and quite warm in the sun. Henry Owens was cremated today. Some very ugly rumours about the way his shift treated him. Death was due to starvation. We receive the Red+ parcels intact and will be able to issue them tomorrow intact. Capt W is able to see the Nip commandant every day and is able to put all his complaints to him.

Thursday January 11
Yasme Day. A very delightful day. A bit cold, temp 3 below zero. Issue of Red+ parcels, one between four men, was very popular. Two doctors, Capt W and I

again shared a parcel. Had bread, butter and cheese with coffee and sugar in the evening. Was unable to go to any of the church services.

Friday January 12
Weather not so bad. Thieving in the camp is terrific. Trying hard to keep it down but great difficulties. I feel very pessimistic these days and wonder if the war will end this year.

Saturday January 13
My unlucky day, nothing untoward. Fryett offers me 50 to 25 that war will be over by Oct. Red+ clothing arrives. Very small issue. 40 articles, pyjamas, hats, socks, blankets, towels etc.

Sunday January 14
Rather cold, slight fall of snow. I feel rather depressed. We had 100 eggs in the camp, the largest number yet. The cooks made a Yorkshire pudding, not so bad. I made a rice pudding today with my milk powder and three lumps of sugar.

Monday January 15
Weather becoming colder, many showers of snow. Fryett gets a Yasme from work with bad feet. Capt W has got a cold. Nip commandant gave him a tot of saki before going to bed.

Tuesday January 16
Very cold, snow showers. I have long talk with Nip commandant and show him all my photographs. Sgt Missen goes sick, means more work for Capt W and myself. News of conference in America, do not put much truth in it.

Wednesday January 17
Snowing continually through the day and freezing. Finish issue of Red+ clothing. I got a towel and two hankies. Capt W and I should have had two shirts but there were two shirts short so we gave up ours. Surprise to get about 300 British Army overcoats that Nips have taken as booty. Very busy day. I feel tired and cold.

Thursday January 18
Missen still ill. Capt W and I distribute British greatcoats. These are very acceptable to the boys at the present moment. We have had a very heavy fall of snow about four to five inches deep. I think it's the coldest day we've had. I work til midnight. The ink in the bottles actually froze while I was in the office.

Friday January 19
By gum it's cold. Stop snowing. Temp 6 degrees below zero. I hope it will become warmer. Letters received, only for new men.

Saturday January 20
Much snow still left, I feel very tired. We get Red+. Tony, boy with broken leg, goes out to work, day after Yasme. Very surprised. Commandant invited Capt W and I to his room in the evening. We spent a very enjoyable evening showing him our photos. Made me feel very homesick. He told us they were still fighting in Europe.

Sunday January 21
Yasme Day. Another Red+ issue. We had another very good parcel. Four butter, very nice. Went to communion and service in the morning. No concert. Still very cold, snow still on the ground. We have issue of Nip socks, about time because very few of the boys have any socks. Capt W looking rather seedy, goes to bed very early. Commandant gives him a good nightcap – eggs and wine beaten up.

Monday January 22
Capt W sick in bed. I am very busy. A memorable day. We receive 1192 letters. I was fortunate to get seven. Two from Babs, two from Joe, two from Dad, one from aunt Ethel. It was smashing news. Everybody in the camp happy. One sad thing is one of the boys very ill. I think he will soon die.

Tuesday January 23
Capt W still in bed. Very busy censoring and issuing letters. The news seems to be all good. Mother, Dad, Ken, Babs all very well. Ken W got a baby.

Wednesday January 24
Capt W still in bed. Another 166 letters in today. I do not get any this time. Perry, the boy who is so ill, I'm afraid will die very soon.

Thursday January 25
Capt W still in bed. Poor Perry is simply a bag of bones. Passing blood all the time. I do not think he will last very long. And yet another batch of letters, 366 this time. I am still unlucky. My last letters are dated March from Mother and Ken and Sept '43 from Babs. I hope everything is OK with Babs. 50 boxes of Red+ arrive.

Friday January 26
Poor Perry will not last very long. He is rapidly sinking. Great rejoicing in camp. Another 50 boxes of Red+ food arrive, making total of 100 boxes. In the absence of Capt W I open with Nip Sgt Major one of the five boxes of toilet requisites that come the same time as the food. All the last letters are dated June, July, Aug, '44 and are very optimistic.

Saturday January 27*
Perry died with his head in my arms at 8.30 this morning. He was conscious to the last. He put up a good fight but it was a losing battle all the way. The weather is better today and a little warmer. Capt W is also better and will probably be up tomorrow.

Sunday January 28
I was disgusted with the attitude of Watson, Number 44. When asked to officiate at the burial of Perry he refused saying he was sleeping at 10 o'clock in the morning. Capt W got out of bed and took the service. It was a very simple service on the parade ground in lovely sunshine. The Nips would not allow any friends time off from work to attend.

Monday January 29
Rumour today that some of the cooks may be changed but I do not think much of it. Capt W much better. Now in harness again. Rumour started again that more men are infected.

Tuesday January 30
Nip commandant returns to the camp much to everyone's pleasure. He certainly is the best commandant we've yet had.

Wednesday January 31
Lovely surprise today. I had four letters on my table for breakfast. Three from Joe and one from Mr B. It was grand.

Thursday February 1
Yasme Day. I was pleased with my letters though they [date from] '43. It makes you feel that you are not forgotten though you have been absent for some time. I have a terrible cold and am feeling lousy but I hope to shake it off with this issue of Red+. One carton between two men is grand. I shared one with Capt W. We had camp inspection to find men that were lousy and dirty. It was very thorough. Short communion service only four present. I go to bed early feeling washed out.

Friday February 2
Still feeling lousy. Terrific cold and off my food. Cannot taste anything. Lovely day, quite warm. We hear that the war may soon be over but I do not feel much reliance on just hearsay.

Saturday February 3*
I am still feeling a little under the weather, also very homesick. I have decided to save some of my Red+ til my birthday and then have a little party. Had a very good evening arguing with Dr Grider and Capt W on a man's conscience.

Sunday February 4
Another Sunday and I go to evening epilogue, only four present. Watson took the service but I wish he had not. Feeling a little better. Weather becoming colder. Snow showers.

Monday February 5
Three years today railway accident at Java. It does not seem so long as that. I am reading Edgar Wallace's life story. Rather disappointing. We hear today that 100 men and two officers are coming to the camp. Capt W, Doc and I have a very good evening over 10 questions of home.

Tuesday February 6
I am feeling better. Boys are becoming more optimistic with rumours of peace becoming prevalent.

Wednesday February 7
Much colder. Another heavy fall of snow. Rumours that the Russians have taken Berlin.

Thursday February 8
A Dutchman died today, very sudden but I think a happy release. Still very cold and snowing. It is much warmer in the office with the fire in an old tin can. We sometimes get smoked out but we put up with these little inconveniences for a little warmth.

Friday February 9
The Dutchman was cremated today. We held a simple ceremony on the parade ground in a snowstorm. The total deaths in the camp now amount to 23. Ten Dutch , 13 English. My foot is still swollen and painful. I ask the doctors if it's serious but do not get satisfactory answer.

Saturday February 10
Still it snows and freezes every day. Frank gets a Yasme with bad feet. The camp
has become very optimistic once again. The general opinion is that we will be
free next month. I give it another six months.

Sunday February 11
Another Sunday passes by without any ceasing of the work. I go to the service
in the evening, usual epilogue service. Capt W and I had a good meal of our
Red+ meat this evening.

Monday February 12
We are having pancakes tomorrow. I spoke to Capt W and told him Shrove Tuesday
was on the 13th and that it would be a good idea if he asked Nip commandant for
a bag of flour for pancakes. He did so and commandant said OK.

Tuesday February 13
The pancakes were a huge success. The Nips gave us 100 eggs with a bag of flour. I
am going to have a birthday cake made tomorrow out of Red+ I have saved. Capt
W has got a couple of eggs so it should be OK. Sensation – Yasme tomorrow.

Wednesday February 14
I am 38 today and this birthday will live long in my memory. It was my intention
to make this birthday a really good day especially when I heard late last night
that it was a Yasme Day and we were going to have a further issue of Red+. I
think I will start at the beginning of the day, giving all the developments as they
occur. I got up at the usual time, 6.15 and was wished all the best by the others
in the room. Went on tenko parade at 6.30 and it looked as if we were going to
have a fine day, the weather being very mild. After tenko I went down dining
hall and stamped men's cards as they went through for their meals. I was rather
surprised to catch a Dutchman using another man's card. I made him tip rice
back in basket and said I would not report him. All the boys were in good spirits
and Capt W made announcement that the Nips had promised Red+ as soon
as the camp was cleaned. We anticipated that we would get Red+ about 9am. I
went to our office about 8.30 and thought I would not eat any breakfast because
last night's pancake made me feel a trifle sick. About 9 o'clock we had message
from Nips to collect Red+ so Capt W took 10 men to collect same while I waited
in Capt W's room to receive. On arriving at stores Capt W found the Nips in
a flat spin. The stores had been broken into. A Red+ carton had been stolen,
also Nips' shirts and blankets. The Nips then said that no Red+ would be issued
unless missing carton was found. Capt W held a conference in the office and
organised search parties to go around the camp while he and I took a general
walk round. We found nothing and we were not surprised because we were all

of the opinion that one of the Nip guards had broken into the store during the night and helped himself to the stolen carton. To make matters worse the Nips found a gas cape in one of the billets, so they immediately said that the man who stole the gas cape must have stolen the Red+. Lunchtime arrived and still no trace of Red+. But Capt W was hoping he would get some in the afternoon because it seemed obvious that the Nips had stolen the food. I had no lunch as I was still feeling a little sick and as the church service was at 2 I went direct to auditorium from our room leaving Capt W and two doctors having their meals. The service had hardly commenced when the bell went for all prisoners to go on parade with their blankets and Red+ cartons. We got everybody on parade and the Nips searched the billets and all the men on parade. A great sensation was caused when we were informed that the missing carton had been found in the room which contains the ashes of the men that had died in this camp. It was now fairly certain that it was either a Dutchman or Englishman that had done it. The Nip Sgt Major threatened to "bash" everybody with his sword if the thief did not own up. The guards also started to take a hand in the affair by hitting and kicking some of the boys who were chewing on parade. Capt W appealed to the man to own up and so did I pointing out that 380 men were being punished because of his thieving. Twas of no avail.

The Nips started cracking on their hitting of the men. I thought I would be the first but they started in the back rank. We also were made to bend our knees and throw our hands up in the air at the same time. It was a great strain. I don't know how long we could've carried on if the Nip commandant had not arrived on the scene. He stopped everything and dismissed all the huts with the exception of 9,10,11 but we were not to have anything to eat. Capt W, doctors and myself, then went and examined some of the suspects and after some investigation it looked as if Billy the Kid had again done the job. Capt W and doctor kept him in the office, took his fingerprints while I for the first time took the camp evening tenko. Some 30 men were kept on parade while remainder of camp went without food. I went back to Capt W and found that Billy the Kid had confessed that he had done it. I had a difficult job to keep myself from hitting him. My blood fairly boiled when I thought how he had allowed the boys to be hit and kept doing PT because he would not own up. We eventually managed to get our meal at 9pm while The Kid was put in the guardroom. We were promised the Red+ tomorrow. I was terribly disappointed at not being able to celebrate my birthday. We (Capt and I) had made such plans for a really cracking meal in the evening. About 9 o'clock we thought we could settle down and have a little meal but it was not to be. Capt W was called up to the Nip office and was there til midnight. I turned in about 11.30 feeling really fed up. I suppose it was the worst day we have yet had in this camp and all through the fault of one man. I hope he will be severely punished. If it was left to the boys I doubt very much if he would live. Well I hope this will be my last birthday in captivity.

Thursday February 15
Billy the Kid was sentenced today. He received five days starvation and to live in jug til the commandant's pleasure. I hope we will never see him again in the camp. Another Dutchman died today making total of 24. 13 English, 11 Dutch. We received the Red+, one parcel between four men, as we expect another Yasme Day before 1st March.

Friday February 16
A lovely day. The Dutchman was buried today. Service held on parade ground. I got weighed today and gained 1kg. I wonder if I shall ever go down the mine again. I do not feel at all certain that I won't.

Saturday February 17
Another beautiful day. This kind of day makes the winter much shorter. Lack of gen making boys very pessimistic. I sometimes wonder whether we will be home this Xmas as I have always hoped.

Sunday February 18
Another 904 letters arrive in camp but I do not receive any. Am rather worried because I have had no news since March last year. The latest letters are dated Oct last year. I go to service in the evening, only four present. Another lovely day.

Monday February 19
Billy the Kid collapses in the jug after four days starvation. Put in hospital and given milk. Another lovely day. I still feel that I may go out to work. Do not feel at all comfortable these days. Nips are becoming interested in my position.

Tuesday February 20
Another scare today when the Nips failed to find my name on any working sheet. I am rather worried about the whole affair. Pessimism is very prevalent in the camp.

Wednesday February 21
I am now put on camp workers' sheet. I do not feel at all happy about it. I will speak to Capt W to try and get on camp staff.

Thursday February 22
Very cold, temp down to 2 degrees below zero. We have further fall of snow. We hear that R are nearing B. I wonder how much longer will Jerry last. I'm hoping it will be over by next month and that we will be free before next winter. I really feel that it will be too much for any of us to do another winter.

Friday February 23
Capt W, two doctors and myself get an egg from Nips, very acceptable. I soft boiled my egg and put it on toast. Delicious. Capt W saw commandant re Frank Fryett and got him out of the mine on to camp work commencing Mar 1. We have issue of two oranges. Capt W was unable to decide whether he would cook his orange in the fire or put it on his rice or eat it as it was. What a state we've got into.

Saturday February 24
I am sorry to see the boys so pessimistic. Some are even thinking that we will be here next Christmas. Much colder today and several falls of snow. I am feeling very unsettled and will be glad when Capt W speaks to the commandant re going on camp staff. More news of 200 men coming next month. Camp garden being extended.

Sunday February 25
The heaviest fall of snow since we've been in Japan, about 4 to 5 inches. Not so cold but very nasty underfoot. Fryett has become pessimistic. Only two Yasme Days next month 1st and 16th. It's very disappointing and very hard. Went to service in the evening.

Monday February 26
96 letters today for new draft, none for us. A lovely day and the sun melts the heavy fall of snow. Alterations in cookhouse for new 200 men.

Tuesday February 27
I hear good news. Am put on camp staff commencing Mar 2nd. Helping Capt W. I am in a spot of bother over some shoes.

Wednesday February 28
The temp today 16 degrees. Very warm. I managed to get out of shoe bother. Fryett also put on camp staff. A really good break for Frank.

Thursday March 1*
St David's Day. Two years ago I lost front teeth playing rugger at Priok. Happy days. We get the Red+ boxes to issue tomorrow, one between two. Much bargaining between the boys. I am going all out for meat and butter. Swapping choc and spam. Our fire has been stopped in the office during the day.

Friday March 2
Yasme Day. It's rained all day but for all the rain it was a grand day with the issue of Red+. I had a good meal in the evening frying spam and making a

Welsh rarebit out of my cheese, milk powder and butter. Capt W, Doc Grider and myself stayed up late drinking coffee and becoming thoroughly intoxicated with coffee. We sang nursery rhymes and other songs but not very loud. It was a grand hour.

Saturday March 3
I went to church in the morning and communion .Only nine present. Much finer and not cold. I have got a frightful cold and am not feeling so good. I am sorry to see so many of the boys feeling depressed.

Sunday March 4
Quite warm. I feel lousy, no doubt due to my cold. Made a hot cup of milk and took some aspirins. Red+ medicine came in today, also about 50 books. The books are very interesting, fiction and non-fiction. Went to epilogue in the evening, six present.

Monday March 5
We are all enjoying our Red+ parcels between two. I do hope we will have more. The man with the broken back actually got out on the side of the bed today. It's a miracle.

Tuesday March 6
Colder. Air raid alarm early this morning about 4.30. Another about 11.30 at night. A Dutchman goes for operation tomorrow for hernia.

Wednesday March 7
Another 50 letters. I was pleased to get nine from Aunt M, Kathleen, Mother and Ken. Disappointment at not receiving one from Babs. One feels very pleased at receiving letters but oh they make you feel very despondent.

Thursday March 8
Three years today we finished fighting and became POWs. How much longer? That is the cry on everybody's lips. Many thought it would be over by this month. But I'm afraid they were too optimistic. I am beginning to wonder whether it will be over this time next year.

Friday March 9
We have in our room a book on psychology which Capt W is reading. It's very interesting and we have many discussions on psychology (Capt W, Doc Grider and myself).

Saturday March 10
Though we are getting some up-to-date gen and it's good the boys are becoming very depressed. My old batman went into doc today. The stupid boy has been exchanging his Red+ for rice. I gave him an egg which I had been keeping for myself and also gave him a good lecture. Notice that there are more men going to work these days than last month.

Sunday March 11
Another Sunday and we keep on working. The weather seems to be more settled. I went to evening epilogue, only four present. The Nips are making swords and lances to defend their homes in case of invasion.

Monday March 12
Weather still warm during the day but cold in the evening. I still sleep with blankets and greatcoat.

Tuesday March 13
Unlucky day but it passes by without any incident. I feel much better and think I have put on a little weight.

Wednesday March 14
Yesterday had a great shock when suspicion turned on a great friend of Capt W and I who is charged with stealing. I think he did it but will have to go thoroughly into the case. I do hope I'm wrong in my suspicion.

Thursday March 15
I got weighed today and am now 82kg. Have gained another kilo. I think I have a touch of beriberi and that has put up my weight. A few of the boys have dysentery but we have now got drugs to combat it, though they are few. It's a great pity that we did not have these drugs a few weeks ago. Poor Perry might have been saved.

Friday March 16
Yasme Day. A rather quiet day. Capt W and I finished off our last tin of spam in the evening. It was delicious. Went to service and communion in the morning, only 10 present. Also had the usual good workers' parade. The boys deplore the non issue of Red+. I think we've had it as far as Red+ is concerned.

Saturday March 17
The air raids have now commenced with a vengeance. The sirens were going all through the night. The Nips are becoming very jittery. We did not go down into the air raid shelter and we heard no planes but there is great activity and the Nips are getting prepared by sharpening their bamboo poles.

Sunday March 18

Last night another night of alarms and also throughout the day. It was the best gen we've had for confirming that the allies are not so far away. The first alarm went early in the morning and we were in the air raid shelter for 2hrs. Then the Nips told us they were expecting more and that the alert was still on. Sure enough the alarm went again at mid-day and we were in the shelter til 5.30pm, the longest yet. We have now been told that a state of emergency is on throughout the island and that we must be prepared to go down into the air raid shelter at a moment's notice. We must sleep with all our clothes on. It seems to me that this is more than an air raid. I think that a convoy must be roaming around and the Nips do not know which way the allies are going to jump. All the boys return from work when the warning goes with exception of the miners which is a good thing except for those who should be sleeping. Last night's nightshift had a bad time. They came back from the mine about 10am, went to bed, were up again at 12.30, and had to go to work this evening. The boys will not be able to stand up to this very long.

Monday March 19

We had another couple of hours down in the shelter this morning but did not go down afterwards. E Williams of my battery has got nephritis and I do not think he will live long.

Tuesday March 20

No shelter today and only one warning. Plenty of rain. I am still in doubt whether these raids are coming from aircraft carrier or not.

Wednesday March 21

Another warning today but did not go down to the shelter. Very cloudy and some rain. I do not doubt that these raids are coming from land bases. Williams is slowly dying.

Thursday March 22

Very heavy rain today. No air raid warnings. I have a small boil on my left breast, also severe pain in my right side which I think is wind. I managed to get a few MB tablets today for emergency. It was actually a year today that I gave all mine away. I'm very sorry to see Williams in such a pitiful state. He's swollen about four times normal size. I cannot help thinking of what he swore some months ago when charged with stealing a bread roll. "If I never see my wife and child again I swear I never took that bread roll".

Friday March 23
No raid today. Very windy, no rain. Em Williams is slowly sinking, he does not know that he's dying. We could do with a few more letters. Have not had any for over a month. Capt W, Doc G and myself spend an interesting afternoon studying psychology and answering a questionnaire on subject dealing with upper and lower classes.

Saturday March 24*
We had a warning during the night but stayed in bed. Williams passed away at midday, very sad. This death makes total of 25. 14 English, 11 Dutch. Mild today and no winds. No gen coming in. This European war keeps dragging on.

Sunday March 25
Palm Sunday. Em Williams was cremated today. A simple service was held on parade ground conducted by Capt W. We sung one verse of Abide With Me. I am feeling lousy today, having severe pains in my tummy. I hope it's nothing serious. No raids today and the Nips think there will not be any more. Sorry to see one of the battery going to TB ward, making a total of five.

Monday March 26
A very fine day. No raids. I have a very bad night with pains in my stomach. Two of the boys wake me at midnight coming in from mine with a paper on which we could see what's happening out here. Rather disappointed over Burma but everything else OK, dated Feb 5. I took evening prayer. Only six present.

Tuesday March 27
Had a better night. Strong rumours of 200 men coming in a few days. Air raid in the morning, saw 31 planes, heard bombing and saw smoke. This is what we want to see. Action. I still feel lousy. Overcoats will not be worn on roll call in morning and evening.

Wednesday March 28
Another raid last night from 10.30pm to 1am. We heard planes going over for one and a half hours. Some of the boys saw them as they flew in line formation. I feel a little better today. Great activity in camp preparing for 200 men. Rumour states they will be here before the end of the month. Warning went at five no shelter. Hear that Lloyd George died two days ago.

Thursday March 29
A beautiful day. Capt W is informed officially 200 men will arrive in this camp in the next 10 days. They will come from main island of Japan. Nationality is not known. I wonder if we shall see some old friends. I doubt it. My tummy

is much better but my foot and leg are badly swollen. We had another air raid warning this evening but did not go down shelter.

Friday March 30
Good Friday. Gee what a day. Very hot and full of surprises. We hear that 300 or 400 letters have arrived in the camp and 131 Dutch and 69 Americans including 7 officers. Terrific panic in the camp as we were not prepared for them, however we manage to get them fed and housed in their billets before 9pm. We hear confirmation of all that we already [believe]. Nearest base is about 350 miles away, the distance between London and Glasgow. No warning today.

Saturday March 31
Easter Saturday. Letters not yet issued. Warning went this morning, all men in shelter for about 2hrs. Very heavy bombing heard in the distance, a lovely day, very warm. The new draft are not being allowed to mix with the rest of the camp. Very stupid action by the Nips. My tummy much better but foot is bad. The eight new officers will sleep in two rooms occupied by camp staff. Office will be kept on. Very good news.

Sunday April 1*
Easter Sunday. Yasme Day. Easter Sunday once again as a POW. This is the 4th Easter. I wonder if it's the last as a POW. It certainly looks as if it may be. I went to church service in the morning and communion. I took part of the service. The Nips are treating these new fellows rather rough and during the mid-day meal I was involved in a nasty incident which put me in bed for the rest of the day. Two tins containing chillies and sauce were left in the dining hall by the new draft after breakfast. I took them in the cookhouse. I waited for the owner to claim them. About midday the draft came in for their dinner and one of the Americans claimed the two tins which I gave him. A few minutes later one of the Nip guards (Singapore Pete) came dashing to me gesticulating and frothing at the mouth, making signs that appeared to mean that I had given him something from the cookhouse. Without waiting for me to explain he just let fly at me with his wooden rifle hitting my left leg with terrific force. I limped away from him telling him I was going to see Nip commandant and with the aid of Sgt Wright and Sgt Windhurst made my way to Nip office where I met Capt W who interviewed Nip commandant who said he would investigate the affair. I was carried to hospital where Dr G gave me a shot of morphine and they carried me to my billet, my leg paining like hell. The incident caused a great sensation in camp. It's to be hoped that the bashing will now cease. I have my doubts. The Nip commandant sent a message that he was very sorry about the whole incident – that's that!

Monday April 2*
Easter Monday. A very fine day. I stay in bed aching in every limb after yesterday's incident. The bashing in the camp continues. I do not go on roll call. We hear that there were many deaths in Thailand where the 77th went after Java.

Tuesday April 3
I get up today but still feel sore. No air raids today. The Yanks are very optimistic re finish of war which they think will be in June. I hope they are right. They also say that our fellows look in poor condition.

Wednesday April 4
Very cold today. No air raids. Very busy with new draft. We get some good gen. I hope it's true. We get 500 letters but I was unlucky. Capt W got two. Hear that all new draft are going down mine.

Thursday April 5
We hear bad news today. Nip commandant is leaving tomorrow. New commandant arrived today. The old commandant has been a blessing to the camp and has helped to make life for all of us more enjoyable than the other two previous commandants. Capt W especially was very intimate with him and was able to get many little grievances straightened out. The new commandant looks very young and inexperienced – a bad start.

Friday April 6*
The old commandant left at midday. We were very sorry to see him leave and I think we shall miss him very much indeed. Capt W made a farewell speech to him in reply to the commandant's farewell speech. It's a funny sensation to hope that the Nip will survive the war. The new commandant has not made a very good impression. It looks as if the Nip Sgt Major will run him.

Saturday April 7
97 boxes Red+ came in today. Not much chance of it being issued for some time. Weather colder. Very interesting conversation with American officers. See very little of new commandant.

Sunday April 8
Still cold. Very busy day making new accommodation lists. Whole camp move billets on Yasme Day. Hear that Nip Sgt Major will be leaving in the next 10 days. I hope that the new one will be better for the camp than the present one.

Monday April 9
Air raid warning last night. Did not go down shelter. Miserable day. Very busy. Accident down mine, two Americans injured.

Tuesday April 10
Still very wet. Guards are becoming very cruel in their bashing. Dutchman hits Nip workman down mine, causes a lot of trouble. He is badly knocked about, also six other Dutchmen. Radiograms came in the camp for six British POW. I hope there may be a few more.

Wednesday April 11
Yasme Day. All the camp changed billets today. Very little fuss or bother. No interference by Nips. Nip Sgt Major tells me that he is leaving tomorrow for [illegible] war. He has not been so bad. A nasty incident occurred during church service. Nip guard passed room and hit Stanton who was taking the service because he did not kiri. This is the first time for the church service to be interrupted in this way. Concert held in the evening was a great success for Dutch quartet. Fryett was not so good.

Thursday April 12
Air raid warning in the night but no shelter. Very warm. Saw American plane this morning, tremendous height. No alarm sounded. Nip Sgt Major left today.

Friday April 13*
A very unlucky day. We hear very bad news. Roosevelt is dead, a big loss to the world but I do not think it will make any difference to the length of the war. Naturally the Nips are very jubilant. Bad day also for the miners. 9 accidents, suspected broken bones in most cases. Saw American plane this morning. Alarm sounded but did not go to shelter.

Saturday April 14
A lovely day. Roosevelt died of a accident. The Americans are having a rough time down the mine. Many are being bashed. One American has gone a bit screwy.

Sunday April 15
Got weighed today. Am now 81kg, losing one last month. The weather is really good and I think we can say farewell to the cold. The Americans are still getting bad treatment down the mine. Quite a number have gone sick. I go to evening service, only six present.

Monday April 16
A few more telegrams arrive but I am not fortunate this time. Gen appears to be good. We are closing in on B. Must be 100km away.

Tuesday April 17
It is rather cold. Doc Grider is sick and has got a high fever, he is afraid of TB.

Wednesday April 18
The American officers want to take a more active part in the camp. One for the cookhouse, one for the library, one for the entertainment.

Thursday April 19
One can see signs of spring everywhere in the camp. Flowers blooming and buds coming on the trees and young birds fluttering around. It makes one think of home. I took the evening service this evening, only six present.

Friday April 20
Much finer and warmer. We are very busy in the gardens and have now extended same. If only the Nips would allow the officers to plant what they wish. Still many accidents down the mine but still they are not very serious.

Saturday April 21
Yasme Day. Very busy. Have now got American officer in the cookhouse. Should make improvement in distribution. I became chief assistant. We have raid in the morning, lasting a couple of hours. Went to service in the afternoon, about 20 present. Concert in the evening was fairly good.

Sunday April 22
Lovely weather. We are closing in on B. Estimate that R forces and ours are about 100 miles from each other. Went to service in the evening, only four present. Doc Grider much better, had bad attack of malaria.

Monday April 23
Camp very busy cleaning up for inspection on the 27th. Lovely day. We get issue of 180 eggs, 200 Red+ books handed into us for issue. Some very interesting books. The Americans are certainly crumbling up on the mine work.

Tuesday April 24
Great shock today. Five American and 1 Dutch have to leave camp tomorrow morning. I am very sorry to see them leave. We held a farewell party in the evening which was a great success.

Wednesday April 25*
The six officers left 8am this morning, only one American officer left with Doc Grider. I move in with Capt W and Lt Hal Fobes (American officer), the two doctors staying in hospital. We get hold of two NT of March, very encouraging. We hear that both R and us have entered B.

Thursday April 26
Air raid this morning. Was in shelter for two and a half hours. Heard no bombs, only planes. Lovely weather. We are now planting a lot of seeds and we should be OK for food in the summer if we are still here. We hear that the six officers left the island by boat. I rather like the American officer who shares room with Capt W and myself. Camp busy cleaning up for inspection tomorrow.

Friday April 27
Inspection went off OK. We had warning about the usual time and were down in shelter for one and a half hours. Heard no bombs but many planes. Weather quite warm. I wonder how much longer. I do hope it will come before next winter. I have my fears that it may go on for another year.

Saturday April 28
Warning went but did not go down shelter. Another lovely day. I feel very homesick when I think that the cricket season is now starting in England. We are building a pigsty for 10 pigs which are supposed to arrive very shortly.

Sunday April 29
Emperor's birthday but we get nothing extra. Another lovely day. A spot of bother with two Americans who tried to double up. The Americans got hold of the two culprits in the dining hall and beat them up. Rough justice which I do not agree with. I went to evening epilogue, about eight present. Warning went this morning.

Monday April 30
Very warm. The gardens are beginning to look green with the veg coming up. We need a little rain. Warning went again this morning.

Tuesday May 1
Yasme Day. Wet and cold. Americans get issued with 2 cigs and soap for good workers. Great excitement when six big sows and 38 young pigs arrive in camp. One sow has broken leg so is killed. We hope that we will have plenty of meat for next few days. Went to service in the afternoon which was taken by American, about 20 present, same number stayed for communion. Concert in the evening was given by the Dutch celebrating Princess Julianna's birthday. Air raid in the afternoon, down shelter for 1hr. We also got vaccinated in the afternoon.

Wednesday May 2*

This is the first day for a week that we have not had an air raid warning. Wet and cold. Very miserable. I feel rather depressed today. We hear that Musso is dead. Shot himself. I think that EW is now practically over. We see the new commandant today. He appears to be OK. The old one leaves in two days after being here only one month.

Thursday May 3*

A lovely day. Much warmer. One of the new men is very ill with pneumonia. We have ARW in the afternoon and go down shelter for 1hr. Old and new commandant make speeches. Hear that H and M are both dead and that EW is finished. I think it is true this time. Some Dutchmen find ingenious way of obliterating stamp on their meal cards.

Friday May 4

We have ARW and go down shelter for 1hr in the morning. Not so warm. News still coming in of G finished, also H and M both dead. I wonder how long now.

Saturday May 5

Capt W's birthday. Gave him a packet of Chesterfields, also had a card made for him. He was delighted. Still hearing that G finished, also H and M are dead. We have ARW and go down shelter for 1hr. The alarm is now a daily occurrence, usually going on 6.30am. The weather is very cold for the time of the year. I now think that we will be another winter here if Nippon is not invaded this summer. Very busy checking accounts.

Sunday May 6*

Still very cold. Heavy hailstorm during the night. Three or four warnings during the day. Did not go down shelter. Saw B29 flying high. Hear rumour that we might all be transferred to Manchuncko in the event of any invasion. Went to service in the evening taken by Fred Woods. We find that we are about 300 Yen deficient in our accounts.

Monday May 7

Still very cold and wet. Rumour still strong of move before invasion. Nip doctor checks people who are crippled and unable to walk.

Tuesday May 8

Still cold, especially in the evening. ARW goes but we do not go down shelter. I have further trouble with my ear.

Wednesday May 9
Still cold. I put extra blanket on my bed. Nips pulling down ceiling in all billets for fear of incendiaries. Inspection by Nip Major passed off without any incident. One of the 77th caught stealing and sentenced to four days in guardroom. A poor type.

Thursday May 10
ARW went at 6.15am and we went down shelter for 5hrs. The longest daylight raid we have had. Heard no bombs and saw no planes. I wonder what will [be] the longest period for us to be in the shelter? Frank admitted to hospital with chicken pox. The American and Dutch miners work on til 8pm but have extra rice sent down the mine. These two shifts are working very hard but are getting extra food.

Friday May 11
Today we had our shortest stay in the shelter – only 15 minutes. ARW went on throughout the day but did not go down shelter. About 38 radio grams came in today but I did not get one. I have a feeling that there is a change coming off, maybe in the camp staff. I am a bit worried.

Saturday May 12
Capt W informs me that part of the Red+ issue will be issued in three days time, probably about six men to one parcel. Cheese, coffee, sugar etc. Still very cold. I take evening service, only four present. Still worried about coming blitz on Yasme Day. I think camp staff and cooks will be changed. My foot is still swollen but I have my doubts whether it will make any difference to my staying in the office. I think they will try and cut it down by 2. Me and probably 302 or 400.

Sunday May 13
Yasme Day. My unlucky day. We go in the shelter thrice. Two hours first time, half hour second time, one and a half hours third time. Well the battle over the office staff has begun. The Nips sent for Capt W and said that we had too many fellows working in the office. Capt W told them that he needed all the staff and that he could not manage otherwise. We must now wait and see the result. I feel that I will probably get pushed out, that is if they decide to put one man out. I don't know what Capt W stood for. I have my doubts. The cooks also had a sort out. Two English, two Dutch and one American put out. Very surprised over Jinty, one of the cooks who has been doing special police duty in the camp. I have found Jinty a great help in tracking down crime and am sorry to see him go. Many others have also gone back to work and we are very busy making necessary alterations for shifts and billets. I went to church and communion in the afternoon about 20 present. No concert in the evening but the alarm went

about 10pm. This time we were in the shelter for 4hrs. Flares were seen, many bombs heard. I think we are in for some heavy raids.

Monday May 14
Gee what a day. We spent most of it down the shelter, starting at 6am and finishing about 6pm. It seems that the planes were operating from carriers. We went down the shelter seven times. We heard many explosions. I saw 33 planes. Nobody goes out to work because of these raids but also nobody gets any sleep. I feel absolutely done in and am going to bed early. I do not think we will have any more raids tonight. I think the carriers have probably moved. Boys are very optimistic but I tell them to [illegible]. No more news of office change. I hope and pray that there will be no change.

Tuesday May 15
A few warnings but did not go down shelter. We see old commandant in the morning. Had a cig plus tea. We hear that the raid was made from 15 to 17 carriers.

Wednesday May 16
A few more warnings but do not go down shelter. The Nips start opening Red+ boxes, keeping all tins, but letting packets out only. It seems a shame that we are not allowed to have our own Red+.

Thursday May 17
No warnings today. Fine but not so warm. We have Red+ issued to us today minus all the tins except coffee. Capt W and I checked all articles and find that the Nips helped themselves to about 16 packets of choc, raisins, sugar and cigs. We were bitterly disappointed because we thought it would not be touched. We will have busy day tomorrow sorting same.

Friday May 18
We had a very busy day issuing Red+. The boys were pleasantly surprised at the issue. We worked everything out to the fraction. Still no air raid. All the boys who work above ground at the shaft have to go down mine tomorrow. Very sorry to see many friends going down mine. We finish issuing Red+ at 10pm. Made ourselves a lovely cup of coffee and smoked a couple of American cigs.

Saturday May 19
What a night. Never slept a wink. The alarm went at 1am and we were down shelter for 2hrs and I couldn't go to sleep afterwards presumably because of coffee. Frank Fryett out of hospital. Many of the boys sick after eating only small portion of their Red+. We will have to be very careful when we are free over our meals.

Sunday May 20
Whitsun. The weather is terrible. Rained all day and very cold. I go to service in the evening, only three present. I am bewildered over F Watson and his attitude over prayer. My idea of prayers and Frank's are not the same. I cannot say who is right, maybe we both are.

Monday May 21
Whit Monday. Another two hours in the shelter last night. Very cold and very wet. Capt W and I spend the afternoon talking about when we arrive in England and what our reaction will be.

Tuesday May 22
Still cold and wet. A very pleasant surprise. I receive a cablegram from Pop saying everybody OK and had received my cards. I was delighted to receive this. Sorry that Capt W did not get one. Only 40 received. Boys are becoming depressed.

Wednesday May 23
Spent another 2hrs in the shelter last night from 1 to 3. Very wet. I feel rather tired. My foot is still swollen and I still have some difficulty in walking. We do not have any further warnings. Nip women are now learning how to use bayonets.

Thursday May 24
Yasme Day. A lovely day started badly when hop-a-long, a Nip who now seems to run the camp (on account of the weakness of the commandant), making the whole camp work half an hour before breakfast. We waited all day for air raid warning but none came. Went to church in the morning, also communion, about 20 present. No concert in the evening. Had a very good meal. One bread roll, spoonful of fried veg and small cup of curry sauce and bowl of soup. Had interesting talk in the evening with Doc Grider and Capt W on cannibalism which later on went to religion. Doc G then retired. We receive 4 Red+ American papers with very little news in.

Friday May 25
We went down in the shelter last night for 3hrs. No bombs or planes heard. I have now put on my shorts but the weather is still on the chilly side. One of the boys had a nasty accident a few days ago when he practically had his foot torn off. He is not doing so good.

Saturday May 26*
Fryett made contact with one of the guards who is a communist. When Fryett told his story to Capt W and I we roared with laughter. It must have been a

very comical sight to see and hear Fryett and guard squatting down singing Red Flag. Fryett told guard that I was also one of them. We hear that there will be a general election in England on July 5th.

Sunday May 27
The bashings have become intolerable. Capt W protested to Nip commandant who says he will investigate. Cold comfort. Guards threatened to kill Capt W when he leaves the camp. Another raid last night. Down shelter for 3hrs, 12 to 3. Did not go to church this evening. Am feeling very tired. I am beginning to think we will be POW for another year.

Monday May 28
Another raid last night. Only 1hr. I went to service in the evening, seven present. Much warmer. We have several warnings but do not go down shelter.

Tuesday May 29
No raid during the night. I get in touch with Nip guard who is a communist. Hope I will be able to get some gen from him. Hear that Les Gardner, the boy who had accident some days ago, will have to have his foot amputated. Very sad. I take the epilogue service in the evening.

Wednesday May 30
The weather now becoming very warm. I wear shorts and shirt. A year today I had my accident. It seems only a few months. We hear that soldiers are arriving here in the next two or three days. No air raid warning today.

Thursday May 31
Had very heavy rain during the night and continues til midday. Nip doctor saw Gardner's foot today and said it was much better and did not think he would have to amputate same. The lack of air raids is worrying me and I am becoming rather pessimistic re our ultimate day when we shall be free. I am beginning to think it may not be this year.

Friday June 1
Busy today with the cut in our rice ration which averages 666kg [sic] each man. We give however 723gr to workers outside camp and 670 to workers in camp. It seems to work OK. 13 soldiers arrive today to take over part of the guard from the civvies.

Saturday June 2
Yasme Day. Very heavy rain during the night. Had another search of the camp by new soldiers in the afternoon. Nothing found. Went to service in the morning,

over 20 present. Twenty stayed to communion. No concert in the evening. Capt W feeling rather depressed. Very few left out of the camp sweep when war will be over. I do hope and pray that this year will see the end of it.

Sunday June 3
Much warmer today. The soldiers have taken over the guard duties and at the moment seem to be OK. I read all my letters from home today and feel very sad. Frank and Capt W are becoming very keen students of psychology. I go to epilogue in the evening, only four present. I have now got the squitters.

Monday June 4
Warm but chilly in the evening. Still have the squitters. No warning, no raids. Makes one wonder what's doing.

Tuesday June 5
We hear that we may expect more letters. Another bad incident of a beating up by one of the guards. They have got a new method of torture, sticking pieces of wood under your nail. Capt W sees commandant.

Wednesday June 6
Cablegrams, letters and postcards arrive today. I received four letters, two from Ken, one from Kay and Aunt Margaret. It's good to hear from them at home and makes one feel very happy. Also had a snap of my little niece Wendy. Looks very good.

Thursday June 7
Slimey, the guard that has been doing a lot of bashing, seems to have got the sack. I hope it's true. Another 300 letters come in today and I get 2, one from Aunt Margaret and another from Kay. I am rather surprised to receive two letters from Kay. No news from Babs. I begin to wonder whether I've left it too late. We kill one of the pigs today and we get one third, the Nips getting other two. Rather heavy thunderstorm and very cold. Much rain.

Friday June 8
We had warning last night, down in shelter for two hours. Raining very heavy. We have our share of the pig this morning and when a [illegible] was made it was very tasty. Still cold and wet. Capt W and I spend the afternoon going through his photographs and enjoy a very pleasant afternoon.

Saturday June 9
We do not go down in the shelter during the day time and I wonder what is the cause. A rather deep depression spread over the camp due to lack of news and

lack of bombing. I am rather pessimistic over the war being over this year. I am beginning to think it will be next year before we are released.

Sunday June 10
We had another warning last night, lasting about 2hrs, but still no daylight raids. The behaviour of the guards continues to be good but Slimey has returned, though it [sic] is rather subdued. I go to epilogue service, only four present.

Monday June 11
Much warmer and little rain. We hear of epidemic of typhus in district. I hope it will not spread to this camp.

Tuesday June 12
Yasme Day. We were in the shelter last night for another 2hrs. Very unusual. Wet, miserable. We have good workers' parade. I went to church service in the morning and communion. The whole afternoon was spoilt by deputation complaining about rations. Have now started a new system of weighing rice before cooking and after cooking. Concert in the evening fair. We have another warning about 9pm but do not go down shelter, though we hear planes and see many flashes in the sky.

Wednesday June 13
Terrible day, very wet. We hear strong rumours that we move from this camp before the end of the month. I think there may be something in the rumour. I spend the afternoon planning my future. Capt W, Lt Fobes, and myself have a delicious supper given to us by the Nips. Fresh egg salad.

Thursday June 14
I am now suffering from the squitters once again. We were down in the shelter last night for 2hrs. Still very wet and miserable. The King's birthday today.

Friday June 15
400 men go on bread today and more flour came in camp. American walks out of mine to the camp because of being bashed by the Nips. Terrible day, very wet. The weather is really atrocious, making the air raid shelter a sea of mud.

Saturday June 16
Still very wet. We went down the shelter last night from 1 til 3 in pouring rain. We heard a few planes overhead. They must be pretty hot in navigating. I make a wager with Capt W that Japan will not be invaded next month. The odds being 2-1.

Sunday June 17*
The sun shone today for first time for six days. We hear of meeting in Berlin of T, C and S. Investigate robbery of 2 loaves from cookhouse and find that Number 3 Dawson was culprit. When Capt W challenged him he immediately admitted his guilt. Both Capt W and myself were surprised. I think he should be committed to guardroom. I went to epilogue, only four present. One of the Americans got struck by one of the guards. Nasty gash on his cheek.

Monday June 18
A real nightmare last night. We spend 5hrs down shelter from 11pm til 4am. Many bombs heard and flares seen. I feel very tired. We were able to buy two thirds of a bottle of lemonade – about a wine glass full.

Tuesday June 19
We had warning last night but did not go down shelter, for which I was truly thankful. A beautiful day. The boys are again becoming optimistic. The guards still continue to do their spasmodic beating up. Number 3 sentenced to three days in the cells.

Wednesday June 20
Gee what a raid last night. We were down shelter for 3hrs, 11 til 2. Planes passed over, heard continually for one and a half hours and when we came up we saw a great red glow in the sky westward. The Nips were rather nasty during the day. We see by the paper that the Nips are afraid of invasion of this island. They say that it's well defended and they have tens of thousands of persons here. We just wait.

Thursday June 21
Longest day. No warning during the night but we go down shelter during the day for one hour, 9am til 10am. Hear only a few planes. Very warm. Strong feeling that invasion will take place next month. I do not think that it can possibly be before August.

Friday June 22
Yasme Day. We had a few warnings today. We went down the shelter twice during the night. First time for 2hrs, 12 til 2, then 4 til 4.30. We heard only a few planes. During the morning the alarm went but did not go down shelter, but we heard in the distance some terrific shelling or bombing, lasting for one hour. It shook all the buildings in the camp. The Nips are very perturbed. I went to service and communion in the morning, about 15 present. We had no concert in the evening. Capt W and I go down the shelter to see if the shelter can be made more comfortable.

Saturday June 23
We had a couple of warnings today and went down the shelter for half an hour. We again had another bombardment lasting for half an hour. I'm convinced it's shelling from the sea. If this is so then we must be prepared for an invasion sooner than what I thought. The weather is very close and I feel very languid.

Sunday June 24
We went down the shelter twice during the night, from 12 til 1 and from 1.30 til 3.30. The weather not so good, very heavy rain during the night. The Nips still continue their beating up of the boys. Number 3 gets stitch put in his face because a Dutchman hit him. He did not have the guts to retaliate. Number 4 Frank's cousin becomes involved in doubling up. I go to evening epilogue, only 4 present.

Monday June 25
A year ago today I received my first letter from home. I shall always remember the date. Weather fine. Two warnings but do not go down shelter.

Tuesday June 26
Very close. I do not feel so good. Have got terrible pains in my stomach. Harold Ratcliffe is dying but does not know. He's in very good spirit. We hear some depressing news. Four of the 38 that left here in Dec are dead, dying of pneumonia.

Wednesday June 27
We go down shelter for 1hr last night. Only heard one or two planes. Weather very sultry. I do not feel so good.

Thursday June 28
Went down shelter last night for quarter of an hour. I feel lousy and go to bed in the afternoon with temp 38.8, which increases in the evening to 39.6, 104F. The American examined me thoroughly but could not find anything wrong, but I certainly have got a high fever.

Friday June 29
I did not go down shelter last night, Capt W having obtained permission for me to stay in bed. The boys were down for two and a half hours. Nothing to report. My temp today normal, no fever, but I feel weak. I will be pleased to see the end of next month and I pray that I may be spared to see same. I stay in bed all day.

Saturday June 30
Went down the shelter last night for two hours. Felt OK in the morning and went to the cookhouse but did not stay as I felt very groggy. Had my temp taken

and found it was 38. Went to bed, got up for sick parade and found my temp was 39.7, pulse 104. Doctors think I have got malaria. But I have my doubts. I am very worried. Nip commandant grants permission for me to stay in bed.

Sunday July 1
The alarm went last night but we did not go down shelter. Am now taking six quinine tablets a day. Am feeling better today. We had two more warnings during the day. The old soldiers left this afternoon and the new ones arrived. I stayed in bed all day but went to service in the evening. I wonder if I will have a fever tomorrow.

Monday July 2
Yasme Day. We went down the shelter twice last night, 12 til 2 and 3 til 5. Saw only a few flashes in the sky. I am feeling better today but I stay in bed all day. Did not go to service. More than 75% of the camp think this will be the month for invasion. I hope they are right. I always think this is my unlucky month.

Tuesday July 3
Did not go down shelter last night. Food is now bad. The soups have very little vegetable in and we have had no salt for weeks. The weather is fairly good. All our winter clothes have been taken out of the camp today. Am feeling better but cannot eat.

Wednesday July 4
Independence Day. We were down shelter last night for 2hrs. Heard a few planes. We also have our first daylight raid when we went down the shelter for half an hour, 9 to 9.30am. No other warnings. Weather very hot and I still do not feel so good. Frank and Capt W are very optimistic and feel certain of invasion this month.

Thursday July 5
No raid last night but we go down twice during the day, 9.30 to 10, 1.30 to 2. The last raid about 15 American fighters came over but we heard no bombs dropped. The weather does not appear to be settled.

Friday July 6
No raid last night and no warning all day. We had a very heavy thunderstorm and it rained all day. We are now having seaweed soup. It's simply terrible. I cannot bear even the smell of it. I still am feeling far from fit and I think I have lost a lot of weight this month.

Saturday July 7
Still no raid last night and no warning during the day. Many of the boys think this is the prelude to invasion but I do not think so. Still raining, the weather is far from being perfect. The food is now very scarce and we run out of rice very frequently. I feel very hungry. We get our issue of tobacco but no cigs. It appears that we will not have any more.

Sunday July 8
Still yet another night without any raid. We had a very cold night, temp dropping to 16 degrees. Great coats have to be handed in and we receive gas capes. I take evening epilogue service. I am trying to swot up my shorthand.

Monday July 9
Still no warning during the night. Weather cold at night, warmer during the day. Boys are feeling rather pessimistic as the months speed by.

Tuesday July 10
We go down shelter last night for 1hr, 11.30 til 12.30. Nothing doing. Still cold. A year today we opened new hospital. The food is really bad, this seaweed soup is terrible and many of the boys have squitters.

Wednesday July 11
Terrific thunderstorms all day. Rain, rain and more rain. The warning went several times but we did not go down shelter. The Nips kill another pig and we get the head and a few lbs of meat. And we managed to scrape some veg from garden. I feel lousy and have again slight fever. Unable to eat.

Thursday July 12
What a night. Terrific thunderstorm and rain and in the middle of it the alarm went at 12.30 and we had to go down shelter for two and a half hours. We hear a few planes and see glow in the sky when we come out. The worse night we've yet had. Terrible day, rained all day. I got very wet and feel lousy. I feel as if I have no energy left. This seaweed soup is terrible.

Friday July 13
Yasme Day. Have got fever again, temp 38.1 in the morning and rose to 40 in the evening. I am very worried. Sgt Hughes came in the evening and gave a sponge to get my temp down. I went to church in the morning and communion, also managed good workers' parade, then went to bed. A glorious day. I hope the weather changes. Capt W got permission for me to stay in bed if alarm goes.

Saturday July 14
Warning went last night. Down in shelter for two and a half hours. I did not go because of my high temp. Temp was down 36.7. Doctors are giving me quinine as they think I've got malaria. Temp up at night, 39.6. I feel lousy and am very worried.

Sunday July 15
Temp down in the morning 37.1. I had a terrible night, did not sleep a wink. I get weighed and find that I've lost 6 and a half kg. Doctors are very perturbed about the health of the camp which is rapidly becoming worse. The weather is still bad. We had two warnings today. My temp in the evening is 37.6. I hope and pray that it will continue to go down to normal. I eat very little. Did not go to church.

Monday July 16
Still raining. Was down in shelter last night for two and a half hours. Also for one hour this afternoon. Temp in morning 37.3 and this evening 37.6. I still feel very sick. Many men are sick and the outlook looks very black.

Tuesday July 17
Still very wet. Down in the shelter for 1hr last night. The shelter is very wet through so much rain. My temp in morning is 37.3, at night 37.6. Still taking quinine. I feel very sick.

Wednesday July 18
Went down shelter last night for 1hr. Very wet. Temp 37 and 37.3. We have issue of cigs which is only two for a week plus a little tobacco. The seaweed soup is finished. What a blessing. I am beginning to think seriously that we will spend another winter as POW.

Thursday July 19
Did not go down shelter last night. I feel very weak. Temp 37 and 37.5. Still it rains and very miserable. The men are looking very ill and we are having a lot of sickness. Three or four cases in hospital are on the danger list and with the food becoming worse so the danger increases.

Friday July 20
Did not go down shelter last night. Still it rains. Temp down 37 and 37. Still taking small doses of quinine. We have long delayed issue of soap. Two tablets a man. It was much needed. I commenced going on roll call this evening. We had practice fire drill this afternoon. Boys seemed to enjoy it very much.

Saturday July 21
No raid again last night. Still rains. I feel sick and really out of sorts. I have no appetite and have to force myself to eat and I am losing a lot of weight. Both Capt W and Frank have colds. The Nips did some more of their torture today when they put stick under a Dutchman's nails because he told Capt W that they had bashed him. The lousy Bs.

Sunday July 22
Another night without any warning. We have a warning this morning but did not go down shelter. Very cloudy and a little rain. We have a few bones in and get half tomato from the garden. I go to epilogue service, only six present. I am feeling better but still rather weak.

Monday July 23
Cold at night. We hear many planes during the night but the alarm does not sound. Was rather amazing as planes were actually overhead with lights full on in the camp. I take evening epilogue service, only six present.

Tuesday July 24
Yasme Day. Did not go down shelter during the night though planes overhead. We went down shelter three times during the day. Saw planes and heard many explosions. We get issued with 11 plums each man. Lovely day. I go to communion service, 12 present. A year ago today poor Norman was killed. I shall be happy when this month is over. I dread this month. I just feel that something is going to happen. No concert. We have a good tea, one tomato each man, egg fruit and curry sauce.

Wednesday July 25
Great shock today when 10 men leave the camp for HQ camp. Five Dutch, five English. Sorry to see Lionel Stanton leave. He was a very good fellow, a real Christian. They left at 1pm just after we had alarm and down in the shelter for one hour. The weather is improving. Joe's birthday today. I wonder how he is. The Nips are rather perturbed over stealing from the garden and have two men watching day and night. The guards are suspected of stealing.

Thursday July 26
Inspection of the camp today by Nip major who inspected all the shelters and gave the Nips some bayonet drill. We went down the shelter last night for 1hr and also this afternoon for 1hr. Much warmer today. The food is a little better. I feel much better and I think I am putting [on] some of the weight that I have lost.

Friday July 27
Went down shelter last night for 2hrs. Very little activity about. We hear that invasion is impending. We went down shelter at 12 noon for half an hour and again at 2pm. I saw 10 planes at one time.

Saturday July 28
Gee what a night and day. ARW went 8pm, 10pm and 12pm. We went down shelter at 11 for 2hrs. Many planes. Alarm went again at 4 and again at 6.30 when we went down shelter til 8.30, going back to the shelter in 10 minutes time til 2.30. We managed to get something to eat and went down shelter at 3.30 for half an hour. We hear many bombs and heavy shelling from ships. I wonder if it's the beginning of the end. We hear that Attlee is PM and that we now have a Labour government in England.

Sunday July 29
Alarm went during the night but we did not go down shelter. We had several alarms during the day and went down the shelter three times for short periods. I saw 10 planes flying very high. We hear more news of election. The weather is now much better. We still have many complaints re cookhouse and Capt W and I have busy time dealing with same. I go to epilogue, only three present. I am feeling very tired.

Monday July 30
A very disturbed night. Capt W taken ill, vomiting and squitters. Alarm went and we were down shelter for one and a half hours. I told Nips that Capt W was too sick to move and asked them for a doctor. When we came out of the shelter at 1.30 Capt W was still extremely sick. Dutch doctor gave him some dope and he was a little better. I had to take Number 3 up to commandant to be punished for stealing two breads. He was sentenced to miss two meals. We went down the shelter twice during the day. Capt W stays in bed.

Tuesday July 31
Warning went during the night but we did not go down shelter. We went down twice during the day, one hour and two and a half hours. Things are certainly looking up with all these raids during the day. We hear that next month will be invasion month. I wonder. Capt W is still sick and keeps to his bed. We are very short of tobacco and cigs.

Wednesday August 1
No raid last night and none during the day. Very dull with occasional rain. Capt W still in bed and looking rather seedy. We have very little veg these days. We are also having a lot of stuff pinched from the garden.

Thursday August 2
Again no raids or alarms during the day or last night. Still wet and miserable. I try to get cigs or tobacco during Capt W's sickness from the Nips but I failed. Promised tomorrow.

Friday August 3
No raid or alarm last night. Still heavy gale blowing. I tried hard to get tobacco or cigs, eventually got them about 7pm. 33 packets short for one packet per man. I took the epilogue service, six present. I think the bad weather has something to do with lack of alarms. We are told further cut in the rice starting tomorrow. The food question is becoming serious.

Saturday August 4
Yasme Day. Bank Holiday. I feel very homesick today. I really thought a year ago that I would be free today but it looks very far away. I go to service and communion in the morning and intended to give a lecture on sport. I was all fixed for it in the afternoon when warning went and we were down the shelter for 1hr. The new rice ration is hellish. The boys will certainly go down the hill with this ration. Spent the evening with Capt W listening to him reading poetry. It was beautiful.

Sunday August 5
Air raid warning during the night. Did not go down shelter. Four cooks taken out of cookhouse. Warning went three times during the day but did not go down shelter. Very busy day. I feel sick once again and have got a temp. The alarm went 10pm and we went down shelter for 3hrs. It was terrible. Capt W went for first time for 10 days.

Monday August 6
Six years today I was called up. I hope it's the last anniversary as a POW. Capt W and I spent the afternoon spring cleaning and rat catching. Our [illegible] bag was one. Many warnings during the day. I still feel a little groggy. Went to epilogue service.

Tuesday August 7
Warning went but did not go down shelter during the night. Went down shelter twice in the morning. Second raid saw many leaflets fall. Guards gathered them up but one of the boys got one worded in Japanese, showing face of clock. Very interesting. The hour has come. I go to bed. Temp 38.8. Doctors say malaria. My temp went down to 37.4 in the evening. Rations cut today. Terrible issue. Nightshift refused to go to work but later decided to go and see if rations improve.

Wednesday August 8
Raid last night. Down shelter for 1hr and during the day we went down for 4hrs and it was some raid. Some of the boys counted about 300 planes and we heard many explosions. It was the largest daylight raid yet. The ration front is still desperate. Receiving about 50% potatoes, 50% rice and beans. We actually get less than a quarter of a pound of potatoes a meal. The men are rapidly becoming weaker and within six weeks there will be many deaths in this camp, of that I am sure. I still feel lousy. Temp 37.3. I hope the Americans will soon arrive.

*Thursday August 9**
The alarm went last night and we were down the shelter for 1hr. We had rather exciting morning, going down no fewer than four times from 7 til 1pm. We saw no planes. I have no temp but still feel sick. A very heavy day. Nips beat up a lot of fellows eventually breaking breastbone of a Dutchman. Stealing from the garden was the offence. An American spilt on the other men. The rations are still bad and we are now starving.

Friday August 10
No raid last night. Long raid in the morning 9 til 1.30. No planes or bombs. I spoke to Hugh Edwards this morning. He's really down and does not think he will see Nov if we are not freed by then. The men are going down rapidly.

Saturday August 11
Warning went last night. Was down shelter for 1hr. Warning went again in the morning, about 9. Was down in shelter for three and a half hours. Had some glorious news from the IT who said that R had declared war on Nippon. R planes had bombed Manchuko [sic]. It's wonderful if it's true. Will try and get confirmation tomorrow.

Sunday August 12
We get confirmation. Saw it in the P. Wonderful. It's bound to shorten the war. Went down shelter last night for 2hrs, also again in the morning for 3hrs. Gee we're certainly hitting them very hard. The civvy guards are leaving on the 15th being replaced by soldiers. Good news. The Nips are still doing a bit of bashing. I am feeling better but a wee bit faint. Weighed today. 77kg gained 1kg. Went to evening epilogue.

Monday August 13
Did not go down shelter last night but had a busy morning. Three alarms lasting from 8.30 til 2. Down the shelter most of the time. Also had another in the afternoon for half an hour. We spend more than half a day down the shelter. Only 14 Americans go to work out of total of 64. Tobacco is scarce. We get

issued with half a packet. No cigs. R seems to be doing OK. The camp has once again become rather optimistic. I do hope and pray it won't be long so that the lives of many men may be saved.

Tuesday August 14

No raid during the night but we have a long session in the shelter during the morning about 5hrs, 8 til 1. Heard very few planes. We go again down the shelter in the afternoon for 15mins. This is very bad for the nightshift who get very little sleep during the day. They all feel very weak. The spirit of the camp is becoming desperate. I feel very weak. I take the epilogue service and pray that we may have a real day of rest tomorrow.

Wednesday August 15

Yasme Day. We go down shelter last night for 2hrs, 11 til 1am. Saw a few flashes. Our prayers were answered, we do not go down the shelter at all during the day though we hear a few planes. Sickness increasing. 35 in hospital, 53 sick in billets. 3 or 4 in a very critical condition. I go to service and communion in the afternoon. Good workers' parade, I hope it's the last. Capt W reads a proclamation on parade to the effect we must obey Nippon orders or be shot. Sensation this evening. We are told that we must rest tomorrow because it's Nippon Christmas. The whole camp is now full of rumours. I'm of the opinion we must wait and see.

Thursday August 16*

What a day. It will live in my memory. We started the day full of excitement. No air raids during the night and still nothing during the day. We are told we will probably rest again tomorrow because our weight has decreased and many men are sick. Later on we are told that the 10 men who left the camp to build air raid shelters will return this evening. We see guards breaking up some of their bamboo poles. All these things, are they just mere coincidences? Can we pray that the war is over, is it too much to think? We hold church service and communion but it's interrupted by Nips. I will write more this evening when we see the 10 men who are coming back.

8pm: I feel sure that the war is over. The men who have just arrived say they have been told it's finished. Stanton also said Dr Goronwy was drowned on his way to Japan. I see JJ, the Nip guard, who told me the war was over and agreement was being signed tomorrow. I cannot just believe it. It's wonderful to think we have waited for three and a half years for this day. I thank God for my deliverance. I just cannot eat, I don't feel hungry or sleepy and will not be able to sleep tonight. The camp is buzzing with excitement and everybody is congratulating each other on being free.

We hear from the guards that one bomb blew up Nagasaki. What a [illegible] the huge cloud [illegible] we saw must have been big oil wells catching fire. We must now take over the camp and out with the Nips.

Friday August 17
We continue to hear that the war is over and at 11.45am this morning the Nip commandant made a speech in which he said the war was over and that today the powers were signing a treaty. Meanwhile we had to be quiet and continue to salute the guards and obey Nippon orders. A lump came to my throat while Capt W was translating commandant's speech. To think we'd been three and a half years waiting for this day. I can imagine what joy they must feel at home over the joyful news. The boys are looking very much better already. We are trying to get the Red+ supplies in the stores. Nips say they will issue tomorrow when more supplies come in today. The Nips will not allow any singing or shouting and we must be in bed by 9 o'clock. I go to epilogue service, about 12 present.

Saturday August 18
I slept very badly last night, was awakened by Nips when the Red+ came in at 1.30am. Had a terrific battle with Nips over issue but Capt W won the day and we got issued with half Red+ parcel for each man. We hear that the treaty has not yet been signed. The Nips are certainly still bombastic and we see a few planes which makes one think that we have given them an easy peace. It does not appear that we will take over Japan like we've done in Germany. We had to fix up a clothing return which had to be ready immediately. Capt W and I and two others worked til 2am before it was completed. I had a very good tea when we opened butter and spam. Official date of peace. 1259 days POW.

Sunday August 19
I feel terribly tired. We hear that the treaty has been signed. We held a thanksgiving service this morning, only 40 attended. The weather these days is glorious. We are very busy in the office getting things organised. Made a lovely dish for dinner with milk, butter and jam. It was delicious. The Nips have cut down our rice once again. I do hope that we will soon leave this camp.

Monday August 20
Rumours that we may move in five or six days time. Weather still glorious. Still do not get the gen on the peace terms. The boys are already becoming impatient. I am very busy organising games etc for the men. I take evening epilogue.

Tuesday August 21
Another beautiful day. Full of rumours but nothing official. We have much trouble with Yanks and Dutch stealing from the garden. We have general parade 5.30pm. Nip commandant makes a speech saying that on the 18th the

war was officially ended. It was a sickly speech full of BS that made me feel I would like to vomit. No news of date of departure. What is our government doing? Letters arrive today. I got postcard from Mother.

Wednesday August 22

We are still having roll calls, Jap fashion. They are a bore. Very busy making lists etc. We hear many rumours. I wonder when we will leave. The guards now patrol outside the fence.

Thursday August 23

The Nips are constantly worrying us for clothing. We get issued with brand new Nip clothing which nobody wants. Concession made that we can go outside camp for two hours in the morning.

Friday August 24

About another 200 cards arrived. I did not get one. Did not have much sleep owing to Nips coming in. We hear that USA planes are expected over this camp tomorrow. We prepare great sign, POW Camp, to be observed from air. Nip roll call finished. Nips are now looking rather sheepish.

Saturday August 25

We saw about 10 planes a good distance away but none came over the camp. We get hold of gramophone and some good records. Another 150 letters come in, received one from Kay. Still no news of departure. Boys are becoming very restless.

Sunday August 26

We received our valuables but several men have had their rings and watches pinched by Nips. The weather not so good. Mob law is coming in this camp. Ugly incident this afternoon. Deputation came to see Capt W re killing of pig. Capt W decides to see Nip commandant re food question. Situation is becoming ugly and serious. I go to church and communion in the afternoon, very few present. I hope we shall kill the pig tomorrow.

Monday August 27

Thank God, we kill the pig late in the afternoon but it's for tomorrow's breakfast. We get rise in rice ration but men are becoming worse and stealing from the garden.

Tuesday August 28

What a day. A day that will always live in my memory. Oh the joy. The morning was uneventful. I had just left our room about 2pm after making arrangement to kill the six small pigs when I saw in the distance a big four-engine bomber flying low. It came over the camp and was followed by five others – a wonderful sight. Well the men rushed out of their billets waving their hands and cheering. After circling the camp two or three times we notice that the bomb doors were open and then from the plane a shower of parachute boxes and drums fell. It was one of the greatest moments of my life. The boys were laughing and crying with joy. I actually saw men with tears streaming down their face. The planes continued to circle around and drop all sorts of bundles, cans, boxes. I remembered the hymn "All Good Gifts Around Us are Sent from Heaven Above" as I saw all this wonderful food and clothing come down. Unfortunately a lot was destroyed by chutes failing to open. The 2.5 gallon drums welded together came down with terrific force. Four Nips were killed and some injured. Some of the boxes crashed through the billets, cookhouse and dining hall but only one was injured. It was marvellous. Choc, sweets, soups, biscuits, cocoa, sugar, shirts, socks, boots, trousers, first aid and drugs, everything which we were starved of. Everybody was happy, a real transformation in 2hrs. I could not sleep at night, in fact I don't think one person slept. The American doctor, Capt W and I had a little drop of liquor to celebrate. It was lovely. I thank God with all my heart and soul for this great day.

Wednesday August 29
What wonderful meals we're having with all this tinned food and tobacco. Pipe tobacco is good and my pipe going all day. We give some food and clothing to the Nips who were injured yesterday. The attitude of the Nips is amazing. They are simply creeping and crawling to us. Only a few days ago they were beating us up. We also receive newspaper and magazines and we are all amazed at the changes all over the world. We will go back to a new world.

Thursday August 30
Red+ delegates arrive in the camp and we hear further interesting news. They do not think we will leave here for another 15 days. American troops are expected here on Sept 3. We had another visit from the planes today. More food and cigs. Not so much damage this time but one or two huts were damaged. It would be very sad if any of the boys got killed by one of these packages. Frank Fryett is in hospital with pneumonia but is now better.

Friday August 31
These days are wonderful. It's just like starting a fresh life. I am very busy being Capt W's second in command and get very tired by the end of the day. Incident took place this morning when Dutch hoisted a newly made flag up flag post in honour of Queen's birthday. The Yanks took great exception to this and one of them made rather a fiery speech. We had another two drops today. More boots, clothes and food. We have three pairs of boots to each man. After the stuff

had been dropped I went for walk in village. It was wonderful to feel sense of freedom. Wherever I went the Nips were bowing to me. I met some of those who had been so cruel down the mine. I just looked through them. Oh boy did I get a kick doing this. The Nip kids get plenty of gum and choc from the boys. Frank Fryett is much better and seems to have got over his crisis. We hear that the Yanks have arrived in Tokyo and are expected here about the 3rd. This new atomic bomb seems to have done the trick but it's a devilish invention.

Saturday September 1*

The weather is putrid. Rain, rain and more rain. It's obliterated all our marking for planes and we had to get cracking on it right away. We are now firing and signalling and hope to get in touch with planes. The camp is now strewn with cans and I have had a busy day getting it cleaned up. We waited for a drop all day but nothing came. Though one plane came over it did not drop anything. Worked very hard during afternoon cleaning camp. Capt W, two doctors and Lt Fobes went to a dinner given to them by Mitsui brothers. It was a two-course dinner and they say that it would have done credit to any English hotel.

Sunday September 2

Another historic day! The weather very bad. Rain and more rain. About 10am in the morning commandant told Capt W that all Nips would leave camp immediately including the guard who would hand over their arms. The full significance of this did not immediately dawn upon us but later we saw the great changeover. About 11am all the Nips who have worked in the camp, the ration waller [sic], the MI orderlies came into our room, numbered off, came to attention and saluted in the approved Jap fashion. The Number 1 then said they had finished working in the camp, did Capt W require any of them to stay? Capt W said he required only one. Two of the Nips were crying and they all looked rather sorry for themselves. I felt rather embarrassed when they bowed to me. It was only a few weeks ago that they were bashing us and even up to a couple of days ago they were still shouting at us. Later in the afternoon we took over the arms and it was a unique moment when the commandant handed over his sword to Capt W, who however returned it to him. Capt W later on got a sword. We are now virtually in control over this area. No longer POW but army of occupation. The transformation is amazing. We now give orders and commandeer anything we require. We have taken over the Nip office. Capt W is now in commandant room and Lt Fobes and myself have got desks in same room. All the other office staff have been put in outer office.

Monday September 3

The weather is terrible. We have now had 48hrs rain. The Americans took over the first guard. The 77th take over tomorrow. We are unable to get any English news over the wireless. Big disappointment. Fryett is much better and will soon be out of dock. We are told to expect a huge storm tomorrow and then it will be fine. I get 90 Yen compensation from the company for my accident. My foot is very painful today. We see many boys from other camp and are told that the sick men will soon be evacuated to Fukuoka, and from there by plane.

Tuesday September 4
Still it rains. The camp is just a sea of mud. Have now arranged for Nips to do all heavy fatigue in camp. Frank Fryett out of hospital today, he looks rather seedy. The 77th took over guard today and were very smart. Sgt Grandon doing NCO in charge. Very little news.

Wednesday September 5
Much finer today. The weather seems to have changed. Capt W, Dutch doctor and American visited other camps today and brought back news of friends. I had rather a busy day doing Capt W's job. We have visitors who hear how fortunate we have been with drops.

Thursday September 6*
I go out today visiting camps by car, driven by Cole. We had to push it up any small incline. I hear news of many deaths with the 77th which come as a great shock to me. One officer said that he thought only 10% of the 77th would get back. I hope this is not true. We are able to get Chungking on the radio and we hear that the world is at least hearing of these little yellow men. The Chinese killed their officer last night by clubbing him to death. He deserved it.

Friday September 7
Another lovely day and what a day. The supply planes came over about 9am and started dropping. We were again very lucky and got about 12 drops. It was a very busy morning especially as Capt W left by car to visit other camps about 11am. I decided to issue one large carton to each man and got cracking with issuing in the afternoon. The boys were gloriously happy. We must send some to other camps tomorrow. I receive a visit from Nip Number 1 down mine. He speaks a little English. He treated us very good. It's very difficult to recognise some of the fellows. They have filled out so much. I actually shook hands with a chap who had been in the camp right from the beginning thinking he was a visitor.

Saturday September 8*
Capt Blakey visits the camp and I get the news of some of the deaths on this island. I am very sorry to see so many good men gone. We close cookhouse down, only cooking for visitors. We pack off 200 cartons to Number 9 camp as they did not have a drop. We go around looking for arms today and picked up 100 rifles.

Sunday September 9
Another lovely day. Capt W and I go for a cycle ride in the afternoon to Number 26 camp. It was very nice. We had a lovely tea there and spot of Nip whiskey. We hear bad news of Number 8 camp. 16 men dead and many in hospital through drinking "saki". We believe it was deliberate.

Monday September 10
We still await news of our departure. We get no official news whatsoever. Thank God we had all that food dropped. The lads are putting on weight, anything up to 10kilos. Capt W and I go for another cycle ride in the evening. I went to epilogue, only three present. I lost my pipe this evening. Capt W loaned me one.

Tuesday September 11
Very wet. Rained all day. About six Americans took off from the camp. How much longer will we have to wait before leaving this camp? I hope it will be this week. We have about 18 Nips working in this camp. Have a visit from officer Number 26 camp. Have a good supper and a lovely piece of pudding from the guard, the best I've yet tasted.

Wednesday September 12
Rained all day. Very little doing. We get issued bottle of beer each man. Have a party with Dutch doctor and then later stayed up til 3am with American doctor, Dai Grandon and Frank Fryett. A very good beer party.

Thursday September 13
A little finer today. We hear rumours that we may move on the 21st. Four USA fighters came over the camp and gave us a wonderful display of aerobatics. I have never seen anything so fast. Went for long walk with Capt W and saw some very pretty scenery. It reminded me of Bavaria. We get some more meat from Nips who are fairly raining food on us.

Friday September 14
Cloudy and dull but no rain. We hear that they are evacuating POWs from other camps. And today we saw a detailed list showing dates of evacuation for all camps. We are last but one, moving on the 21st. The boys are going around beating up some of the Nips who ill-treated them down the mine, also some of the guards. Capt W and I take no notice and we are pleased to see them taking the law in their own hands.

Saturday September 15
Finer but no drops. Capt W, Lt Fobes, Doc Grider and myself went to a concert and meal about six miles away. It was a show given by Geisha girls, about 30 to

40 officers present and officials of the mine including mayor of city. They (Nips) did all they could to be hospitable. What a difference a month has made. The Geisha girls were not so bad nor were some of the girls who waited on us. I was sorry that the party broke up so early. I was feeling OK.

Sunday September 16
We hear that American recovery team is at a camp near here so I cycle over in the afternoon in pouring rain. I find out that they will be in our camp Monday or Tuesday. They seem to be in a chaotic state. The weather is becoming worse. Later in the afternoon, American officers arrived and said team was coming over in two days time. Went to service and communion, only five present.

Monday September 17
What a day. Exactly a year ago we had similar weather. It blew a typhoon wrecking half of the camp. We had no lights or water. It rained incessantly for 36hrs. I am glad we are not on the sea today, it would be just too bad. Gee the boys are getting fat, they are still gaining weight.

Tuesday September 18
The storm continued last night, finishing this morning. The American relieving force got bogged and put three lorries into a rice paddy. We eventually got cracking on getting men through at 10am, finishing about 3pm. We all sent message home. Ten words. Capt W and two doctors went to dinner. I turned it down, felt tired, drank couple of beers with Fryett. American officers and three others leave for Nagasaki.

Wednesday September 19
Had a lovely day. Went for a walk with Fryett across country, came to small village where we gave sweets and chewing gum to the children. Later we had a spot of tea with these people. Came back and went to a party. I gave away several snaps.

Thursday September 20
Last day in camp. Very busy day making lists and arrangement for train party. Fryett goes to village over mountain in the afternoon. I follow later, have a really good time. Disturbances in camp when the boys beat up few Nips. The Nips were in a hell of a state, bleeding from nose and mouth. Investigate the matter and found that two or three boys set on one Nip. I gave them good lecture and told them beat Nip up as often as they like, but one for one. Very heavy party at night. I put Fryett to bed after hectic walk over mountains. Dai Grandon and [illegible] start fighting 1am.

Friday September 21*
We left camp today. Capt W, two doctors and all Americans, Dutch personnel left at 5am. I left at 8am in charge of 215 English. The whole village turned out to see us off. I was the last man to leave the camp and the first to come in. We had uneventful train journey to Nagasaki and then we saw the result of the atomic bomb. It was simply astounding, nothing left standing for miles, everything flat and burnt out. When we arrived at station I met Capt W, also USA officers. There was a band at the platform playing modern music and all men had doughnuts and coffee. We then had to be deloused and medical inspection in the course of which I lost my pipes and jacket and tobacco. I lost most of the 240 who went on a destroyer. Capt W and I get in an aircraft carrier called Chenango. We share a cabin with Dutch doctor. Went to movie show in the evening. Had a lovely tea and feel that we are still Alice in Wonderland. Feel very tired and sleepy. Morning off tomorrow.

Saturday September 22
Had a wonderful night's sleep. Slept like a log for 10 hrs. We moved off 10am. Exactly two years ago at the same hour we left Singapore. A lovely ship this is. Does not roll or pitch and you can hardly tell that you are moving. Weather rather dirty, sea choppy. I went to sleep in the afternoon for three hours. Went to see another flick in the evening. Rather stupid stuff. Made conversation with US officer who gave Capt W and myself a shirt each.

Sunday September 23
Another grand night's rest. Weather horrible. 9am breakfast then went for tour of the ship with Capt W. It took us one and a half hours and was good fun. The US officer who took us around was the same one that gave us the shirt. We arrived at Okinawa at noon and anchored in a bay with hundreds of other ships. We do not know when we will disembark. It looks as if it will be tomorrow. Did not go to church service in the morning. Went to see another flick in the evening, was a bit better than the previous night. Bed 10pm tired.

Monday September 24*
Another wet day. We have many rumours of moving but we do eventually leave the carrier at 4pm by LTC. We passed hundreds of vessels of all descriptions. We landed Okinawa about 5pm. Owing to some bad arrangements we were on the quayside for over an hour. We then transferred by trucks to the other side of the island. The camp reminded me of Manorbier, all mud. Picked up Dai, Frank, and rest of the boys who said they had grand time on cruiser. Slept in tents. Pouring with rain.

Tuesday September 25
This camp reminds me very much of Manorbier. Nothing but mud, mud and more mud. We hear that we may leave tomorrow by plane. Went to the flicks with Capt W this evening. Not too bad. Tired.

Wednesday September 26
We were awakened 2am this morning and taken by lorries to aerodrome. I got split from Capt W, Fryett and Grandon and got on a plane, a C46 Douglas transport with 14 others. We had a splendid trip. It was a wonderful experience looking on the other side of the clouds. There were four crew and they had a primus stove in the cabin to cook breakfast. We left at 8.30, arriving Manila 12.30. It was just like riding in a car. We arrived at a large camp 20 miles outside Manila about 3pm. Lost all touch with Capt W, Dai and Frank. They are in another part of the camp, about 1 mile away. We are 12 in a tent. There must be at least 10,000 POW in the camp. Went to cinema show in the evening.

Thursday September 27
Very quiet day. Very warm. I send cablegram and airmail letter to Mother and Joe. We can collect from canteen three bottles of beer a day, two packets of cigs, one packet tobacco, four cigars, hot and cold drinks. We do not get medical examination or interview but Dai, Frank and all others get done.

Friday September 28
Receive two letters from Mother and Ken. Get medical examination, not very impressed. See a good flick – Salome.

Saturday September 29
I meet a fellow named Dai Evans from Penarth, get a lot of gen, also had letter dated March, also had two letters from aunt Ethel and Margaret.

Sunday September 30
Very wet and stormy. Went to communion in the morning. Still waiting for interrogation. Maybe tomorrow. Capt W drops in for a chat. The boys are becoming rather fed up.

Monday October 1
Terrific weather. Just caught edge of typhoon. Got paid and finished interrogation. Now waiting for move which cannot come too soon.

Tuesday October 2
Aussies left camp today but returned later. Weather too bad. This is the second time. Still no signs of moving.

Wednesday October 3
Aussies left again today but returned later. Grub not so good. I go to dentist and have remainder of my top teeth taken out. I was in the chair for one and a half hours. He took about one hour to take one tooth out. However it was painless. I feel rather lousy.

Thursday October 4
Do not feel so good. My gums are very painful. We hear that some of the English move tomorrow. Aussies left today.

Friday October 5
Still very wet. I go to the pictures with Dai and Frank. Hear rumours of departure. I see Capt W and he looks much better.

Saturday October 6
We go to Manila for the evening. Lot of bomb damage. Did not have a drink, very quiet. Still rumours of a move.

Sunday October 7
Move on. Dai and Frank are on but I'm off. I take the matter up, get little satisfaction. Went to early communion, only 10 present. Morning service about 1,000 present. Hear news of another draft. Went to theatre in the evening. Poor show.

Monday October 8
On draft but not on same boat as Dai or Frank. Move tomorrow via America.

Tuesday October 9
Arrive onboard Marine Shark, a troop ship. 3,500 onboard. Very crowded. 200 nurses. Unfortunately I get a bottom deck. Phew it's hot.

Wednesday October 10
We left harbour 9pm. Anchored in bay. Weighed anchor 4pm. Now for San Francisco. Phew it's hot though much rain.

Thursday October 11
Heavy rain. Ship rolls, slight groundswell. I see Capt W who is onboard. We still see the Philippines.

Friday October 12
Much finer but it's very hot. We are very crowded down in our hold, in fact the whole ship is crowded out. The food is only fair.

Saturday October 13
We hear many rumours of our destination. I think it's Frisco. I am sleeping on top bunk, the hottest in the hold.

Sunday October 14
Went to service in the morning, also communion and service in the evening. Quite a good number present. Still unbearably hot.

Monday October 15
We are doing about 400 miles a day. Should get to Frisco about 29th. We hear that we may call at Honolulu.

Tuesday October 16
We have had a couple of cinema shows but only about 200 can see it at a time. We are able to buy some drinks but not many.

Wednesday October 17
Still very hot. Sea calm. Best part of the day is in the evening, much cooler then.

Thursday October 18
Going slow, engines not so good. Many complaints re food. Went to service in the evening.

Friday October 19
We are near the dateline and tomorrow will be another Friday 19th. We are told we will arrive Honolulu Tuesday.

Friday October 19
This is second Friday and we cross the dateline ship going extremely slow, everybody fed up.

Saturday October 20
The lousy ship stopped at 11pm last night and drifted for 12 hrs. We are now going dead slow. This is supposed to be a new ship. It makes you long to be on a British ship.

Sunday October 21*
Rain spoilt service on deck but we held service in dining hall in evening and communion. Syd Perkins went into hospital, infection in the mouth. Still going slow.

Monday October 22
We are told we arrive in Pearl Harbour tomorrow, 10am and we will then put engines in order. May be for few days.

Tuesday October 23*
Arrive at Pearl Harbour 10.30am. Not allowed to land. Bands play on our arrival. Nurses come aboard. I send letters to Babs, Mary, Ken and Dad. Pearl Harbour looks OK from the ship.

Wednesday October 24
We pulled out 5pm this evening. Engines said to be OK. Now full speed to Frisco.

Thursday October 25
Well I'm darned. B ship stopped 2am this morning and was drifting for 4hrs. No light, no ventilation. I got up and slept on deck. Ship is now doing half speed.

Friday October 26
Due to one of the crew neglecting his duty the boiler burst and that was the cause of yesterday's mishap. Started to blow a gale towards evening.

Saturday October 27
Gale terrific. Storm lasted all day. Ship engines just turning over. Many seasick and to make our life more unpleasant oil poured on the decks making them just like ice. This is a terrible ship and we have just been told our destination is now Seattle. At least one or two days more onboard and food is now scarce.

Sunday October 28
Very rough. Ship just plunging and rolling continually. Went to service in the morning, also communion. Went to recital in the evening. We hear food running short. Decks still slippery with oil. Went to cinema show in the evening.

Monday October 29
Terrible night last night. Hardly slept a wink. Nearly thrown out of my bed three times. Ship rolled and rolled and rolled. I sometimes wondered whether we should ever see Seattle.

Tuesday October 30
Much calmer seas, not so rough. We are now told we are going to Frisco. Running short of food. English engineers work in engine room.

Wednesday October 31
We are due to arrive tomorrow. Weather beautiful. We are going very slow. Very cold at night.

Thursday November 1*
Arrived San Francisco about 10am. Wonderful sight coming under the Golden Gate. Boat met us with band and crowd on board, waving and cheering. Saw Alcatraz. We are put on island in middle of bay, Angel Island, where we meet English officer who made plans for us to leave. We are treated very well and plenty to eat and drink. I will get to Frisco before we leave. Feeling tired.

Friday November 2
Very hot, lovely sunshine. We get issued with our own khaki uniforms and berets which look very smart. I go out in the evening with Bill Fleming to Frisco. Have a wonderful time, arriving back to camp 8.30 this morning, Saturday. We were about the only two that managed to get out of the camp.

Saturday November 3
I feel very tired after last night's do but managed to crack along. We left in the afternoon for Seattle in hospital train which was very comfortable. We laid in beds all the time we were on the train and I went to sleep very early.

Sunday November 4
Quite a nice day and we travel all day arriving at a place called Fort Lewis about 10pm where we saw our first snow.

Monday November 5
We stay here 2 days and then away across Canada. This place, wonderful camp, enormous but very cold. I go with Bill Fleming to town called Olympia and buy stockings to take home. Got back about 1am.

Tuesday November 6
Give interview to press reporter and then on to Olympia. Had a grand time. Americans were rather decent.

Wednesday November 7
Left on second train about 11am. So started our long train journey across Canada. I manage to get [illegible] car with two other WOs and I'm very comfortable. We have our beds in the salon and they are put down for us by attendants. We have about 300 onboard, 12 dining cars. I go to bed early.

Thursday November 8
I slept badly last night. Could not keep my mind off crash in Java. We passed through wonderful scenery as we went across Rockies but is it cold when 30 below zero!

Friday November 9
Another bad night. Hardly any sleep. This train just bumps along. We stop at Sasketchuan and have quite a good time. Still cold, heavy snow. Food is very good on the train.

Saturday November 10
We arrive Winnipeg 9am. 16 below, very cold. Not a very good reception. Ten hours late.

Sunday November 11
It is not so cold and the snow has stopped. We observe two mins silence on train. Very impressive. We have great reception at Ottawa and was met by the mayor. We get onboard Queen Mary tomorrow.

Monday November 12*
We arrive onboard Queen Mary 3 o'clock. Can see nothing of New York. Very thick fog. I meet Dai Grandon and rest of "glory" boys. Frank Fryett left behind in hospital. We are due to sail midnight. Everybody excited.

Tuesday November 13
Did not leave til midday owing to fog. Saw Statue of Liberty in Manhattan skyline. Very comfortable onboard.

Wednesday November 14
I received five letters today. Very good. Pleased to see that Babs is still waiting. I hope that she will accept my proposal. Lovely day, beautiful sunshine.

EPILOGUE

L es Spence and the other former prisoners who travelled from New York on the 'Queen Mary' arrived in Southampton on November 18, 1945.

A reporter from the Southern Daily Echo caught up with some of the men a few days later as they waited around in a transit camp. "Home," he wrote. "It was the word on every man's lips. Home, the wife, the kids, the local (if they ain't run out o''ops"), the back garden and the dog."

There were no names in the article but Les had been one of the dreamers. His diaries show how much he had missed his fiancée, Babs.

Wishing they had married before the war, he had proposed in a letter. Hearing nothing, he had feared he had left it too late.

He was wrong.

On his return to Cardiff, Babs was waiting. They married in 1947. His best man was his former team-mate and prison chum Wilfred Wooller. Les and Babs had two sons, Jeremy, who has always wished to see these diaries in print, and Michael, who sadly predeceased his father.

As well as running the family china and glassware firm, Les returned to his love of sport.

He was to become chairman of Cardiff Rugby Club and joint secretary of Glamorgan County Cricket Club, and was awarded the MBE.

By the time Les died in 1988, aged 81, he had become one of the leading administrators in Welsh sport. Memorial gates were installed at Cardiff Arms Park in his name.

It had been in perhaps his greatest role, as president of the Welsh Rugby Union, that he had helped take a small step to heal the wounds opened between the UK and Japan during World War 2.

In 1973 he had formed a firm friendship with Shiggy Konno, manager of the visiting Japanese rugby side. And two years later he led the Welsh rugby team on a tour of Japan.

As the South Wales Echo reported: "[Les] learned to forgive if not forget the tragedy of war."

ACKNOWLEDGEMENTS

Many thanks to the committee and members of the Java Far East Prisoners of War Club 1942 for their help with this book. In particular, I'd like to thank Lesley Clark and Margaret Martin for their support; Nowell Peach, Pete Truelove and Ken Holland, Tony Cowling, Vic Herman, Dr Geoffrey Lees, Amanda Johnston and Frank Williams, who kindly responded to appeals for information; the late Rev Hugh Edwards, John Baxter and Stanley Roberts whom I interviewed regarding their recollections of the days described in Les Spence's diaries; thanks also to Rev Edwards' son Peter and Mr Baxter's son John.

Special thanks to Kathleen Booth and Mary Sharkey for proofreading the manuscript. Kathleen was also a great source of information regarding the 77th. My wife, Moira, spent many days deciphering the handwritten diaries with me, a task which took us through her pregnancy with our son Evan and our daughter Caoimhe.

It had been Les Spence's wish that his diaries were one day published. His family tried to fulfil that wish shortly after his death but when the diaries were entrusted to a third party they were lost. The books, which Les Spence had risked his life to write, had hidden successfully through almost four years of incarceration, and had kept safe for 40 more years, were almost lost forever. They were discovered years later in the back drawer in a newspaper office and passed to me. When I contacted Les' son, Jeremy, to say the diaries had been found and that I hoped to publish them he was delighted: he had thought he would never see the diaries again but now his father's wish for them would be fulfilled. Jeremy has supported the project from the beginning and my final thanks go to him.

Greg Lewis, Cardiff 2012

REFERENCE
NOTES

January 1, 1942
For further information on the convoy which took Les Spence to Java see the webpage **www.naval-history.net/xAH-WSConvoys04-1941B.htm**
In his e-book 'The Diary of a Japanese POW', John Baxter describes the Warwick Castle, a former Union Castle boat, as being decorated "in regulation grey paint with the number HMT.Z16 on her bows".

January 17 and 18, 1942
The Batemans were the family of Les' fiancée Babs. Ken was Les' brother, who he also sometimes refers to by a nickname Joe. Ken later moved to the Midlands and became a public health inspector.
Les' parents were Magnus Spence, an engineer, and Mary Simon.

January 19, 1942
The Ramillies. HMS Ramillies was a Revenge-class battleship of the Royal Navy.

January 23, 1942
According to Rev Hugh Edwards (letter to editor, January 26, 2011): "Our convoy having left South Africa, we assumed we would head north to the Middle East but one morning the convoy turned and travelled east to Java - we regularly watched the sun's position."

January 24, 1942
Although the name of the island is difficult to make out, it is likely that the convoy called at the Maldives, as stated by John Baxter in his e-book 'The Diary of a Japanese POW'.

January 25, 1942
Bombardier Frank G Fryett. According to an online article by Mr Neville Dunn, Fryett "had been a streetwise, Fleet Street reporter before the war and was very daring". He was from London. His cousin, Frank Dunn, would also become a prisoner in Java, having been serving as a wireless operator/air gunner with No 34 (B) Squadron. Mr Neville Dunn writes that Fryett helped save his older brother's life in Batavia by bartering for food to help build up his strength when he went down with dysentery. Frank Dunn, who appears in Les Spence's diaries on September 30, 1944, stayed on in the RAF after the war.
Reference: **www.bbc.co.uk/ww2peopleswar/stories/23/a2035423.shtml**

January 26, 1942
E of A. The 'Empress of Australia' was a former ocean liner which had been converted into a troopship at the outbreak of the Second World War.

February 3, 1942
On disembarkation, 239 Battery was ordered to remain at Batavia to mount an air defence of the port. The docks were a hub of activity with troops and supplies being unloaded and transport ships bringing civilian evacuees from Malaya and Singapore.
The other two batteries, 240 and 241, were instructed to move by rail to defend Surabaya, another port several hundred miles away on the eastern coast of Java. Surabaya was the headquarters of the Dutch Naval Fleet.
Spellings for Surabaya vary, and Les sometimes uses Sourabaja.

February 4-7 1942.
The train crash and its victims.
According to Brigadier RJ Lewendon in an article called 'Gunners in Java, 1942' which was published in the Journal of the Royal Artillery (March 1981), "After their arrival in Batavia 77 HAA Regiment RA, less 239 Battery, moved by road and rail to Soerabaja in Eastern Java... In the early hours of 6th February 1942 (0300 hours) a troop train carrying part of 77 HAA Regiment RA was involved in a train accident just outside Soerabaja when it smashed into an ammunition train on a single track on a bridge over a ravine. Some thirty members of 77 HAA Regiment RA were killed in the accident and nearly one hundred were injured."
According to John Baxter (interview with editor, April 16, 2009), the train "had been deliberately sabotaged, a signalman who they never found again had switched to another train containing oil and explosives on the same line and there was a head-on collision".
Ronald Williams notes in his memoir, 'Under The Poached Egg' (Ronald Williams and Frank Williams), that the cause of the crash was "probably an accident due to brake failure, though some suspected sabotage, as the stationary

train's driver was missing and the area was known to be rife with Japanese collaborators. There were also likely to be Japanese agents on the island, as the Japanese had free access to Java up to the declaration of war."

The officers killed included:Captain HMR MacMillan; Lieutenant JK Ainsley; Lieutenant JA Boxall and Lieutenant JH Stoodley. (Source: South Wales Echo, September 12, 1945).

Ken Street, the Battery Sergeant Major (BSM), was a well-known Welsh rugby forward and champion swimmer in the British Army. He had played alongside Les Spence and Wilf Wooller for Cardiff Rugby Club.
He had also captained Penarth Water Polo Club.
According to Rev Hugh Edwards (interview with editor, April 28, 2009), Ken Street was the sergeant major with 240 Battery.
Following Street's death Les Spence became acting BSM.
Each battery had eight 3.7in heavy anti-aircraft guns, although 241 only had four at Tjilitjap as the other four had been sent back to Surabaya.

February 13, 1942
HRH. The commanding officer of the 77th was Lieutenant Colonel HR Humphries, who before the war had been a telephone official at Cardiff Post Office. He survived to return home, his photograph appearing in the South Wales Echo. (Source: South Wales Echo, September 12, 1945).

Wilf. Lieutenant Wilfred Wooller. Born in November 1912, Wooller has gone down in history as one of Wales' greatest all-round sportsman. Before the war he had not only captained Wales at rugby, he had played cricket for Glamorgan, briefly played up front for Cardiff City and represented his country at squash. After the war, he went on to captain Glamorgan to its first County Championship in 1948 and to become a test selector for England. He also became a distinguished writer and broadcaster. He died in 1997.

February 16, 1942
Major G. Major George Frederick Gerald Gaskell, (known as Gerald) an officer of the 77th who had worked at Hancock's Breweries before the war. Despite becoming part of the infamous 'H' Force sent to work on the Thai-Burma railway (see note, February 9, 1943), he would survive to return home, his photograph appearing in the South Wales Echo (September 12, 1945).

February 17, 1942
Johnny Probert. John T Probert, of Brook Street, Barry, had been a sergeant in 240 Battery. He was promoted to 2nd Lieutenant and posted to 239 Battery following the rail crash. Probert replaced 2nd Lt WL Wallis who was transferred

to 240 to replace one of the crash fatalities. (Source: Kathleen Booth, letter to editor, October 10, 2011)

February 22, 1942
Brig Colonel. Brigadier HDW Sitwell, Commanding Officer 16th AA Brigade.

February 27, 1942
It is hard to make out Les Spence's spelling here but he is referring to the port of Tjilatjap.
The Dutch island of Java possessed only three deep-water ports, Tandjong Priok, the port for the capital Batavia, Sourabaja on the northern coast, and Tjilatjap in the south.

March 3, 1942
Ted Sumption. According to Kathleen Booth (letter to editor, January 26, 2011): "Edward Sumption was born on February 28, 1891, and was the husband of Florence Sumption, of 13 Market Place, Pentre, Rhondda, He was Battery Sergeant Major, 241 Battery. Sadly, he was one of the 548 prisoners on board the hellship 'Suez Maru' which was torpedoed by US submarine 'Bonefish' on November 29, 1943, north of Bali. Many had survived the torpedo attack but were subsequently machine-gunned in the water by the Japanese. There were no survivors."
Further reading: 'The Suez Maru Atrocity – Justice Denied', by Allan Jones, who is campaigning for an apology from the Japanese government for the killings. Mr Jones' father Lewis died on the 'Suez Maru'.

March 7, 1942
The crossroads was at Wangon Cross. Tasikmalaya is a town and airfield to the north west of Tjilatjap.
(Source: Lieutenant Colonel Humphries comments recorded here **www. reocities.com/dutcheastindies/java.html**)

March 9, 1942
Following the surrender the remains of the regiment were at first quartered in lorries and estate buildings at Tjisompet.

March 13, 1942
Battery Headquarters and Regimental Headquarters.

March 14, 1942
Magazine. This probably refers to a first issue of the 'Jungle Journal', a magazine created by prisoners.

March 16, 1942
G. Garoet.

March 19, 1942
Lieutenant-Colonel Humphries was to reconstruct regimental records after the war. They had been destroyed to keep them from falling into enemy hands. In them, he records that the regiment moved on March 21 to "Trogong where a halt was made for the night".

March 29, 1942
Arrives in Boei Glodok. From 'Under The Poached Egg' by Ronald Williams and Frank Williams: "(This was) a nasty, filthy camp and former civilian prison for murderers and hardened criminals, with high walls, watchtowers and cramped, bug-infested cells with concrete floors. There was very poor sanitation and water supply. Dysentery was rife. Little medication was available and regular heavy work parties were organised to repair local airfields, such as Kemajoran."

March, 30, 1942
OM. Officers' Mess.

April 6–8, 1942
Charlie Hawkins. According to the Commonwealth War Graves Commission casualty list this is most probably Gunner Charles Hawkins, of 240 Battery, 77th HAA Regiment. He was the son of Charles and Mildred Hawkins of Guernsey, Channel Islands. The CWGC records his death as falling on April 7. He is buried at Jakarta War Cemetery.

April 12, 1942
This was Gunner Charles Thompson, of 240 Battery, 77th HAA Regiment. He was from Smethwick in Staffordshire and had a wife, Pat. He is buried at Jakarta War Cemetery.

April 19, 1942
Captain Birch. Stanley Roberts, who served in 239 Battery, 77th HAA, believes Captain Birch may have been a regular officer in the 3rd Hussars (Interview with the editor, August 13, 2011).

May 13, 1942. Priok.
Tandjong Priok was the largest transit camp in Java. It was near Batavia. According to John Baxter (interview with editor, April 16, 2009): "Alongside the harbour there was an open space with a few shanty sort of buildings which had been used as a standby place for coolies when they used to unload the ships

there... The coolies would come off the ships and go under these shelters which were just tiled roofs held up with big teak beams and that was it, no side walls or anything like that.

The only sort of concession to modernity was at the end of each of these long huts – there was about six of them - there was a primitive urinal which was a short piece of pipe, about six feet long, with about a dozen holes in it and water was dribbling out into a channel which again went into a concrete channel which was nine inches by 12 which ran right through the camp.

Between us and the sea there was an actual mangrove swamp which nobody went into, of course, because there was all sorts of horrible reptiles, sea snakes and spiders and whatnot there...

There were 3,500 men, mixed nationalities, mixed units in that one camp."

May 19, 1942
The docks. According to John Baxter (interview with editor, April 16, 2009): "The docks [had all been] heavily bombed... We had to clear all the damaged buildings and salvage as much stock from the docks as possible, not for us... Anything any good, if it was a whole package or sack of anything, that went on the ships and was shipped off by the Japanese to their battle areas."

Food. According to Mr Baxter: "On the warehouse floors, there was about six to nine inches deep of rubbish, which was partly food, partly stones, bits of steelwork, burnt wood. We had to shovel all that up in sacks and take it back to the camp and take all the bits of wood and stones out... The cooks had already made some improvised cookers out of 40 gallon oil drums... And the system was that they would tip a sackful of this into a drum full of water in the hope that all the solids would drop to the bottom, all the bits of paper, string and coconut fibre, anything like that, old packets of food, they'd float to the top... What we have got there is a liquid, where the bottom layer is solids, either metal, stone or whatever, so you'd pour that into another drum, it was like a weak porridge by then and they'd boil it... It used to taste horrible. The only thing that they gave us in any solid form was rice but they only gave us rice in bags that had either been saturated by fire hoses, diesel oil or something else in the docks. We had to sort that out. You couldn't do anything with the ones that had oil in. You just had to dump that or use it for fuel for the fire."

May 23, 1942
Doc Lloyd. According to Kathleen Booth (letter to editor, January 26, 2011): "Herbert 'Doc' Lloyd was a lieutenant in 239 Battery, subsequently promoted to captain and appointed adjutant to Lieutenant Colonel Humphries."

May 24, 1942
According to the Commonwealth War Graves Commission casualty lists Sergeant Stanley Street, of 240 Battery, 77th HAA Regiment, died sometime on February 12 or 13, 1942. He was 22. He is buried at Jakarta War Cemetery.

May 27, 1942
Les' spelling of Tasikmalaya varies. Here he appears to write Tasikmala.

June 4, 1942
Lieutenant Griffith George Davies, 241 Battery, of William Street, Cardigan. He was recommended for the Military Cross by Lt Col Humphries for his brave action under fire at Tjilitjap on March 5.
Alan Reardon Smith was a lieutenant in the 77th and the son of Sir William Reardon-Smith, a Welsh ship-owner. Les Spence sometimes refers to him as Alan R Smith and spells his name as both Alan and Allan.

June 8, 1942
Ice cream. This is part of Les' secret code. It appears to refer to news from outside camp, presumably through a secret radio. An online article by Ted Marriott about Far East prisoner of war Dennis Riley states that in Riley's camp an illicit radio was also known by the code 'ice cream'. See http://www.far-eastern-heroes.org.uk/Life_of_Riley

June 27, 1942
French 75. A French 75mm field gun, one of the main French artillery pieces from the First World War.

June 28, 1942
Les Spence refers to the currency, more often spelt guilder, as gilder or G throughout.

July 10, 1942
Veteran Stanley Roberts told the editor: "One of the toes went under the other one, curled under the other. I don't know why. We used to wear the Japanese type boots like boxing gloves. They laced up at the back. Everybody wore them." (Interview, August 13, 2011.)

July 20, 1942
JJ – 'Jungle Journal', a magazine created by prisoners at Tandjong Priok. Editions of this magazine were kept by Les Spence but went missing with the diaries following his death. Some editions of the magazine are held by the Imperial War Museum.

July 23, 1942
The asterisk here is Les', as is the spelling 'swen'.

July 24, 1942
Knight. The Commonwealth War Graves Commission records the death of Gunner William Knight, of 240 Battery, 77th HAA, on July 23, 1942. He was 33. He was the son of George and Louie Knight, and his wife, Edith, lived in Staffordshire. He is buried in Jakarta War Cemetery.

July 26, 1942
According to Rev Hugh Edwards (interview with editor, April 28, 2009), the prisoners built the chapel and two officers made the stained glass windows. The church has "been since destroyed but happily they've saved two of the stained glass windows". The windows contained a little joke which the Japanese never realised: incorporated in the stained glass design was a "Royal Lion (with) the face was of Churchill smoking a cigar!"
In 'Prisoners in Java', Rev Edwards states that the chapel was only 20 feet by 15 feet but that it "signified faith and hope" and indicated a "moral defiance".
Both 'Prisoners in Java' and John Baxter's e-book 'The Diary of a Japanese POW' record that the windows were made by Lieutenant Commander HC Upton). Mr Baxter writes: "The finished chapel was a labour of love by a small band of dedicated Christians who produced marvels of carved woodwork." He adds that Tandjong Priok camp was bulldozed after the war to make way for development but the windows were salvaged and are now in the Anglican Church in Jakarta. (There is a replica at the National Memorial Arboretum in Staffordshire.)

August 2, 1942
Padre. Rev Phillips, of the 77th (Source: Prisoners in Java.)

August 8, 1942
Ernie Curtis. A former Cardiff City player, who had been the youngest member of the club's 1927 FA Cup winning side. He also played for Birmingham City, Coventry City and Wales. After the war, he was a member of Cardiff City's coaching staff and later ran a pub. He died in 1992, aged 85. (Source: http://news.bbc.co.uk/sport1/hi/football/7328650.stm)

August 10, 1942
Big battle in the Pacific. This could refer to the opening offensive carried out by US forces on the island of Guadalcanal.

August 29, 1942
241 Battery had among its players former Cardiff City and Wales centre half Billy James and Cardiff City goalkeeper John 'Jackie' Pritchard, who was later killed on the 'Suez Maru'.

September 4, 1942
Lieutenant John Rutter, son of Edgar J Rutter, of Cardiff. He survived to return home. (Source: South Wales Echo, September 12, 1945.)
After the war he resumed his studies in law and was called to the Bar in 1948. He became a stipendiary magistrate in 1966 and a senior circuit judge in 1990. He died in 2009, aged 90. (Source: obituary in The Times, July 7, 2009; Kathleen Booth.)

September 12, 1942
Sapper row. According to John Baxter (letter to the editor, January 8, 2011), this was a gambling game "played originally by Royal Engineers (Sappers) but it was also called a number of other names, being a peacetime gamble in the building industry and elsewhere using tin cans or other receptacles and a variety of items including a dice".

September 13, 1942
Les Spence was correct in his assumption that large scale movements of prisoners out of Java were now to begin. Similar movements of prisoners out of Singapore were already taking place, mainly by rail northwards through Malaya, to build the Thai-Burma railway.
But for those who had been captured on Java, their ultimate destination would be more uncertain and their mode of transport more hazardous. They were to be shipped overseas in vessels which became known as "hellships". Conditions on board were primitive, disease was rife and US submarines were lurking.

September 15, 1942
The 500 arrived at Changi camp, Singapore, on September 18 and subsequently departed on October 9 for Borneo. (Source: 'The Story of Changi' by David Nelson)

September 19, 1942
Colonel Charles Malet Lane was the senior British officer at Tandjong Priok. He was an officer in the 2nd Battalion, 15th Punjab Regiment, Indian Army.

September 22, 1942
This party of prisoners arrived at Changi on September 26 and joined the group mentioned above (note, September 15, 1942) to depart for Borneo.

The two groups were joined by other prisoners from across Java bringing the total number of prisoners on that journey to 1,886. All were British. 1,048 disembarked at Kuching and the remainder at Jesselton (now Kota Kinabalu). Hundreds of these men were to die on Borneo, mainly as a result of the forced marches to Sandakan.

September 25, 1942
One of the prisoners who had left on the Borneo draft had been breeding pigeons while in Tandjong Priok. Two of these arrived back in Priok on September 23 bearing news that Borneo was the destination. (Source: 'Notify Alec Rattray...' by Meg Parkes)

September 28, 1942
Java balls. This probably refers to an itching or reddening of the scrotum, common among prisoners in the tropics. It is referred to as scrotal dermatitis in 'Singapore Diary, The Hidden Journal of Captain RM Horner' (Spellmount).

October 3, 1942
Badung. Les is probably referring to the town or prison camp at Bandoeng.

October 9, 1942
The name of the place here is hard to read. However, the 77th was split up for a few weeks during October 1941. 239 Battery was at Crewe, 240 Battery at Hawarden in North Wales and 241 Battery was at Donnington, Shropshire. At the end of the month they all moved up to Glasgow for their final preparations before deploying overseas. Les was with 241 at the time; however, the word in his diary does not appear to be 'Donnington' and it is unclear where he spent his "10 happy weeks".

October 11, 1942
Dusty Forge. In the addresses section of his 1942 diary Les lists a 'John Forge, of Ashford'. This was Sergeant John Bliss Forge, of 240 Battery, 77 HAA. He would be later held in Ohama Camp, Japan, with Harry Hamer, father of Kathleen Booth, of Derbyshire, who has done extensive research on the 77th. Forge would survive the war.

October 21, 1942
This draft of 1,000 men left Java on the 'Yoshida Maru' for Singapore, before being transferred to the 'Singapore Maru' for the onward journey to Japan.
"Conditions on board the 'Singapore Maru' were terrible and there would be many deaths during the voyage and afterwards, mainly from dysentery. The neglect of the prisoners by the Japanese was to become the subject of a War

Crimes Trial." (Kathleen Booth, letter to the editor, October 10, 2011)
On arrival at Moji, Japan, at the end of November, the men were split into four groups and sent to Ohama, Motoyama, Higashi Misome and Okinoyama, neighbouring coal-mining camps along the southern coast of Honshu Island between the towns of Onada and Ube. Mine shafts there extended two miles under the sea.

Les mentions a number of people on this draft.

Weeks. Battery Quartermaster Sergeant Maurice Arnold Weekes, of 240 Battery, had survived the Java rail crash. He was taken to Ohama camp where he died on December 7, 1942 of dysentery. The Commonwealth War Graves Commission website states that he was 31 and the son of James and Catherine Weekes. His remains were among those removed to Australia after the war and interred at Sydney War Cemetery.

Hunt. 2nd Lieutenant Leslie George Richard Hunt, of 240 Battery, was a mining engineering graduate of Otago, New Zealand. He died at Ohama Camp on January 19, 1943. He was 29 and the son of George and Annie Hunt, of Otago.

2nd Lieutenant John Probert was taken to Ohama Camp. He was to survive the war.

Fawcett. Lieutenant Frederick Siddell Fawcett, of Cardiff, was one of the prisoners who would become very ill during the voyage of the 'Singapore Maru'. He was taken to Simonoseki hospital camp where he remained until February 1943 when he was transferred to Kokura and then Yawata steel mill where he remained until the liberation in September 1945.

Mitchell. Lieutenant Stuart Digby Mitchell, of 240 Battery, was taken to Moji Number 4 hospital camp, where he remained until the liberation.

November 8, 1942
Dengue fever, a mosquito-borne infection causing pain and swelling of the joints.

December 13, 1942
OO. Orderly Officer.

December 24, 1942
Pc. Postcard.

December 30, 1942
The eyesight of many prisoners deteriorated due to a lack of vitamins in their diet.

January 3, 1943
Kiri. A kiri was a salute or a bow.

January 23, 1943
Taylor. Lieutenant Kenneth Langdale Taylor, of 239 Battery, who was from Southport, Lancashire. He died on November 3, 1943, at Kanchanaburi hospital camp, Thailand, aged 31.

February 4, 1943
Pat Cox. Lieutenant DP Cox died of injuries sustained in the February 1942 train crash. He was "one of the best known of South Wales golfers". (Source: South Wales Echo, September 12, 1945)

February 9, 1943
This draft of 1,000 men (704 British from various Royal Artillery regiments and the RAF; 296 Dutch) arrived at Singapore on February 13. 505 of the British left Changi for Thailand on May 5, 1943 as part of 'H' Force, a working party led by Lt Col Humphries, which was to work on the Thai-Burma railway. (Source: 'The Story of Changi' by David Nelson)
The death rate on 'H' Force was high. 112 men from the 77th died and are buried at either Kanchanaburi or Chungkai.
Ernie Curtis (see note, August 8, 1942) was on this draft.

February 10, 1943
Sergeant Dai Grandon, of Cardiff, would be in the same camps as Les Spence throughout. He survived to return home.

March 11, 1943
Girls. These, of course, were men in drag.

April 16, 1943
This draft travelled overland to Surabaya before boarding hellships on April 22 and April 24 which would take them to the Mollucan islands of Ambon and Haruku. Here they were forced to build airstrips.
Many deaths occurred among the group, some at various camps and others during shipments back to Java. 548, including 91 members of the 77th, died in the sinking of the 'Suez Maru' (see note, March 3, 1942).
Three Cardiff City footballers were on this draft. Billy James and Jackie Pritchard (see note, August 29, 1942), and Billy Baker who, like James, would survive the war.

April 17, 1943
Les Spence is moved from Tandjong Priok to Cycle Camp, also near Batavia, Java. It was named after a cycle-mounted unit of the Dutch East Indies who had formerly used it as a barracks, and is sometimes referred to as Bicycle Camp.

John Baxter writes in his e-book 'The Diary of a Japanese POW' that, "The buildings were more substantial single storey barracks complete with latrines and wash places... The one snag was the hopeless overcrowding as some 2,000 prisoners were housed in accommodation intended for 500 peacetime troops." The commandant Les refers to was Lieutenant, later Captain, Kenichi Sonei. He would later take charge at Tjideng internment camp where women and children were beaten and mistreated. After the war he was tried by the Far East War Crimes Tribunal. He was executed by a Dutch firing squad in December 1946.

April 24, 1943
Working parties. According to 'Under The Poached Egg' (Ronald Williams and Frank Williams): "Work parties [at Bicycle Camp] were organised for planting castor oil seeds, salvage work and sisal (string) making. Other duties included burial parties and latrine digging."

May 2, 1943
MB. 'Cure-all' cream, or more often tablets, made by the company May & Baker.

May 8, 1943
Serang, a town in west Java, about 70 kilometres from Batavia.

May 10, 1943
Les Spence is moved back to Boei Glodok prison in the northern part of the city of Batavia where he had been held for almost six weeks a year earlier.

May 18, 1943
North Africa is ours. The news received from the Japanese was accurate: Axis forces in North Africa surrendered on May 13, 1943.

July 10, 1943
Glass rod. A form of screening for amoebiasis or dysentery which involved taking rectal smears from prisoners.
The following description of the glass rod test is taken from 'Hard Way Back', the online memoir of American prisoner Frank Hoeffer: "This dysentery wasn't very pleasant as the Japanese medical attendants had a long glass rod about ten inches long and about the thickness of a thermometer with a small hook on the bottom, which was pushed into the rectum, twisted and then withdrawn. The end of the rod was then rubbed back and forth on round glass slides which were numbered and placed in large wooden boxes. At every port where we stopped this test was applied with much discomfort." (Source: http://www.wtv-zone.com/califPamela/memorial-Page-14.html)

According to John Baxter (letter to the editor, January 8, 2011): "The glass rod treatment was the standard Japanese treatment in diagnosing dysentery. The cellophane was simply a kind of plastic envelope or other container into which the glass rod was dipped to indicate, probably by chemicals, whether the insertion proved positive or otherwise."

According to Kathleen Booth (letter to editor, January 26, 2011): "Before departing from Java on overseas drafts, the prisoners were required to provide a sample for a dysentery test. They were given a piece of cellophane each on which to deposit a stool."

July 11, 1943
Les Spence moved back to Cycle Camp.

July 17, 1943
Les Spence moved to a camp at Tjimahi in west Java.

July 28, 1943
Old Musso drops out. Once again the prisoners have received pretty accurate information. The Allies had invaded Sicily on July 10. Popular support for the war in Italy began to fall and on July 25 the Grand Council of Fascism voted to limit Benito Mussolini's power. However, although Mussolini was then imprisoned and control of the armed forces given over to the King Victor Emmanuel III, Italy did not surrender to the Allies until September 1943.

September 1, 1943
Les Spence returns to Cycle Camp.
In an interview with editor (April 16, 2009), John Baxter, who followed the same route through the camps as Les Spence, explained why they had been moved about: "All the drafts used to go first of all from Tandjong Priok to Bandoeng in the centre of Java [for a] so called medical course. You would then go back to Bicycle Camp where they said you would be kitted out for transit. Their idea of kitting you out was to give you a small pair of highly coloured shorts, a pair of rubber shoes like plimsolls... that was it, no warm clothing or anything like that, because the first few drafts never did go to Japan, they sent them all up on the dreaded railway. When it came to our turn, which was in September 1943, the call was for more labour in Japan. We did the tour. We went up to Bandoeng for two or three weeks until we got back a few calories, a bit better food, one or two bits of equipment replaced - usually tatty stuff, not worth giving us really - and then we assembled back at Bicycle Camp which was used as a transit camp before we went onboard ship."

September 10, 1943
Les Spence leaves Java.

September 12, 1943
The Sunda Strait between Sumatra and Java.

September 14, 1943
Les Spence arrives in Singapore and is moved to a transit camp, a former army barracks near Changi jail. According to Changi prisoner David Nelson, who kept a tally of the drafts in and out of Changi and later recorded his memories in the book, 'The Story of Changi Singapore', there were 519 men in the party that arrived at Changi that day. Three hundred and sixty were British; 159 were Dutch.

Burma draft refers to those who left Java on February 9, 1943, bound for Singapore and then the Thai-Burma railway. Of the original 704, 199 remained at Changi as they were too sick to be sent onwards.

September 20, 1943
Five hundred and seven prisoners left Changi that day (Source: 'The Story of Changi Singapore', David Nelson).
Les Spence was on the same ship as Stanley Roberts who recorded his memories in the book 'Prisoners in Java'. He names the ship as the 'Ussuri Maru'.
Les Spence would not see his friends Wilf Wooller and Alan Reardon Smith again until after the war.
(Wooller's later presence in Changi gaol is referred to in 'Singapore Diary, The Hidden Journal of Captain RM Horner' (Spellmount), p128 (June 1, 1944).

September 22, 1943
Les Spence leaves Singapore.

September 24, 1943
DV. Deo volente, God willing

September 25, 1943
The ship alongside us was torpedoed and sank in 5 mins. The ship had been sunk by a US submarine. In an interview with editor (April 16, 2009), John Baxter, recalled: "I was lying on this hatch cover drying off with a pal of mine looking at this ship alongside us - it was about quarter of a mile away I suppose. And you could see all the drums loaded on the deck and you could see a torpedo wake coming... Now the whole convoy was zigzagging. The torpedo blew the bows off this one with the high octane on... They blew the whole front of the

ship off and the whole ship exploded and in less than five minutes all you saw was a blazing patch of oil. No survivors."

October 12, 1943
The 'Ussuri Maru' arrives in Japan. Stanley Roberts states in 'Prisoners in Java': "It was a depressing sight that met us in the morning as we divided into two parties and marched off through the drab streets of Moji, amidst the curious stares of the local populace... A brief respite ensued when our party, consisting of about 250 men, one officer (Captain Peter Williams) and one senior non-commissioned officer (Sergeant Major Les Spence) arrived at the railway station, to be handed our first meal since leaving ship."
Captain Williams, from Sussex, was the commanding officer of the 48th Light Ack Ack Regiment and would be the senior British officer at Camp 8 in Japan.

October 13, 1943
New camp. This is Camp 8 Kamo (sometimes Kamoo), which was near the village of Inatsuki or Inatsukimachi, in Kyushu, Southern Japan.
Stanley Roberts, in 'Prisoners in Java', describes the complex as being about 20 yards square "with an earthen ramp at the entrance gate, dominated by the guardroom". The huts were "the low-weather boarded type with felted roofs and raised floors of 'tatami' straw matting... Partitions divided the huts into separate rooms, housing four, six or eight men, depending on size, and each was lit by a single light bulb."
According to Rev Hugh Edwards (interview with editor), "there was a very high wall around [the camp] and down in the dip there were these huts where we stayed. I was in number one hut. [Captain] Peter [Williams] and Les [Spence] were number one, and I was in another room, along the same hut. They were divided into rooms. They were really straw mats on the floor and rice paper windows..."

October 18, 1943
The mines.
Camp 8 consisted of two mines which were approached by drifts driven into the mountain. "Conditions were primitive, in the extreme, due to poor ventilation, inadequate propping and indifferent pumping, the last resulting in long stretches being deep in oily black sludge." (Stanley Roberts, 'Prisoners in Java'.)
According to Rev Hugh Edwards (interview with editor, April 28, 2009), it was "very dark... We had our head lamps which we had to collect on our way down... but they were acid battery which we had to have on our backs and if these things were leaking you could get a burn, believe me. But they were the only lights that we had...

"What we were given was a basket, an open-ended basket, for carrying but we had a short-handled tool with a flat blade to scrape it. You'd scrape it and then carry it.

"The Japanese would work on the faces. Sometimes we would help to drill the holes into the face, probably about a yard or metre-worth into the face, several holes, and then they would put in explosive and then we would have to come back when they'd blew the faces out. Then we'd have to go gather it all up and put it in the trucks.

"[We were] only supposed to put coal in – but sometimes we put bits of rock and bits of bolt and whatever."

October 20, 1943
Rev Hugh Edwards stated that because of the cramped conditions down the mine life was particularly difficult for taller prisoners who had to crouch for hours on end. Les Spence was more than six feet tall.

October 28, 1943
The shaft.
"The Shaft Party…probably faced the most gruelling and thankless task of us all… This project, which had been abandoned pre-war by Swedish contractors, was now opened by the Japanese in an endeavour to strike a new seam of coal. Originally some 25 feet in diameter and 800 feet deep, it was relentlessly driven downwards by luckless working parties of POWs until it reached the awesome depth of 1,500 feet by the time of our release." (Stanley Roberts, 'Prisoners in Java'.)

October 31, 1943
Yasme Day. A rest day. Les Spence sometimes spells this Yasume and other sources also use both spellings.

November 17, 1943
Norman. This is probably Lance Bombardier Norman Welsford. See note for July 24, 1944.

November 24, 1943
M&Bs. A reference to May & Baker tablets.

January 22, 1944
Woolley. The British Roster for Camp 8 lists a Gunner AA Woolley or Wooley, of Southend-on-sea, Essex. 77th veteran Stanley Roberts remembered him: "He was a nice chap. Everyone liked him. Lots of laughter, knockabout. He boosted everything. He never stopped talking." (Interview with the editor, August 13, 2011)

A Corporal Gibson is not listed, however, the roster is known to be incomplete. Gibson does appear on the Commonwealth War Graves Commission casualty list. It appears he was Walter Gibson, from 211 Squadron, RAF, who was from Lanarkshire. He was 23 and is buried in Yokohama War Cemetery.

Monday, February 14, 1944
Les Spence has written entries for the first six weeks of 1944 at the end of his 1943 diary. Les now starts his third book of diaries in what appears to be a Dutch accounts book. This book will feature all his writings until the end of the war.

February 17, 1944
Gunner Francis Henry Wood (not Woods), of 240 Battery, 77th HAA Regiment. According to the Commonwealth War Graves Commission casualty list, Wood was from Pontefract, Yorkshire and was 34. He is buried in Yokohama War Cemetery.

February 24, 1944
According to the Commonwealth War Graves Commission casualty list, this refers to Sergeant Alfred Owen Burrlock, of 84 Squadron, RAF. He is buried in Yokohama War Cemetery.

March 6, 1944
Joe Smead. Les Spence spells the surname wrong. This refers to Signalman Joseph Robert Cecil Smeed, of the Royal Corps of Signals. He was the son of Cecil and Violet Smeed, of Tottenham, and the husband of Alice Smeed. He was 30 when he died and he is buried at Yokohama War Cemetery.

March 9, 1944
According to the Commonwealth War Graves Commission casualty list, this refers to Gunner Michael O'Hara, of 49 Battery, 48th Light AA Regiment. He was 29 and had a wife, Nora, in Glasgow. He is buried in Yokohama War Cemetery.

March 19, 1944
According to the Commonwealth War Graves Commission casualty list, this refers to Gunner Sidney Charles Brandon, of 15 Battery, 6 HAA Regiment. He was 24 and is buried in Yokohama War Cemetery.

April 7, 1944
According to the Commonwealth War Graves Commission casualty list, this refers to Gunner John Wilfred Musson, of 78 Battery, 35 Light AA Regiment. He was from Leicester and was 23. He is buried in Yokohama War Cemetery.

April 9, 1944
It is possible that this is Corporal Ellis Sutcliffe, of the RAF, who was from Bradford, Yorkshire, and is buried at Yokohama. However, the Commonwealth War Graves Commission lists his death as September 9, 1944.

April 20, 1944
The British Roster for Camp 8 lists a Sergeant LA Missen, from Surrey.

April 22, 1944
Five years today I was at Twickenham. A big day in the history of Cardiff Rugby Club. The club was invited as guests to the Middlesex Sevens at Twickenham. Although the team had never played Sevens, it won the tournament. Les Spence was a forward in the team; Wilf Wooller was its captain. (Source: 'Cardiff's magnificent Sevens remembered!', South Wales Echo, March 1, 2011.)

May 5, 1944
The British Roster for Camp 8 lists a Gunner LH Stanton, of Exeter.

May 10, 1944
The Commonwealth War Graves Commission casualty list includes Gunner Simon Rabinovitch, of 48 Battery, 21st LAA Regiment. He was from Clapton, London, and was 32. He is buried at Yokohama War Cemetery.
In a letter to the editor (April 30, 2009) John Baxter stated: "The shaft party were engaged in the drilling and concreting of a new shaft some 1500ft deep under continuous cold water conditions to which the work party was lowered in a large bucket holding 9 persons. It was considered one of the worst jobs served by our camp. Rabinovitch fell through a gap in the staging covering the access to the shaft which was in darkness at the time due to an airraid alert."

June 8, 1944
The camp hears rumours of the invasion of France, which had occurred two days earlier.

June 15 and 16, 1944
The raid Les Spence records was the first by the USAAF on the Japanese home islands and the first launched from staging bases in China. Its primary target was an iron and steel works in the north of Kyushu.

June 18, 1944
The British Roster for Camp 8 lists a LAC Frank Arthur Watson, of Kent.

June 24, 1944
Dear old Stan. Les is probably referring to Stan Street who had died more than two years earlier. See the note for May 24, 1942.

July 7, 1944
According to the Commonwealth War Graves Commission casualty list, this refers to Craftsman Reginald John King, of the Royal Electrical and Mechanical Engineers. He was from Enfield, Middlesex, and aged 33. He is buried in Yokohama War Cemetery.

July 21, 1944
Hear that Tojo has been pushed out. General Hideki Tojo had been Japan's prime minister since before the attacks on Pearl Harbour. On July 18, 1944, with his popularity falling, he was forced to resign. After the war, he was tried by the International Military Tribunal for the Far East and found guilty of war crimes. He was hanged in December 1948.

July 24, 1944
According to the Commonwealth War Graves Commission casualty list, this refers to Lance Bombardier Norman Outram Welsford, of 48 Battery, 21 Lt AA Regiment. He was from Palmers Green, Middlesex, and aged 27. He is buried in Yokohama War Cemetery.

August 31, 1944
Gunner Ronald Gosney.

September 30, 1944
Doubling up. Here refers to "the practice of joining the ration queue to falsely obtain extra food" (John Baxter, letter to the editor, January 8, 2011).
Sergeant Hugh Edwards, of 240 Battery, 77th HAA Regiment, was one of the men injured in the train crash. Originally from the Rhondda, he was a lay preacher before the war. After the war he trained as a Baptist minister. Rev Edwards, of Newport, south Wales, was a great help in compiling the notes for this book.
In John Baxter's e-book 'The Diary of a Japanese POW' he states: "Late in 1943 all padres were deported to Formosa (now Taiwan) to work in the copper mines and we were left without any religious influence except for one or two dedicated lay preachers who remained in our ranks". One of these was Rev Hugh Edwards.
Fryett and Frank. See note for January 25, 1942.

October 13, 1944
Bento. A tin lunch box.

November 26, 1944
Nasi goreng is a fried rice dish. It was a staple food for many POWs in Indonesia and Malaya, but is now available in the world food section of most modern supermarkets.

December 3, 1944
J Lewis. Staff Sergeant John Lewis, 240 Battery, from Trealaw, South Wales. He died on November 29, 1942, at Moji Number 4 camp, aged 59. He had a wife Sarah at home. He had arrived in Japan with an earlier group of prisoners in dreadful conditions on board the 'Singapore Maru'. His name is on Yokohama Cremation Memorial.
Major L Street was the second-in-command of the 77th.

January 2, 1945
According to notes made by Les Spence after the war 'Billy the Kid' acquired his nickname because of his ability to keep a flick-knife secret from camp searches.

January 9, 1945
Henry Owens. The death of Gunner Henry Owens, of 144 Battery, 35th LAA, is recorded on the Commonwealth War Graves Commission casualty list. He was 34 and is buried at Yokohama War Cemetery.

January 27, 1945
Perry. The death of Gunner Harry Perry, of 239 Battery, 77th HAA, is recorded on the Commonwealth War Graves Commission casualty list. He was 28 and the son of Joseph and Mary Ann Perry, of Pye Green, Hednesford, Staffordshire. He is buried at Yokohama War Cemetery.

February 3, 1945
Captain (later Major) James A Grider, an American. According to a report prepared on July 31, 1946 for the Allies, Grider was from the US Public Health Service and was Medical Officer for the American detail in the camp. (Source: **http://www.mansell.com/pow_resources/camplists/fukuoka/fuk_08_inatsuki/fuku_08_gibbs.html**)

March 1945
According to a report prepared on July 31, 1946 for the Allies, the camp population reached its peak during March 1945 when there were 590 prisoners housed there.

March 24, 1945
According to the Commonwealth War Graves Commission casualty list, this refers to Gunner Emrys Williams, of 240 Battery, 77th HAA Regiment. He was 38 and had a wife, Gladys in West Bromwich. He is buried in Yokohama War Cemetery.

April 1, 1945
The British Roster for Camp 8 lists a Lance Sergeant A Wright, of Suffolk.
Sergeant Windhurst. Les Spence writes the surname as 'Windhurst' and John Baxter's list of Royal Engineer personnel at Tandjong Priok notes a "Sergeant RC Windhurst, trade: fitter, of The Grove, Rumney, Cardiff". However, 'Prisoners In Java' has an unattributed story from Camp 8 which mentions a 'Sergeant Windust' and, in conversation with the editor (August 13, 2011), Mr Baxter and fellow 77th veteran Stanley Roberts both agreed they believed that the sergeant's correct surname was Windust.

April 2, 1945
Deaths in Thailand. News on this would be coming from the camp's new arrivals, some of whom might have worked on the Thai-Burma railway. After it was completed in October 1943, the Japanese gradually moved most of the surviving prisoners back to Singapore. Then, during 1944, around 8,700 of these men were shipped to camps in Japan to work in mines, factories and on the docks.

April 6, 1945
According to a report prepared on July 31, 1946 for the Allies, "1st Lt Toda was commandant from Nov 1944 to April 1945. He was pronounced to be gentlemanly toward and personally considerate of the prisoners, but unfortunately the operation of the camp was left largely in the hands of a Sgt Maj who was cruel, cunning, thieving and vindictive".

April 13, 1945
President Franklin D Roosevelt died on April 12, 1945, following a stroke.

April 25, 1945
1st Lieutenant (later Captain) Alfred E. Fobes.
NT: Nippon Times. R: Russia. B: Berlin.

May 2, 1945
Mussolini was executed by Communist partisans in Mezzegra, near Milan, on April 28, 1945, after being caught trying to flee Italy.

May 3, 1945
Hear that H and M are both dead and that EW is finished. Hitler committed suicide in the Führerbunker in Berlin on April 30, 1945. The Allies would formally accept the unconditional surrender of Nazi Germany on May 8, 1945, ending the European War.

May 6, 1945
Manchuncko. Les is referring to the Japanese colony of Manchukuo.

May 26, 1945
We hear that there will be a general election in England on July 5th. Once again the PoW information is correct.

June 17, 1945
We hear of meeting in Berlin of T, C and S. President Truman, Churchill and Stalin. This information was incorrect. Some leaders had been meeting in San Francisco during May and June to discuss the creation of the United Nations. The Potsdam Conference, which all three leaders did attend, did not start until July 16, 1945.

August 9, 1945
We had rather exciting morning, going down no fewer than four times from 7 til 1pm. We saw no planes.
This was the morning of the dropping of the plutonium bomb on the city of Nagasaki. Only four planes flew on the raid. The bomb exploded at 11.02am. Les' camp, which was near the present day city of Kama, Fukuoka Prefecture, was less than 100 miles from the explosion.

August 16, 1945
A recorded speech by the Japanese Emperor was played to the people at noon on August 15, 1945. It stated that the war was over. Japan's formal surrender took place on September 2.
Captain John W Goronwy. According to Rev Hugh Edwards (letter to editor, January 26, 2011): "Doctor Goronwy's parents kept a butcher's shop in High Street, Pontypridd."
According to Kathleen Booth (letter to editor, January 26, 2011): "Dr John W Goronwy was a member of the Royal Army Medical Corps, 174 Field Ambulance, accompanying the 77th HAA. He was one of those injured in the Surabaya rail crash. He was one of 772 mixed nationality prisoners who departed Singapore on June 5, 1944 on the 'Bijou Maru'. On arrival at Taiwan, they transferred to the 'Tamahoko Maru' which departed on June 20 for Japan. On June 24, in Nagasaki Bay, the 'Tamahoko' was torpedoed by US submarine

Tang with the loss of 560 lives. Of the 196 UK people on board, only 44 survived. Sadly, Dr Goronwy was one of those who died. He was 28."

Ronald Williams notes in his memoir, 'Under The Poached Egg' (Ronald Williams and Frank Williams), that Goronwy was being transferred to Japan following a request for British doctors. He describes Goronwy - his best friend - as a "mischievous little Welshman from Pontypridd, never averse to playing tricks on people" and that he was known as "Doc Grony".

September 1, 1945
Les Spence's writing is not clear here but the name is almost certainly Mitsui or Mitsue brothers, and probably relates to a family from the Mitsubishi company for which many prisoners of war had been forced to work.

September 6, 1945
The British Roster for Camp 8 lists a Driver S Cole, from Dudley.

September 8, 1945
Capt Blakey. According to Kathleen Booth (letter to editor, January 26, 2011): "Captain George Blakey had been a lieutenant in 241 Battery but was promoted to captain and transferred to 240 following the rail crash. He replaced Captain MacMillan who was one of the rail crash casualties. Blakey departed Java on October 21, 1942 on the 'Yoshida Maru' to Singapore then 'Singapore Maru' to Moji, Japan. The survivors of this terrible voyage were split into four groups and sent to neighbouring coal mining camps on the coast at the southern end of Honshu Island. Blakey was the senior army officer in Ohama camp until July 29, 1943 when he, along with other officers from neighbouring camps, was transferred to Zentsugi camp on Shikoku Island. Zentsugi camp closed in June 1945 and Blakey transferred to Miyata camp on Kyushu Island, about two miles from Inatsuki which was Les Spence's camp. Thus, after the Japanese surrendered, Blakey was able to visit Inatsuki and vice versa."

September 21, 1945
Chenango. Built as a tanker by the Standard Oil Company, the USS Chenango was acquired by the United States Navy in 1941 and converted into an escort carrier. It carried 1,900 Allied prisoners of war and 1,500 civilians from slave labour camps back to the United States.

September 24, 1945
Landing craft tank: an amphibious assault ship.
Manorbier: a TA training camp in west Wales.

October 21, 1945
The British Roster for Camp 8 lists a Gunner SW Perkins, from Shepherd's Bush London.

October 23, 1945
Arrive at Pearl Harbour. The San Antonio Express for October 24, 1945, includes a short article from the Associated Press: "Honolulu. Oct 23. The transport Marine Shark docked Tuesday with 2,442 passengers, including 70 American Army officers and 623 enlisted men, and 140 officers and 1,550 soldiers of the United Kingdom, all of whom had been prisoners of the Japanese in various Asiatic camps."
Interestingly, the American contingent on the boat included a national hero, Major Arthur Wermuth, who had been celebrated as the "One-Man Army of Bataan".

November 1, 1945
According to the website of the California State Military Museum the army post on Angel Island was called Fort McDowell. It states: "When the war with Japan ended... Fort McDowell was almost swamped by the number of servicemen returning from overseas duty in the Pacific Theater. As the troop transports brought soldiers home from the Pacific, they were processed at Fort McDowell, ferried across the bay to Oakland or San Francisco, loaded on trains and sent off to be discharged at their original induction centers. During this hectic activity twenty-two troop trains were loaded in one day; twenty in Oakland and two in San Francisco. It was thought to be a record of its kind." (Source: **www.militarymuseum.org**)

November 12, 1945
'Glory' boys. The aircraft carrier HMS Glory was used as a transport ship for the repatriation of former prisoners of war. It left Manila on October 9, 1945 and went direct to Vancouver, from where the men took the same route as Les Spence across Canada to New York.

INDEX